365
FOUR-STAR
VIDEOS

★ ★ ★ ★

YOU (PROBABLY)
HAVEN'T SEEN

LESLIE HAMILTON

CONTEMPORARY BOOKS
A TRIBUNE COMPANY

Library of Congress Cataloging-in-Publication Data

Hamilton, Leslie.
    365 four-star videos you (probably) haven't seen / Leslie
Hamilton.
        p.   cm.
    ISBN 0-8092-3219-7
        1. Motion pictures—Catalogs.   2. Motion pictures—Evaluation—
Catalogs.   3. Video recordings—Catalogs.   I. Title.
PN1998.H44   1996
016.79143'75—dc20   95-48228
                                                                              CIP

Front-cover design by Amy Nathan
Interior design by Nancy Freeborn

Copyright © 1996 by Leslie Tragert
All rights reserved
Published by Contemporary Books, Inc.
Two Prudential Plaza, Chicago, Illinois 60601-6790
Manufactured in the United States of America
International Standard Book Number: 0-8092-3219-7
10   9   8   7   6   5   4   3   2   1

*To my girls—Meghan, Emma, and Cassie—without whom
watching shooting stars wouldn't be half as much fun.*

★ ★ ★ ★

*To my husband, Bob Tragert, who was always there,
and always will be.
As Kirstie Alley might put it,
"Thank you . . . and I love you very much."*

Acknowledgments

My first, and deepest, words of thanks must go to the staff of the Ipswich Video Barn, in Ipswich, Massachusetts. There is a rare kind of video store: the small-town establishment that really is willing to track down anything you want. The Video Barn is such a place. It's a tiny, eclectic spot filled at all times with people who know and love movies. Here you are blessedly free from that insipid, distracted clerk who only stares at you vacantly when you pose the all-too-complex question, "Is *His Girl Friday* in?" Often this person will respond after some minutes, brain cells dying with each snap of gum, with a retort like "I don't think that's out on video yet."

The town of Ipswich is blessed to have a rare oasis where film lovers can gather without having to endure such traumatic exchanges. The conversations you encounter when you first walk in are as likely to concern spicy local gossip as they are to touch on the latest efforts of the Dalai Lama to free the people of Tibet. When you make your way to the counter, you find that these people know movies inside and out and can answer any question you pose with lightning speed and awe-inspiring accuracy. Even more remarkably, given enough lead time, they will locate any and every video you care to name.

I thank Michele Shibley McGrath, and all the women of the Video Barn (including Denny Eldridge, Janna Kinney, Angela Rollins, and Sue Maniates), for having the best choices, for providing invaluable insight and assistance throughout the project, and for sharing their extraordinary knowledge of movies with me. When I say that this book would never have come into existence without the help of these intelligent women, it comes from the heart.

My grateful thanks also go to the wonderful people of Golden Retriever Way for rooting me on and keeping an eye out for the girls while I worked and for making me laugh and offering constant words of encouragement; to the women of Sip and Sew—Tracee Kneeland-Swanson, Mary Toropov, Anne Cote, Margaret Geoffrion, and Kathy Geoffrion Scannell—for their suggestions and for their unfailing support as I faced obstacles large and small (remember our motto: To Sip, To Sew, To Eat Cake); to Donna Basset, Michael Geoffrion Scannell, and Suzanne Tragert, who are old friends (the best kind); to Peter and Tasia Knudsen, and to Will Silvio, for always coming through at the last minute, whether that meant a movie quote or a cup of milk; to Brandon Toropov, who had enough on the ball to know when it was "Duck Season" and trusted me enough to know when it was "Rabbit Season"; to my editors, Linda Gray and Craig Bolt, for all their help and support; to "all" the Tragerts; to Frances McHugh, for making me laugh, for the ducks, and for being there for mom and me; to my mother, Leslie Hamilton, for teaching me to love books; and to my father, Robert Hamilton, for teaching me to love movies.

Introduction

If you're determined to never again leave the video store frustrated and empty-handed because all the new releases have been snatched up . . .

If you've ever stared helplessly at the thousands of video boxes lined up on the walls, silently pleading for one good film to leap off the shelf and into your waiting hands . . .

If you're beginning to suspect that you've already seen every single decent movie ever made . . .

If you've ever rented two "B" movies hoping they'll add up to an "A" movie, only to fall asleep halfway through the first rental . . .

If you just can't bring yourself to watch *The Three Amigos* one more time . . .

Congratulations! You've picked up the right book. *365 Four-Star Videos You (Probably) Haven't Seen* is your guide to more than 300 truly great, entertaining, worthwhile videos available today. Many of them never found the audience they deserve at the corner cineplex—and now you can use that to your advantage, because every one of these films is a winner, and every one of them is probably on the shelf, right now, at your local video store.

From comedy, action, documentary, and horror to cartoons, romance, silent films, and drama, every movie category is here. There are even a handful of completely watchable foreign films and musicals that won't have you feeling you've somehow mistaken your dentist's drill for a VCR. Think of this book as your own personal video clerk: a dedicated film buff with varied and eclectic, always entertaining, tastes who's here to guide you in the right direction toward whatever kind of movie you're in the mood for.

Each entry in this guide contains succinct plot descriptions, memorable quotes, trivia questions, and a listing of the film's director and lead actors. You'll also find suggestions on what to rent if you've already seen a particular movie but are in the mood for something similar, as well as recommendations for companion films if you're up for a double feature. With this book, you can watch *at least* one terrific new flick every single night for a year. You can also impress the guys behind the video counter with your rental choices, your mastery of cool movie facts and trivia, and your ability to actually walk out of the store with a video rental *every single time you come in.*

And speaking of video clerks . . . If you happen to *be* a video clerk, or if you own a video store, why not keep a copy of this book behind the counter? That way, when all the new releases have been rented for the night and customers are gazing at the shelves in despair, you can pull this out and offer up some intriguing alternatives. Your customers will be happy, you'll do some business, and, hey, you'll be doing me a favor by promoting the book.

Pass the popcorn, and have fun!

The Abominable Dr. Phibes

*He may be gross,
but you can't say he doesn't have style.*

Vincent Price (Dr. Phibes) is very upset. His wife has died on the operating table, and now someone is going to have to pay. As a matter of fact, several people are going to have to pay. Sure, Price is insane; but he's such a clever madman that you take a strange pleasure in watching him. He's come up with more weird ways to knock people off than anyone this side of the Penguin on an old "Batman" rerun. Actually he succeeds where the Penguin and all the rest failed; he's smarter, and he usually manages to carry out his sick plans. What's more, he *knows* just how crazy he is, and the movie knows it, too.

Every scene in this picture is a wink and a nod to the audience; you're in on the joke, and you appreciate the film because it's brave enough to mix horror and humor. It takes nerve, and more than a little talent, to gross an audience out and make it laugh at the same time. You're never quite sure what's going to happen next in *The Abominable Dr. Phibes*, because the rule book has obviously been thrown out the window from the get-go. At any given moment you find yourself wondering whether the movie will get funnier or scarier. And I'm not telling.

★ 1971, 94 minutes, color, not rated.

★ With: Vincent Price, Joseph Cotten, Hugh Griffith. Director: Robert Fuest.

★ True or false: *Vincent Price recorded a song that earned a gold record.* (Answer on page 58.)

"Love means never having to say you're ugly."
—Vincent Price, tense as usual after yet another bad hair day

For a great double feature, rent it with *House of Wax.*

Seen it but in the mood for something similar? Try *Dr. Phibes Rises Again.*

Answer to page 285 trivia question: Rod Serling.

Horror

1

The Adventures of Buckaroo Banzai Across the Eighth Dimension

Remember: No matter where you go, there you are.

Buckaroo Banzai is a hip, relentlessly bizarre send-up of *The War of the Worlds* and *Flash Gordon* that boasts a topflight cast. (John Lithgow has almost too much fun as Emilio Lizardo, a Mussolini-inspired mad scientist.)

As our picture opens, the handsome, famous neurosurgeon Buckaroo Banzai (Peter Weller) is finishing up a breakthrough brain operation. But he has to hurry—the government's waiting to see just what Banzai's latest experiments in particle physics have turned up. Also, his rock band has a gig tonight. Buckaroo and his band of hard-rocking scientists walk a very thin line between the outrageous and the silly, but by the middle of this movie you're willing to follow Weller down whichever side of that line he chooses to go.

Director W. D. Ritchter goes for—and gets—a hilarious futuristic garage-sale aesthetic here. Watch it twice (or more); the movie features a nonstop background of intricately layered vocal gags that emerge only after repeated viewings. Some films are fun; some films are weird; very few films are *as* weird and *as* much fun as *Buckaroo Banzai*.

★ 1984, 103 minutes, color, PG.

★ With: Peter Weller, John Lithgow, Ellen Barkin, Jeff Goldblum, Christopher Lloyd. Director: W. D. Ritchter.

★ *What instruments does Buckaroo Banzai play during the course of the film?* (Answer on page 88.)

The Adventures of Rocky and Bullwinkle—Mona Moose

Parental advisory:
Pun-sensitive viewers should avoid this.

Actually, any volume of this twelve-cassette package will do quite nicely indeed, but the first in the series features a favorite episode of mine, in which Mr. Peabody and his boy Sherman go back in time to visit Robinson Crusoe. So I picked this one. These are crystal-clear, commercial-free versions of the sixties cartoon classics; they work both as crowd pleasers for the younger set and as a relentlessly loopy trip down memory lane for those of us who were glued to the set during the show's original run.

This one will make you laugh, but it may also make you cry at what has been lost when it comes to decent kids' entertainment. The animation is as cheap as it could possibly be, and it's all the more hilarious as a result. Why then must today's kids sit through the equally cheap yet relentlessly cheesy "Captain Planet"?

★ 1991, 46 minutes, color, not rated.

★ With: Rocky, Bullwinkle, Boris, Natasha, Mr. Sherman, Peabody, Dudley Do-Right (voices of June Foray, Bill Scott, William Conrad). Director: Jay Ward.

★ *What is the name of Dudley Do-Right's horse?*
(Answer on page 117.)

"Have you forgotten the plot again?" "In a word, you said it."
—Bullwinkle is, as usual, a little slower on the uptake than his winged friend.

For a great double feature, rent it with

one of the 11 subsequent volumes (your call).

Seen it but in the mood for something similar? Try

Speed Racer: The Fire Race.

Answer to page 341 trivia question:

Beats me. Budget problems? Lack of imagination? Or maybe they figured cars just couldn't get any cooler.

Family

After Hours

Computer dating never looked better.

"Different rules apply when it gets late. You know what I mean?"

—The proprietor of a diner, setting Griffin Dunne straight. Gee, all he wanted to do was make a phone call.

For a great double feature, rent it with

Barton Fink.

Seen it but in the mood for something similar? Try

The King of Comedy.

Answer to page 139 trivia question:

Alec Baldwin and Kim Basinger.

Every move Griffin Dunne makes in this movie gets him in deeper trouble, starting with the ill-fated visit he makes to a local diner after work. There he runs into Rosanna Arquette, who makes it clear she would like to get to know him better. He's young, he's single, it's New York: what could happen if he follows her lead? Plenty.

Like many nightmares, *After Hours* admits a number of interpretations; those who are inclined to find Freudian interpretations in Martin Scorsese's surpassingly weird comedy about an endless night in Manhattan can certainly have a field day doing so. But the fun lies in watching computer operator Dunne's worst fears come to life with clocklike regularity: every woman he meets turns against him, every gay man is out to persecute him, and the unpleasant prospect of emasculation looms uneasily for much of the film. In any hands other than Scorsese's, the unusually dark material would make for exhausting going, but the direction is so strong, and the cast is so perfect, that you buy in.

It takes a fateful encounter with an older woman and some symbolic egg hatching for Dunne to complete his rough journey toward day.

★ 1985, 97 minutes, color, R.

★ With: Griffin Dunne, Rosanna Arquette, Teri Garr, Linda Fiorentino. Director: Martin Scorsese.

★ *What is the title of the book in which Dunne writes Arquette's number?* (Answer on page 185.)

Agatha

I don't know about you, but I wouldn't go out of my way to get Agatha Christie mad.

In 1926, not long after Agatha Christie found out that her husband was leaving her for a younger, prettier woman, she disappeared for eleven days. She never gave an explanation as to where she went or what she was up to. This movie takes that factual event and asks an intriguing question: what if the world's most famous mystery writer had been up to murder? We follow Agatha, played with a haunting, intellectual regality by Vanessa Redgrave, to the Yorkshire health spa where her husband's mistress has gone to preen. It's not the young woman's good health that concerns Redgrave; it's whether or not to exact revenge.

Dustin Hoffman is an American reporter who finds Redgrave and watches with awe and trepidation as his idol ponders whether she should set another perfect crime to paper—or try the real thing. Redgrave pulls off one of the toughest acting challenges here, that of portraying a genius; there's no doubt in your mind that if she wanted to kill someone, she could. By the way, did you ever notice that after 1926 the murderer in her stories often turned out to be a young, pretty girl?

★ 1979, 98 minutes, color, PG.

★ With: Dustin Hoffman, Vanessa Redgrave, Celia Gregory. Director: Michael Apted.

★ *What play was the movie* And Then There Were None *based on?* (Answer on page 209.)

"I admire your driving style. And may I say that what you said about philodendrons needed saying."
—Dustin Hoffman has an odd set of literary criteria, but, hey, it works for him.

For a great double feature, rent it with
Love from a Stranger.

Seen it but in the mood for something similar? Try
And Then There Were None (1945).

Answer to page 177 trivia question:
Emmanuelle Beart.

Suspense

Alice

So rich yet so bored.

"You have a nice personality, and, you know, sweaters."

—The comforting response elicited by Mia Farrow, who has just asked whether or not she's been wasting her life

For a great double feature, rent it with

Another Woman.

Seen it but in the mood for something similar? Try

My Life.

Answer to page 212 trivia question:

They bound her chest flat. Ouch!

Mia Farrow is Alice, a woman who lives what might at first glance appear to be the perfect life. She has more money than she can spend. She has beautiful children who love her and an au pair who is always ready to whisk them away should caring for them become tiresome. Her successful husband is handsome but detached from the small world that Farrow finds herself inhabitating. Farrow finds the key to her fulfillment in the unlikeliest of places: a Chinese doctor who gives her magical herbs, for instance. After she consumes them, she is visited by the ghosts of past loves and imbued with a new sensual bravado.

This picture marked a welcome return to comic form for director Woody Allen, who manages to make some serious points about lost opportunities and rack up enough laughs to keep us hooked (especially in the finale). The picture's use of color is masterful; Allen uses soft romantic tones to return to the romance and magic that he achieved in movies like *Manhattan*.

★ 1990, 106 minutes, color, PG-13.

★ With: Mia Farrow, Alec Baldwin, Blythe Danner, William Hurt. Director: Woody Allen.

★ *Who played Mia Farrow's obstetrician in* Rosemary's Baby? (Answer on page 249.)

All of Me

Talk about a two-for-one deal.

As if to confirm, once and for all, that great comic performances generally go unrecognized at Oscar time, Steve Martin's hilarious work in *All of Me* went without a nomination when the 1984 list was unveiled. This despite his having been awarded the Best Actor prize from the New York Film Critics! I guess the academy figures that making people laugh doesn't really count as, you know, work.

Martin teams up with dream partner Lily Tomlin in this inspired gender-war comedy. Tomlin has recently died, but due to a double-talk-laden slipup of some kind during an attempt to transfer her soul into the body of the young and nubile Victoria Tennant, she finds herself stuck in Martin's body. The two have to share a single set of wheels, so to speak, even though he hated her while she was alive.

They fall in love, of course. The double-barreled squabble for control of one body is priceless; Martin's superlative physical comedy makes this one a must.

★ 1984, 93 minutes, color, PG.

★ With: Steve Martin, Lily Tomlin, Victoria Tennant. Director: Carl Reiner.

★ *What Steve Martin film is a valentine of sorts to Victoria Tennant, whom he met during the filming of* All of Me *and later married?* (Answer on page 277.)

"I'm sorry I made you being dead an unpleasant experience."

—Steve Martin, a little testy with Lily Tomlin, whose quest for immortality he has interrupted

For a great double feature, rent it with

Dead Men Don't Wear Plaid.

Seen it but in the mood for something similar? Try

The Man with Two Brains.

Answer to page 247 trivia question:

It's the name of the pizza restaurant where the young women work; the town in which the film takes place is Mystic, Connecticut.

Comedy

American Dreamer

Or, An American in Paris with a Headache.

"I ran into some trouble—or, should I say, it ran into me."

—Would-be novelist JoBeth Williams's florid explanation of how all her problems started

For a great double feature, rent it with

Compromising Positions.

Seen it but in the mood for something similar? Try

Shirley Valentine.

Answer to page 176 trivia question:

The *Star Wars* movies.

This is a silly romantic romp in which JoBeth Williams, bored with the world of housewifery, enters a contest in which the aim is to mimic the style of one Rebecca Ryan, a famous romance writer who stars in her own novels. Through a series of plot complications far too intricate to be detailed here, Williams wins the contest, goes to Paris alone, gets amnesia, becomes Rebecca Ryan, speaks many languages, acts like a glamorous worldly sophisticate, charges things to the hotel at which Ryan is supposedly staying, and finally encounters a befuddled Tom Conti.

Conti resolves to get to the bottom of things, and in the process he finds himself increasingly fascinated by the mystery woman who has assumed the character he created. Williams turns in a marvelously over-the-top performance, and Conti is his usual charming self.

★ 1984, 105 minutes, color, PG.

★ With: JoBeth Williams, Tom Conti, Giancarlo Giannini. Director: Rick Rosenthal.

★ *What does JoBeth Williams make out of Jell-O in this film?* (Answer on page 326.)

Comedy

An Angel at My Table

Square peg, round hole, really red hair.

W ho needs Harvey Keitel? Director Jane Campion won worldwide acclaim for her 1993 film *The Piano,* but before that mainstream success had proved elusive for her. This picture, which immediately preceded Campion's best-known film, is a powerful, mature adaptation of the autobiographies of the New Zealand writer Janet Frame, who overcame incredible odds—a troubled childhood, sadistic teachers, and the incorrect diagnosis of her extreme shyness as mental illness—to create a noteworthy body of written work. The picture follows Frame through one male-dominated hierarchy after another; none of them can make much sense of the talented, unusual young lady with the plain features and fiery red hair. Whose fault is that, I'd like to know?

An Angel at My Table uses a confident, assured visual style, a surreal, backcountry setting, and a bare-bones script to tell a familiar story: that of an artist whom the rest of the society has trouble pigeonholing. With exquisite subtlety Campion paints a picture of a world that refuses to accommodate extraordinary, creative people because it's obsessed with order, dominance, and control—ideas that are not, typically, female fixations. The movie is not, however, a feminist treatise; it's a striking, carefully rendered portrait of a memorable character.

★ 1990, 158 minutes, color, R.

★ With: Kerry Fox, Alexia Keogh, Karen Fergusson. Director: Jane Campion.

★ *What was Jane Campion's first feature film?* (Answer on page 337.)

"I'm not allowed to speak to you ever again."
—See what happens when you teach a friend a dirty word?

For a great double feature, rent it with *My Brilliant Career.*

Seen it but in the mood for something similar? Try *The Piano.*

Answer to page 211 trivia question: Garry Marshall, actor/director Penny's brother.

Drama

9

Anatomy of a Murder

Probably the only Hollywood courtroom drama you could watch with a lawyer—and still have a good time.

For a great double feature, rent it with

Witness for the Prosecution.

Seen it but in the mood for something similar? Try

Call Northside 777.

Answer to page 246 trivia question:

The Princess Bride.

Don't worry; the action in this fascinating re-creation of a real-life case is compelling enough for us non-lawyers, too. A serviceman trained to become a ruthless killing machine discovers that his wife has been raped—and kills her attacker. Everyone knows the serviceman pulled the trigger—but is there a defense that will save him from the electric chair?

Director Otto Preminger went above and beyond the call of duty to maintain crackling authenticity for this story. He ordered an exact replica of the courtroom in which the actual trial was held and shot some scenes at locations of the original case. The result: a film that exudes realism in every frame, yielding a nearly documentarylike feel, but never drags for a moment.

In only her second role a smoldering Lee Remick oozes danger and sexuality. Ben Gazzara serves up some electrifying work as the avenging soldier in probably his finest screen role. Both of them are trouble with a capital *T*. Jimmy Stewart is Jimmy Stewart, and that's more than enough for this film buff.

★ 1959, 160 minutes, B&W, not rated.

★ With: Jimmy Stewart, Ben Gazzara, Lee Remick. Director: Otto Preminger.

★ *What song does Jimmy Stewart play as a duet with Duke Ellington?* (Answer on page 210.)

Suspense

The Andromeda Strain

A (literally) blood-curdling experience.

Something in Piedmont, New Mexico, is making people keel over, dead in their tracks. The strange, unparalleled epidemic causes human blood to turn into powder within the body—and if that doesn't put a crimp in your day, nothing will. The biohazard is the subject of a superpowered research effort by a team of topflight scientists.

Why has the virus—if it is a virus—spared 2, and only 2, of the town's 68 inhabitants? Will the team come up with a way to stop the epidemic in time to spare the rest of humanity? How the heck are the doctors going to get anything done stuffed inside the antiseptic confines of that massive, multilevel, high-security complex where a good chunk of the film takes place? For the answers, check out this classic sci-fi survival yarn—one of the best in a much-mangled genre. One cautionary note: although this is rated G, for some inexplicable reason, it's grisly enough to consider it a PG—at least—flick.

★ 1971, 130 minutes, color, G.

★ With: Arthur Hill, James Olson, David Wayne. Director: Robert Wise.

★ *Who wrote the book on which the film was based?*
(Answer on page 253.)

"Boy, that's one dead burg."
—An unsuspecting soldier's bewildered report as he makes his way toward the unlucky town

For a great double feature, rent it with
Altered States.

Seen it but in the mood for something similar? Try
Soylent Green.

Answer to page 284 trivia question:
"Hooperman."

Anne of Green Gables (1985)

Next week: Little Orphan Annie meets Anne in a battle to the death to determine the cutest redheaded orphan of all time!

"Oh, Miss Cuthbert, did you really say that perhaps you would let me stay at Green Gables?"

—Looks like Colleen Dewhurst might relent and let Megan Follows stick around for a while after all.

For a great double feature, rent it with

Anne of Avonlea.

Seen it but in the mood for something similar? Try

Polyanna (1960).

Answer to page 158 trivia question:

Elizabeth Taylor.

Have your kids seen this one? Based on the works of Lucy Maud Montgomery, this account of the early years of the spunky, fast-talking orphan with the red pigtails was produced for Canadian television in the eighties. Young Anne (Megan Follows) lands on Prince Edward Island and either infuriates or captures the hearts of everyone she meets. Sometimes she does both. Most of the time she brings a little sunshine to the lives of the two kindly old folks who take her in.

The crusty lady who pretends she's not falling in love with the kid is played by Colleen Dewhurst; her brother, who knows he is, is played by Richard Farnsworth. Outstanding family viewing. This was followed by *Anne of Avonlea*, which beats the sequel jinx and is just as much fun to watch as the original.

★ 1985, 195 minutes, color, not rated.

★ With: Megan Follows, Colleen Dewhurst, Richard Farnsworth. Director: Kevin Sullivan.

★ *Who played Anne Shirley in the 1935 film version?*
(Answer on page 214.)

Family

Another Woman

Gena Rowlands vents.

Yes, this is one of those "serious" Woody Allen movies that he made when his public was begging for more funny movies, like his early work. Not surprisingly, it got lost in the shuffle, but it's well worth tracking down.

Once again Allen tries his hand at a Bergman classic, making it his own and giving it an essentially American feel; he pulls it off, keeping his homage to Bergman believable without losing sight of his trademark themes of paranoia and insecurity. Thankfully there's also a dash (but just barely) of humor.

Gena Rowlands plays a woman who, upon turning 50, takes a year off from work to write a book, but the voices creeping through the air vent in her new apartment—those of the patients on the couch of the analyst next door—keep distracting her from her task. Pretty soon she's revisiting the scenes of her own life, reviewing places where she could have taken risks and made emotionally fulfilling decisions rather than practical ones.

Emotions would be the key word here: Rowlands has always known that they can be messy and that they're not always rewarding, so she's simply skipped them. But the voices through the vent won't let her forget what might have been.

★ 1988, 84 minutes, color, PG.

★ With: Gena Rowlands, Gene Hackman, Sandy Dennis, and Mia Farrow. Director: Woody Allen.

★ *In what film did Dennis portray the young wife of a college professor attending a late-night party from hell?* (Answer on page 189.)

"While I'll admit that eavesdropping on the intimate revelations of a psychiatrist's office might be fascinating to some people, it was not exactly what I had in mind when I rented the place."
—Gena Rowlands finds herself in possession of a little more information than she needs.

For a great double feature, rent it with *Wild Strawberries.*

Seen it but in the mood for something similar? Try *Interiors.*

Answer to page 193 trivia question: Bruce Lee.

Drama

*One of Dreyfuss's
most memorable wiseasses.*

"It's war, Duddy, it's war. If you want to be a saint, go to Israel and plant some trees."
—Duddy gets a lesson in pragmatism.

For a great double feature, rent it with
The Goodbye Girl.

Seen it but in the mood for something similar? Try
Goodbye, Columbus.

Answer to page 229 trivia question:
White Fang.

Duddy Kravitz (Richard Dreyfuss) is going places. He's one nervous ball of pent-up energy. He can't sit still because he's got to find some way to get ahead—it seems he's convinced that he's wasting every moment not spent scheming.

This witty, biting look at Jewish life in Montreal in years gone by is one of Richard Dreyfuss's first leading roles and certainly one of his best. A modestly scaled movie, it manages to make us care for Dreyfuss even if he does get on our nerves a bit. (Not all of his starring vehicles, alas, have succeeded in this effort.)

The snappy, irreverent screenplay, adapted by Mordecai Richler from his own novel, moves along nicely and is, like its lead actor, just this side of too smart for its own good. The film was shot entirely in Canada, a touch that adds to its authentic feel.

★ 1974, 121 minutes, color, PG.

★ With: Richard Dreyfuss, Jack Warden, Randy Quaid. Director: Ted Kotcheff.

★ *In what Oscar-nominated Jack Nicholson film did Randy Quaid play a supporting role?*
(Answer on page 121.)

Drama

Arsenic and Old Lace

"A Halloween tale of Brooklyn, where anything can happen and usually does."

A potentially risky combination: equal parts screwball farce and black comedy. A delicate balance indeed! Thankfully, nothing slips.

Cary Grant is a once-confirmed bachelor who's about to get married. He's stressed out already, but when he discovers that his two sweet, saintly old aunts are dosing the home-brewed elderberry wine they serve to lonely old gentlemen, he's mortified. Wrinkled guys are kicking the bucket left and right.

Supposedly Grant had trepidations about his ability to handle the broadly scaled comic material in *Arsenic and Old Lace;* the numerous double takes and bug-eyed realizations he engages in here are certainly hazardous territory for a wary actor, but Grant's technique is, as usual, unassailable, and he pulls it all off winningly.

A frame from this picture should appear in any dictionary next to the listing for black comedy; the genre can't hope to get much better than this. The whole cast seems to know it, too.

★ 1944, 118 minutes, B&W, not rated.

★ With: Cary Grant, Priscilla Lane, Peter Lorre. Director: Frank Capra.

★ *Who was Cary Grant's last wife?* (Answer on page 92.)

"Charge!"
—Lunatic ascending staircase

For a great double feature, rent it with
Harvey.

Seen it but in the mood for something similar? Try
Bringing Up Baby.

Answer to page 267 trivia question:
Leslie Howard, whose telegram read "No Bogey, no Leslie."

Comedy

Nobody, but nobody, takes a bath in the sink like Susan Sarandon.

"I only do business with the people I do business with. The people I do business with . . . find out I do business with the people I don't do business with . . . I can't do business with you."

—Big-time crook explaining to small-time crook why plans for fast money aren't always as easy as they look

For a great double feature, rent it with

The Lemon Sisters.

Seen it but in the mood for something similar? Try

Tough Guys.

Answer to page 319 trivia question:

Goodfellas.

This is a satisfying character-driven story of Atlantic City at a time when it was beginning its renaissance as the Vegas of the East after decades of decline. As with all renewals, some of the old has to make way for the new. Not everyone will achieve prosperity; some will fall between the cracks.

Burt Lancaster gives a funny, poignant performance that has to be regarded as one of the highlights of his career. Susan Sarandon, in her breakthrough role as a casino worker who gets caught up in a drug deal, shows the first indications of the top-level acting that would follow from her.

Each of the picture's stories is compelling on its own terms; each of its principal characters sticks with you for a long time after the film's over. If you're like me, once you watch this movie, you won't be able to hear the words *Atlantic City* without wondering just how they're all getting along now.

★ 1980, 104 minutes, color, R.

★ With: Burt Lancaster, Susan Sarandon, Kate Reid. Director: Louis Malle.

★ *What did Burt Lancaster do before he became a film star?* (Answer on page 193.)

Drama

The Atomic Cafe

Rent, duck, and cover.

Even people who don't like documentaries will probably find it tough to stop watching this one. It's a collection of classic film clips from the height of the cold war, some of them unintentionally hilarious, alerting the populace to the new rules of the game in the Atomic Age. The era's nearly indescribable levels of anti-Red hysteria are on display in all their glory, as are some pretty graphic scenes of postnuclear destruction. (The movie is, in a few sections, probably a little too intense for younger children.)

When it's not making you wonder how we made it through the fifties without setting off a nuclear holocaust, the assemblage of clips is a laughable reminder of exactly why people decided to rebel against the Establishment in the next decade. If you're looking for proof that news events are sometimes far too bizarre in their own right to parody, look no further.

★ 1982, 88 minutes, B&W, not rated.

★ With: Richard Nixon, Lloyd Bentsen, Lyndon Johnson, and a cast of thousands, some, no doubt, still glowing. Directors: Kevin Rafferty, Jayne Loader, Pierce Rafferty.

★ *Why does Richard Nixon ring a bell in this film?*
(Answer on page 258.)

"And by the way, do you know exactly what your family would do if an attack came, say, at ten o'clock tomorrow . . . ? Good question, isn't it?"
—As if you hadn't thought of a good reason to build a bomb shelter yet.

For a great double feature, rent it with
Invasion of the Body Snatchers (1956).

Seen it but in the mood for something similar? Try
The Thin Blue Line.

Answer to page 340 trivia question:
Both traveled around the world in 80 days; Palin's exploits were the subject of a memorable television documentary.

Documentary

Au Revoir, Les Enfants

That's "Good-bye, Children" to you.

In this memorable Louis Malle film, the acclaimed director weaves an affecting story based on a painful incident from his own past; it took him years to confront the tale on-screen.

During World War II a young Jewish boy is hidden away from the Nazis when the priest-headmaster of an elite boarding school agrees to take him in under a gentile name. One brilliant young boy (clearly based on a childhood Malle) at first sees the new boy as a threat—he's the only other fellow in the place who can match him intellectually—but the two soon become fast friends. When the young refugee and the priest who protected him are betrayed to the Germans, our heart breaks along with Malle's, and we can't help imagining what the insightful youngster might have become had the war never intervened.

An unforgettable tale of friendship and loss that never veers into grim solemnity—like *Europa, Europa* (see page 116), which offers some interesting parallels, *Au Revoir, Les Enfants* is a compelling look at the human costs of war that can be watched by just about any member of the family.

★ 1987, 103 minutes, color, PG.

★ With: Gaspard Manesse, Raphael Fejto, Philippe Morier-Genoud. Director: Louis Malle.

★ *Name Louis Malle's father-in-law.* (Answer on page 330.)

Foreign

Autumn Sonata

A Bergman masterpiece—and that goes for both of them.

There are a lot of great reasons to rent this movie, and one of the most important has to be that you can confuse the names *Ingmar Bergman* and *Ingrid Bergman* when you're discussing the work and stand a decent chance of getting away with it. Both cinematic giants turn in masterful work in this somber study of the perils of adulthood. Liv Ullmann is a conflicted, late-30s daughter who has a series of issues to work out with her concert pianist mother—Ingrid Bergman, in a particularly memorable cosmopolitan incarnation. Ingrid manages to find fault in nearly everything Liv does—it's an old instinct she can't seem to control, even after a seven-year gap in the relationship, and her exasperated daughter decides it's time to lay everything out on the table. Some have dismissed this film as a whine fest, but the work is far more complex than that. Bergman (Ingmar, that is) shows us two women trapped in bonds of their own creation; the portrait is something that will resonate for just about anyone whose family doesn't quite measure up to Norman Rockwell standards.

★ 1978, 97 minutes, color, PG.

★ With: Ingrid Bergman, Liv Ullmann, Lena Nyman. Director: Ingmar Bergman.

★ *What Bergman film is parodied in* Bill & Ted's Bogus Journey? (Answer on page 344.)

"I could always live in my art. But never in my life."

—Ingrid Bergman, reflecting on her maternal instincts, which are few and far between

For a great double feature, rent it with

Cactus Flower.

Seen it but in the mood for something similar? Try

Interiors.

Answer to page 328 trivia question:

Women in Love (1970) and *A Touch of Class* (1973).

Drama

1930s divorce, Hollywood style.

"I'm a great teacher, not a great lover."
"That's right, Armand, no one could ever accuse you of being a great lover."

—Irene Dunne isn't having an affair . . . yet.

For a great double feature, rent it with
Bringing Up Baby.

Seen it but in the mood for something similar? Try
His Girl Friday.

Answer to page 349 trivia question:
Tad Mosel.

As much fun as this film is, it does merit a word of warning: In it Irene Dunne sports the single most hideous collection of hats in Hollywood history. If you can get past that, you're in for a great hour and a half. Cary Grant and Irene Dunne get a divorce so that they can hook up with other partners; then each one sets out to spoil the romantic objectives of the other. The two stars are magnificent, as is Ralph Bellamy, who provides his usual effectively befuddled counterpoint to Grant's suave, sophisticated man of the world. One of the funniest screwball comedies Hollywood ever produced, complete with a risqué reconciliation in a secluded cabin that uses a tissue of elaborate legal double talk to make it past the Hays Commission.

★ 1937, 92 minutes, B&W, not rated.

★ With: Cary Grant, Irene Dunne, Ralph Bellamy. Director: Leo McCarey.

★ *In what other film with a similar plot did Grant and Dunne star?* (Answer on page 264.)

Comedy

Babette's Feast

Life is a banquet.

This whimsical morality tale, based on a short story by Isak Dinesen, introduces us to two Danish sisters in a very devout Lutheran religious order. The creed of the group demands that members deny their senses to become closer to the spirit of God. When the sisters plan a dinner party for a visiting general, Babette, the new cook, is given the job of preparing the meal. As the dinner draws nearer, however, the two sisters begin to fear that Babette's feast may be an unhealthy temptation or even an excess that could earn them condemnation in the eyes of the Lord. They can't cancel, however—important guests are on the way—so the entire group convenes and decides that its members will eat but will studiously avoid enjoying the dinner. Think they'll pull it off?

Suffice it to say that getting to the finish line without a smile proves to be a pretty challenging undertaking. As Babette is preparing the much-debated meal, director Gabriel Axel makes sure we feel the same revulsion as the good sisters, but his movie is, in the end, just as sumptuous a spread as Babette's. By the time it ends, we, too, have decided to settle in and enjoy ourselves for a moment.

★ 1987, 102 minutes, color, G.

★ With: Stephanie Audran, Birgitte Federspiel, Bodil Kjer. Director: Gabriel Axel.

★ *What does this film have in common with the 1942 classic* Casablanca? (Answer on page 352.)

"Mercy and truth have met together."
—That's all very well for the general to say, but where are the after-dinner mints?

For a great double feature, rent it with *Out of Africa.*

Seen it but in the mood for something similar? Try *Like Water for Chocolate.*

Answer to page 169 trivia question: *Naked Lunch.*

A 12-pack of disposable diapers and a laptop, please.

For a great double feature, rent it with

Crimes of the Heart.

Seen it but in the mood for something similar? Try

Bachelor Mother.

Answer to page 203 trivia question:

121. Yeah, that was a gimme.

Diane Keaton stars in a sweet, lighthearted comedy that doesn't ask anything from the viewer beyond sitting back and enjoying a good old-fashioned romantic movie. The twist is that the romance is between career-obsessed Keaton and the baby girl she inherits.

The Tiger Lady, as Keaton is known around the Manhattan office she rules, receives custody of the child of some never-before-seen distant cousins. Keaton, who was complete and happy (well, *occasionally* happy) with her yupped-out life, is utterly bewildered when it comes to caring for a baby. So is her anal-retentive live-in lover, played with unerring deadpan charm by Harold Ramis. (Yes, he did something besides the *Ghostbuster* movies.) Soon Keaton finds herself willing to learn how to incorporate the new arrival into her life—even if she has to do it alone. She gives up her job and makes her way to a new life in rural Vermont, leaving behind the world she so easily commanded. Now she owns the pond, but she's still a fish out of water.

There is a bright side, though. Local doctor Sam Shepard is a very good kisser. This one's cute as heck. Enjoy yourself.

★ 1987, 103 minutes, color, PG.

★ With: Diane Keaton, Sam Shepard, Harold Ramis. Director: Charles Shyer.

★ *In what film did Sam Shepard play "the fastest man in the world"?* (Answer on page 334.)

Comedy

Badlands

Life on the lam.

Check this one out if only to see Martin Sheen put his name up there with Brando, Presley, and Dean as a modern icon: the Disaffected Young Man Not to Be Trifled With. (Truth be told, Sheen's entire memorable performance is an homage to James Dean.) The film is a study of a ruthless series of real-life 1950s killings; Sheen picks up a young teenage girl (Sissy Spacek) and sets off on a cold, remorseless path of murder and destruction. Sounds fun, huh? The amoral approach the two bring to the business at hand only mirrors the moral emptiness of the society in which they live.

OK, it sounds grisly and pointless, but Sheen does something remarkable in this film; he brings a strange, otherworldy poise to the inhuman acts he undertakes, and you can't stop watching him even if you want to. As for Spacek, remember the uncanny age range she showed off in *Coal Miner's Daughter*? She does the youngest end of it for the whole movie here, and it's pretty darn cool.

Not for the faint of heart, perhaps, but well worth watching if you're willing to put up with a few rough spots.

★ 1973, 95 minutes, color, PG.

★ With: Martin Sheen, Sissy Spacek, Warren Oates. Director: Terrence Malick.

★ *During the filming for what Francis Ford Coppola film did Sheen nearly kick the bucket?* (Answer on page 263.)

"You want to go for a ride?"
—Martin Sheen's big line to Sissy Spacek. Talk about an offer you can't refuse. . . .

For a great double feature, rent it with
The Sugarland Express.

Seen it but in the mood for something similar? Try
Bonnie and Clyde.

Answer to page 239 trivia question:
Rosemary Clooney.

Drama

Bagdad Cafe

Jack Palance
as the romantic lead?

"I like that word . . . vision."
—Marianne Sägebrecht starts seeing life in a new light.

For a great double feature, rent it with

Stranger than Paradise.

Seen it but in the mood for something similar? Try

Rosencrantz and Guildenstern Are Dead.

Answer to page 277 trivia question:

Twins and *Junior.*

What happens when a large German woman leaves her husband in the middle of the American desert? That's what the vacationing Marianne Sägebrecht does after an argument with her husband—she just walks out of the car and makes her way on her own to the tiny town of Bagdad, California, where a rundown cafe-motel is being run (barely) by CCH Pounder, who hasn't been in a good mood for a *really* long time. Her family is driving her nuts, her guests are at best odd, and, with the addition of Sägebrecht, who has no ladies' clothes (she grabbed the wrong suitcase), things are about as strange as Pounder wants things to get.

This fanciful tale has some moments of real magic, both literally and figuratively. Jack Palance is great; he seems almost tranquil, given the supremely oddball surroundings in which he's placed. From what we've all seen of Jack over the last few years, we know how much talent that takes to pull off.

★ 1988, 108 minutes, color, PG.

★ With: Marianne Sägebrecht, CCH Pounder, Jack Palance. Director: Percy Adlon.

★ *Name the comedy that reintroduced Palance to a new generation of moviegoers.* (Answer on page 197.)

Comedy

Barbara Stanwyck and
the Eight Dwarfs

Barbara Stanwyck carries away the award for Best Character Name in a Non–James Bond Film in this one. She's known as Shuga Puss O'Shea, and we'll leave it up to you to figure out what nickname she goes by.

Eight monastic professors are completely sheltered from the distractions of modern-day existence within the walls of the Daniel S. Tooten Foundation. One of them, Gary Cooper, is working on an exhaustive dictionary of American slang. When he heads outside the walls of the foundation to do some firsthand field research, he comes across Stanwyck, a showstopping nightclub entertainer. After listening to her speak, Cooper realizes she's a walking, talking—and then some—slang sourcebook in her own right. He gives her his card—and when Stanwyck's connections to her gangster boyfriend land her in hot water, she shows up at the door of the foundation.

This engaging, offbeat parody of *Snow White and the Seven Dwarfs* asks whether an unlikely pair—fuddy-duddy Cooper and white-hot Stanwyck, can find true love. They can, and as if that weren't enough, Gene Krupa plays a drum solo on a box of matches. That's entertainment!

★ 1941, 111 minutes, B&W, not rated.

★ With: Barbara Stanwyck, Gary Cooper, Dana Andrews. Director: Howard Hawks.

★ *When the gangster wets his gunsight, claiming to have seen the maneuver in a movie once, to what film is he referring?* (Answer on page 357.)

"She's root, zoot, cute, and solid to boot."
—The busboy's description of Shuga's attributes

For a great double feature, rent it with *Meet John Doe.*

Seen it but in the mood for something similar? Try *The Lady Eve.*

Answer to page 147 trivia question: *The Lion King.*

Comedy

Ready for the show?

Robert De Niro made his first major splash in this film. The future Oscar winner plays a less-than-brilliant catcher for the big-league New York Mammoths who learns that he has a terminal disease and is, in all likelihood, playing his last season. Although it's easy to get sidetracked watching De Niro because (a) he's really, really good and (b) his first important screen role carries tantalizing hints of the accomplishments to come, the main attraction of the film is still Michael Moriarty. He plays the star pitcher whose outlook on life changes as a result of his decision to serve as De Niro's protector and confidant. When he puts the interests of the longtime benchwarmer ahead of his own, something changes for both of them: De Niro's game improves, and Moriarty begins to see outside himself. Its locker rooms, dugouts, and pennant races are only backdrops; *Bang the Drum Slowly* is really the story of Moriarty's progression from a big-time hotshot to a caring human being who figures out that the real game has to do with finding meaning in the face of mortality—and that its duration is short indeed.

★ 1973, 97 minutes, color, PG.

★ With: Michael Moriarty, Robert De Niro, Vincent Gardenia. Director: John Hancock.

★ *Can you name the Emmy-winning World War II miniseries in which Michael Moriarty costarred with Meryl Streep?* (Answer on page 143.)

The Bank Dick

*Pass the remote and the martini shaker, my dear.
I feel the need to move things into slow-motion for a spell.*

The credits for this, the greatest of W. C. Fields's feature-length comedies, list the screenwriter as one Mahatma Kane Jeeves. Sounds a little suspicious, doesn't it? OK, you guessed it: Jeeves is none other than Fields himself, and his, shall we say, *eccentric* story spins together enough in the way of improbable, side-of-the-mouth shenanigans to keep this effort rolling along with unceasing, side-splitting insouciance. And if that's not a line worthy of Fields, I don't know what is.

The red-nosed one plays a bystander who stops a bank robbery without meaning to, then makes a fateful career move by becoming a bank guard. At this point things get pretty silly, which is, I trust, exactly what you were hoping for. During the course of the movie Fields tees off on nagging relatives, movie studio idiocy, and, yes, even the incivilities of beefsteak mining. The great comedian's legendary misanthropic streak never found better comic expression than in this picture. Thank you, Mr. Jeeves, wherever you are.

★ 1940, 73 minutes, B&W, not rated.

★ With: W. C. Fields, Cora Witherspoon, Una Merkel. Director: Eddie Cline.

★ *What disease did Fields suddenly come down with when he realized, during his vaudeville days, that he had been scheduled on the same bill with the Marx Brothers?* (Answer on page 269.)

"I shall repair to the bosom of my family— a dismal place, I must admit."
—Fields assumes his customary role of understanding family man.

For a great double feature, rent it with
Brain Donors.

Seen it but in the mood for something similar? Try
Never Give a Sucker an Even Break.

Answer to page 218 trivia question:
Shakira Caine (she is Michael Caine's wife).

Comedy

Barbarians at the Gate

That town ain't big enough for the two of them.

As a boy, he could outsell any paper boy in the neighborhood. As a teenager he could sell baby pictures to the parents of the ugliest children in town. Wait till you see what he does with the Nabisco corporation as an adult.

This docucomedy about one of the most notorious takeovers of the eighties is told with wry humor and plenty of delicious withering sarcasm; the script comes courtesy of inspired "M*A*S*H" writer Larry Gelbart, and you can tell. The lines are nearly all beauties; everyone talks on cellular phones, even when the other party is in the car in the next lane. If the wheeler-dealers aren't exercising on their home gyms or having their money ironed by the maid, they're schmoozing it up at a costume ball where the players, heedless of the irony, dress as Marie Antoinette and Superman.

Yes, these folks see the occasional homeless person, but not for long enough to bother anyone. As James Garner's character puts it, "I am not worried about being homeless . . . or planeless either, for that matter." Garner is superb.

★ 1993, 120 minutes, color, R.

★ With: James Garner, Jonathan Pryce, and Joanna Cassidy. Director: Glenn Jordan.

★ *What actress is most famous for not being married to James Garner?* (Answer on page 218.)

I love you.
I want a divorce.

Let's face it, Jane Fonda and Robert Redford are the two most attractive Caucasians ever to be put in a film together. But don't hate them because they're beautiful. These are two stars who are young and fresh-faced enough to get away with anything; fortunately, what they try to get away with are some of Neil Simon's funniest lines, so there's no problem mowing down any audiences that may be in the vicinity. This is a sweet, funny film about a charmingly naive outlook on love and life that doesn't quite work in the real world these two inhabit. (Did it ever?)

The two newlyweds spend their first days getting to know each other on a full-time basis. You see, they didn't live together first. No, really, people used to do that; they actually got married, *then* had sex and tried to figure out what it was going to be like to live with their partner for a lifetime. Surprise! Redford learns that Fonda is a flibbertigibbet; Fonda discovers that Redford is too uptight.

Maybe their upstairs neighbor, Charles Boyer, can help them out. And just maybe Boyer and Fonda's mother can find true love themselves. But hey, they've got an advantage. They've had sex before. Not with each other, though.

★ 1967, 105 minutes, color, not rated.

★ With: Jane Fonda, Robert Redford, Charles Boyer. Director: Gene Saks.

★ *What landmark 1960s role did Robert Redford lose to Dustin Hoffman?* (Answer on page 205.)

"I am not getting sarcastic. I'm getting chapped lips."
—No matter how warm Jane Fonda is willing to keep Robert Redford, the snow is beginning to pile up in the living room.

For a great double feature, rent it with
He Said, She Said.

Seen it but in the mood for something similar? Try
Fun with Dick and Jane.

Answer to page 286 trivia question:
The Clan of the Cave Bear.

Comedy

Or would you rather have what's in the box?

**For a great double
feature, rent it with**

Golden Boy.

**Seen it but in the mood
for something similar?
Try**

The Player.

**Answer to page 321
trivia question:**

The Cough Drop
Queen.

John Turturro and John Goodman each turn in a spell-binding performance in this Joel and Ethan Coen paranoia fest. Turturro is a 1940s playwright whose work celebrating the common man is the toast of Broadway; when he gets an offer to work in Hollywood, he heads west—and promptly encounters the most horrific case of writer's block known to man.

The picture is visually adventurous in the extreme, and the script zooms from point to point with almost unimaginable speed; this is a video that you'll probably enjoy watching twice, because the first time is a little like standing in front of a fire hose. Enjoy yourself; lean in. You have to hand it to a pair of filmmakers who can take something as passive as a writer's inability to come up with an idea and build a race car of a movie around it.

The less said about the specifics of John Goodman's role, the better; let's just say he has a lot to offer to Turturro's research. By the way, the entire picture is a thinly veiled parody of the ornate hell that awaited the playwright Clifford Odets upon the sale of his soul to Hollywood.

★ 1991, 117 minutes, color, R.

★ With: John Turturro, John Goodman, Judy Davis. Director: Joel Coen.

★ *In what film did Turturro try his hand at Groucho?* (Answer on page 348.)

Beau Geste (1939)

The first—and best—remake of Beau Geste.

From a stark fortress in the middle of a vast desert, dead men stare from every parapet, guns clasped in their still, cold hands. A lone gunman fires. One man is left to fight off an Arab horde—impossible odds. Or . . . so it would seem.

Flashback to 15 years earlier: Three plucky young brothers, full of mischief and brotherly loyalty, play at war games. Their family is rich, but not as wealthy as it would have been if it weren't for the black sheep of an uncle who seems intent on gambling away the family fortune. Only one great treasure remains: the Blue Water, a massive paperweight of a sapphire. It bears a dire curse that everyone in the family shrugs off without a thought.

Bad move. The boys grow up, and the jewel is stolen; each brother, in succession, runs off to join the French Foreign Legion, claiming that it was he who stole the gem. Who, if anyone, is telling the truth?

If you've followed this so far, congratulations. Trust me. It all pays off spectacularly.

★ 1939, 114 minutes, B&W, not rated.

★ With: Gary Cooper, Ray Milland, Robert Preston. Director: William Wellman.

★ *Who plays the young Michael?* (Answer on page 273.)

"Where would you go if you wanted to disappear completely—and still have some excitement?"
—When one brother mysteriously disappears, can adventure be far behind?

For a great double feature, rent it with *Gunga Din.*

Seen it but in the mood for something similar? Try *The Four Feathers.*

Answer to page 342 trivia question:
He carried her diamond earrings in a locket around his neck for the rest of his life.

Casting coup of the sixties:
Raquel Welch as Lust.

**For a great double
feature, rent it with**

*The Secret Policeman's
Other Ball.*

**Seen it but in the mood
for something similar?
Try**

The Magic Christian.

**Answer to page 306
trivia question:**

The Exorcist.

Don't think of it as a conventional plot-first comedy; think of it as a rare chance to see the legendary comic team of Peter Cook and Dudley Moore in a series of unforgettable vignettes. Their strength was always sketch material anyway, and this movie has the good sense to move on when a gag has pretty much played itself out. (Well, *most* of the time it has the good sense to move on, but the same can be said for the Python movies, right?) Cook plays the devil, Moore an unkempt cook; the guy from down below is—you guessed it—after an average Joe's soul, and he's got a bounty of seven wishes to bestow in hopes that they'll help him snare the cook.

This picture provides a good opportunity to see this hugely influential comic duo in action at the peak of their career, before professional and personal rifts intervened—and before Moore reaped the solo Hollywood windfall that struck many of the original act's devoted fans as just a little bit surreal.

Cook is worth watching particularly closely here: his timing is, dare I say it, supernaturally good, and he's cast in a role that he was clearly born to play. I'm not sure exactly what it *says* about him, but he seems to have had one hell of a time as Lucifer.

★ 1967, 107 minutes, color, not rated.

★ With: Peter Cook, Dudley Moore, Raquel Welch. Director: Stanley Donen.

★ *What parody of thirties Hollywood moviemaking did Donen direct?* (Answer on page 223.)

Being There

*Life is like a box of chocolates . . .
no, wait, wrong movie.*

Let's say you're one of the folks who liked *Forrest Gump* well enough but thought it was a little, well, light. You're in for a treat if you haven't yet seen Hal Ashby's superb 1979 film adaptation of Jerzy Kosinski's novel. This film lets comic Zen master Peter Sellers use the same basic idea behind the Hanks picture to put on a seminar in perfect timing; his work in this film ranks with some of the very best work of Chaplin or Buster Keaton, and he does it all without ever cracking a smile . . . or any other facial expression, for that matter.

Sellers plays a vacant shell of a man who's spent his entire life cooped up in a small apartment with only a television for companionship; there's nobody, but nobody, home upstairs, so people tend to see themselves when they run into him. Naturally the Nowhere Man makes his way to the highest levels of the federal government. (You could see *that* coming a mile away, couldn't you?)

This is Sellers's finest screen performance, which is saying something. Do not miss this movie under any circumstances.

★ 1979, 130 minutes, color, PG.

★ With: Peter Sellers, Shirley MacLaine, Melvyn Douglas, Jack Warden. Director: Hal Ashby.

★ *When Sellers and MacLaine finally kiss, what movie is playing on TV in the background, serving as a prompt for their every move?* (Answer on page 201.)

"I like to watch."
—Once again, Peter Sellers finds himself misunderstood.

For a great double feature, rent it with
Dr. Strangelove.

Seen it but in the mood for something similar? Try
Dave.

Answer to page 153 trivia question:
The Clash; the album was *London Calling.*

Comedy

The Big Easy

Stop what? That?

"I never did have much luck with sex."
"Your luck's about to change."

—Dennis Quaid thinks a lot of himself, huh? And she buys it, too.

For a great double feature, rent it with

The Drowning Pool.

Seen it but in the mood for something similar? Try

D.O.A. (1950).

Answer to page 361 trivia question:

The Whales of August.

Dennis Quaid plays a handsome rogue of a cop who has followed in the shoes of his father and his father before him; they've all received free meals here, a free parking spot there, and quite a few dollars donated to the local policemen's Widows and Orphans Fund (uh-huh). Enter Ellen Barkin, a district attorney who believes in pursuing the letter of the law. She's far too uptight for her own good, but then Quaid is far too loose.

If you guessed that these two will meet somewhere in the middle, you're right. Quaid's broad, wicked grin meets its match in Barkin's erotically twisted smile; you know, the one that looks like there's something she'd really *like* to control but can't? The surprise in *The Big Easy* is that after these two succumb to the passion that positively crackles between them, the story doesn't slow down. It picks up. Together they may just clean up the force and figure out who's trying to kill them. Along the way Barkin may learn to have a little more fun. OK, she has a lot more fun. And good for her.

★ 1987, 108 minutes, color, R.

★ With: Dennis Quaid, Ellen Barkin, John Goodman. Director: Jim McBride.

★ *In what film did Ellen Barkin play Penny Pretty?*
(Answer on page 96.)

A Big Hand for the Little Lady

Who says women and poker don't mix?

What happens when the biggest, brassiest, cigar-chompingest, once-a-year poker game this side of the Mississippi runs into a little roadblock? That's what the beefy frontiersmen in this picture find themselves asking when compulsive gambler Henry Fonda is carted off to the hospital after suffering what appears to be a serious heart attack.

The game continues, with Fonda's wife (Joanne Woodward) sitting in with her husband's "inherited" hand. She's a novice when it comes to poker; she says she'd rather take the money—their life savings—and head home, but that's not an option. The question then becomes: Exactly how good is Woodward's hand?

The strong cast makes all the difference in this exercise in the proper deployment of cinematic charm: Henry Fonda is great in the relatively small role he's given; Burgess Meredith, as the doctor, squawks and grumbles with more than his usual agreeability. A slick, well-told story with a nifty twist or two up its sleeve, this engaging comedy transcends its predictable layer of 1960s sexism and offers Woodward the chance to showcase her comedic talents, which are considerable.

★ 1966, 95 minutes, color, not rated.

★ With: Henry Fonda, Joanne Woodward, Jason Robards, Jr. Director: Fielder Cook.

★ *In what film did Woodward first appear with Paul Newman?* (Answer on page 59.)

"All right—how do you play this game?"
—Just the sort of question Joanne Woodward's new companions were afraid might be coming up.

For a great double feature, rent it with
Cat Ballou.

Seen it but in the mood for something similar? Try
Maverick.

Answer to page 294 trivia question:
Himself.

World War II,
one man at a time.

*"That's a monument
from the last war."
"But the names are
the same?" "They
always are."*

—Same as it ever was for Lee
Marvin's men

**For a great double
feature, rent it with**

*They Were
Expendable.*

**Seen it but in the mood
for something similar?
Try**

Battle Cry.

**Answer to page 329
trivia question:**

Montgomery Clift.

This World War II picture is the polar opposite of something like *A Bridge Too Far;* it tells its story not on an epic scale but from the foot soldier's point of view. We follow a small band of men as they go from one dangerous situation to the next. They face small battles and win small victories; they're never able to forget that another battle lies waiting for them at the next foxhole and that the grim process will probably repeat itself until the war ends or the men themselves are driven to exhaustion, death, or both.

The film is based on the personal experiences of director Samuel Fuller; Robert Carradine plays Fuller's screen alter ego, Zab. Mark Hamill turns in the kind of performance that would, if this were a just world, make people forget the whole *Star Wars* thing; Lee Marvin, as the sergeant who must lead the rookies into battle, turns in one of the greatest performances of his career.

We don't see the now-stereotypical chorus lines of tanks churning their way across enemy turf; we don't, for that matter, see much evidence at all of the rest of the war that is going on around our heroes. But the guys in the platoon are so interesting that you never mind that you're seeing only the tiniest sliver of the war. After all, that's all *they* have to look at.

★ 1980, 113 minutes, color, PG.

★ With: Lee Marvin, Mark Hamill, Robert Carradine. Director: Samuel Fuller.

★ *For what performance did Lee Marvin win an Oscar?*
(Answer on page 90.)

Bill & Ted's Bogus Journey

No, really, I'm quite serious about this one.

The plot line for this surprisingly strong sequel is nothing particularly unusual. You know the classic story line: oblivious teenage space cadets die at the hands of their respective evil twins, meet Death, beat him at Battleship, journey to heaven, return to life, and save the planet. This is a film that would collapse in an instant if the script, the director, or the actors gave the merest hint of even *thinking* about taking anything seriously. Fortunately, no one does. Think in terms of a top-notch Warner Brothers cartoon script—one of the really wild ones, where the characters make fun of the fact that they're stuck in a cartoon—and you'll have a hint of why this movie works, despite giving every indication of being, well, insipid. Which, actually, it kind of is, but it doesn't pretend *not* to be. So it's, like, insipid in a most funny way, dude.

★ 1991, 98 minutes, color, PG.

★ With: Keanu Reeves, Alex Winter, George Carlin. Director: Peter Hewitt.

★ *What was the working title of this movie?*
(Answer on page 118.)

"Be excellent to each other."
—Could it be so simple? Sure.

For a great double feature, rent it with
The Seventh Seal (no kidding).

Seen it but in the mood for something similar? Try
Bill & Ted's Excellent Adventure.

Answer to page 350 trivia question:
The left.

Comedy

Billy Budd

The Love Boat it ain't.

"Good-bye to you all . . . good-bye to you too, old Rights of Man."

—Could this line be intended metaphorically?

For a great double feature, rent it with

The Sand Pebbles.

Seen it, but in the mood for something similar? Try

Mutiny on the Bounty (1962).

Answer to page 174 trivia question:

The Lost Weekend (1945).

This is the tale of a young innocent pressed into service on the British warship *Avenger*. Try as he might, handsome Billy Budd cannot avoid coming under the sway of the evil Mr. Claggart, master-at-arms. Why is Claggart determined to destroy Budd? The answer is revealed in an intricate tale with many themes: the ongoing struggle of good against evil; the difficulty of balancing the rights of the individual with those of the society in which he lives; and, last but certainly not least, the whole repressed sexuality thing. I could go on all day here. But I won't.

Ustinov not only directed the fine cast, he adapted the script and (perhaps unwisely) cast himself as the captain, a role for which he was not particularly well suited. Terence Stamp, in his film debut, does a nice job of getting Budd's angelic character across without a trace of narcissism.

★ 1962, 119 minutes, B&W, not rated.

★ With: Terence Stamp, Peter Ustinov, Robert Ryan. Director: Peter Ustinov.

★ *In what film did Terence Stamp play an aging transvestite?* (Answer on page 186.)

Bird

If you have to ask, you'll never know.

Clint Eastwood has always been a devoted jazz buff. This finely crafted film is proof that he's no casual fan and that he has an abiding respect for the genius of Charlie Parker. Parker, also known as Bird, was a postwar musical giant whose life ended at thirty-five but whose legacy continues to this day.

Bird does not portray Parker as a saint (which would be difficult, given the circumstances of his life). What it does do is give us a glimpse into the world of a mind perceptive and daring enough to have created bebop—and a soul big enough to feel pain more keenly than most of us will ever feel it. Parker emerges as a modern tragic hero, epic in his virtues and his flaws.

The story is framed by the last few days of Bird's life and uses a series of flashbacks and nearly instantaneous repeated images to move the film forward. It's a technique that risks calling too much attention to itself, but it works: we see who Parker was, what haunted him, and how he changed the world of music.

Forest Whitaker convinces us that Parker, for all his excesses, was in the end forgivable. The supporting cast is outstanding. Bud Powell, Dizzy Gillespie, and Parker's wife, Chan, all contributed to the film, and it shows.

★ 1988, 140 minutes, color, R.

★ With: Forest Whitaker, Diane Venora, Samuel E. Wright. Director: Clint Eastwood.

★ *What actor was originally slated to star as Charlie Parker?* (Answer on page 211.)

"Charlie Parker? I knew him when he couldn't play 'Come Home to Jesus' in whole notes."

—An older musician delivering the ultimate jazzer's insult when reminiscing about a young Charlie Parker

For a great double feature, rent it with
Paris Blues.

Seen it but in the mood for something similar? Try
Round Midnight.

Answer to page 209 trivia question:
Charlie Chaplin.

*You won't find this one
hard to swallow.*

*"I shall convert a
missionary."*

—Nils Asther stakes out his
position with regard to
Barbara Stanwyck.

**For a great double
feature, rent it with**

Ball of Fire.

**Seen it but in the mood
for something similar?
Try**

*The Enchanted
Cottage.*

**Answer to page 245
trivia question:**

Prick Up Your Ears.

The rich, exotic look of this Frank Capra movie is as much the star as the actors themselves. A missionary (Barbara Stanwyck? *OK . . .*) finds herself drawn to a Chinese warlord, here played by Nils Asther, who's Swedish (*OK . . .*). Confused? Don't worry. Both actors are surprisingly convincing in their unlikely roles, and Asther is downright hypnotic. Stanwyck, never one to fade into the woodwork, is positively dazzling once she's decked out in her Chinese gown to please Asther, who promptly kidnaps her. Political correctness alert: he then shows her the meaning of love, forgiveness, and sacrifice. Sure, it's melodramatic and sentimental, but heck, it's Capra. We wouldn't want it any other way, right?

It's hard to say exactly why this bombed so spectacularly upon its initial release; maybe the audiences had a problem with the interracial romance. How do you suppose *Jungle Fever* would have gone over during the Depression?

★ 1933, 89 minutes, B&W, not rated.

★ With: Barbara Stanwyck, Nils Asther, Gavin Gordon. Director: Frank Capra.

★ *What famous New York theater did this movie open?*
(Answer on page 250.)

Romance

Black Adder III, Parts One and Two

The butler steals the show—and everything else he can get his hands on.

Here's an interesting solution to the perennial problem of how to keep a situation comedy from becoming stale after a season or two. The gifted British comedian Rowan Atkinson decided to set each season of his "Black Adder" series in a different historical period. One batch of episodes, for instance, is set in the Elizabethan period, and another takes place during World War I, but Atkinson plays a character named Edmund Blackadder throughout.

In *Black Adder III*, arguably the best outing, Atkinson plays a snide, scheming manservant to Hugh Laurie, the impossibly dim-witted prince of Wales. The standout episode in the collection is probably "Amy and Amiability" in which Miranda Richardson plays a wealthy merchant's daughter with a vocal range that corresponds roughly to the fingernails-on-the-chalkboard sequence in *Jaws*. A fast-paced, delightfully improbable farce with a kick, Atkinson's landmark series suggests an encounter between the Monty Python troupe and a tenured professor in English history—on acid.

★ 1989, approximately 90 minutes each, color, not rated.

★ With: Rowan Atkinson, Hugh Laurie, Miranda Richardson. Director: Mandie Fletcher.

★ *In what movie did Rowan Atkinson portray the unforgettable Nigel Smallfaucets?* (Answer on page 278.)

"She is famous for having the worst personality in Germany—and, as you can imagine, that's up against some pretty stiff competition."
—Ever diplomatic, Rowan Atkinson assesses the merits of a potential royal companion.

For a great double feature, rent it with
Start the Revolution Without Me.

Seen it but in the mood for something similar? Try
Black Adder IV.

Answer to page 283 trivia question:
Goodbye, Mr. Chips.

Comedy

41

Black Like Me

Some of my best friends are . . .
wait a minute. . . .

"I sure appreciate you putting me wise."
—A "black" James Whitmore, relying on the kindness of strangers

For a great double feature, rent it with
Do the Right Thing.

Seen it but in the mood for something similar? Try
Map of the Human Heart.

Answer to page 157 trivia question:
A Face in the Crowd.

You want to talk about acting range? Enter James Whitmore. This is the true story of a white journalist who had his skin treated chemically and wrote of his experiences as a black man in a white-dominated society. The premise may not be quite as explosive as it was when *Black Like Me* was released in 1964, but this movie's observations are every bit as pertinent to today's racially divided world as they were to the period in which the film is set. At a time when most media ducked difficult racial themes, *Black Like Me* tackled them head-on. It's a well-crafted examination of the fundamental ugliness of racism, and it's still tremendously affecting. A sobering watch but not preachy; expertly done from beginning to end. Whitmore is, as usual, terrific.

★ 1964, 107 minutes, B&W, not rated.

★ With: James Whitmore, Roscoe Lee Brown. Director: Carl Lerner.

★ *Whose book inspired the film?* (Answer on page 327.)

Blow Out

Things are seldom what they seem.

Man, sometimes I think I'd rather be *anything* than an innocent bystander in a suspense film. John Travolta plays a cinema sound-effects technician who rescues a young woman (Nancy Allen) from a car crash. He has taped the accident without meaning to; when he plays the tape back, he realizes he may be holding on to evidence of a murder. Travolta and Allen are terrific in this powerful, well-assembled Brian DePalma thriller. The director is, as usual, paying tribute to Alfred Hitchcock in nearly every scene—this time, though, he's also paying tribute to Michelangelo Antonioni's 1966 picture *Blow-Up*, which features a similar plot. *Blow Out* offers strong characters, a solid, turn-hugging script, and lots of spooky political intrigues to get paranoid over. A great ride, but it's not for the kids.

★ 1981, 107 minutes, color, R.

★ With: John Travolta, Nancy Allen, John Lithgow. Director: Brian DePalma.

★ *Who plays the female lead in Antonioni's* Blow-Up, *which inspired this film?* (Answer on page 338.)

"It's a good scream."
—Actually, it may be a little *too* good. Just ask John Travolta.

For a great double feature, rent it with
Body Double.

Seen it but in the mood for something similar? Try
The Conversation.

Answer to page 192 trivia question:
Jeremy Irons, in 1988's *Dead Ringers.*

Suspense

Blue Chips

It shoots, it scores!

From a distance, it looks like another forgettable product of some uninspired Tinseltown conference call. "OK, *Hoosiers* was a big hit; Shaquille O'Neal is an NBA superstar and all-purpose marketing juggernaut; let's toss Nick Nolte in as the coach of a college team, put O'Neal in a supporting role as a player, and get a couple of big-time basketball faces to show up for cameos. Maybe we'll end up with a crossover hit." It all looks just a little contrived on the box cover, but surprise, surprise: *Blue Chips* checks in as a winner.

Nolte is the coach who loves basketball for its own sake and is content to take care of the on-court business without bothering himself with too much of the financial stuff. He's as surprised as anyone to learn that he does in fact have a conscience. After the big game Nolte delivers himself of a postgame press conference that shows he's capable of personal growth—and puts the movie squarely in the "who'd have thunk it?" category. (And, yes, in case you were wondering, O'Neal is up to the acting demands of his modest role.)

Blue Chips shows us a guy who realizes he has to add a moral component to a life that had never much bothered with questions of right and wrong; when a story like that is told well, as it is here, it deserves to be recognized.

★ 1994, 101 minutes, color, PG-13.

★ With: Nick Nolte, Mary MacDonnell, Shaquille O'Neal. Director: William Friedkin.

★ *What 1973 picture directed by William Friedkin really turned some heads?* (Answer on page 221.)

Blue Collar

A side of Richard Pryor you may never have seen before.

The barely veiled Marxism in Paul Schrader's study of three struggling Detroit autoworkers may or may not get your dander up, but there's no denying this underrated film's emotional impact. Harvey Keitel and Yaphet Kotto turn in top-notch performances, which is exactly what you'd expect from these two fine actors, but you may be a little bewildered at first to find Richard Pryor holding court in a gritty, realistic study of honor and betrayal among working men. Pryor is remarkably good, and he resorts to schtick only once or twice; for the most part his is a solid, carefully crafted piece of acting that will make you wish the great comedian had chosen to make a few more serious dramas over the course of his career.

The picture is an intense portrait of workers facing exploitation and abuse of power; it's got a distinct point of view when it comes to the inherently oppressive and exploitative nature of the capitalists who inhabit its little world. Although the picture's perspective in this regard is a minority one in this society, it's one Schrader never apologizes for; thankfully, *Blue Collar* has the good sense not to shortchange character development in favor of its social message.

★ 1978, 114 minutes, color, R.

★ With: Yaphet Kotto, Richard Pryor, Harvey Keitel. Director: Paul Schrader.

★ *What 1970s media sensation was the subject of a 1988 film from the director of* Blue Collar? (Answer on page 255.)

"The black against the white . . ."
—Richard Pryor, Harvey Keitel, and Yaphet Kotto face forces that will sow division.

For a great double feature, rent it with *El Norte.*

Seen it but in the mood for something similar? Try *The Grapes of Wrath.*

Answer to page 266 trivia question: Bob Hoskins.

Drama

The Blue Kite

Banned in Beijing.

"Uncle, why can't a goldfish blink?"
—A question with an answer not to be found in that little red book

For a great double feature, rent it with

Hope and Glory.

Seen it but in the mood for something similar? Try

Farewell, My Concubine.

Answer to page 140 trivia questin:

Blood and Swash.

The *New York Observer*'s Andrew Sarris called this film "the most amazing act of political courage and defiance I have ever seen in the cinema." And he's right. The subject is life in China before and during the Cultural Revolution; through the eyes of a young boy, Tietou, we follow a "middle-class" family in a supposedly classless society. They're *trying* to be good Communists; the problem is, the rules keep changing. Tietou's mother is a teacher and his father a librarian; these, as it turns out, are dangerous jobs indeed to hold in China at this point in the country's history.

The subplot involves the boy's uncle, a pilot who is slowly going blind, and the young actress with whom he falls in love. The darker demands of the party—all the more ominous because they are only implied—serve to doom the emerging love affair. A poignant, unforgettable film, it is every bit as memorable as Sarris suggests. Don't miss it.

★ 1993, 138 minutes, color, not rated.

★ With: Yi Tian, Zhang Wenyao, Chen Xiaoman. Director: Tian Zhuangzhuang.

★ *What rock band took its name from the group of accused Cultural Revolution conspirators that included Chairman Mao's wife?* (Answer on page 215.)

Body Double

Ever wonder what a Hitchcock movie would look like if the director could have gotten away with anything he wanted to?

This slick, finely crafted Brian DePalma film is easily one of the most disgusting movies I've ever enjoyed. It's gratuitously violent, it flaunts a graphic, in-your-face sexuality pretty much from beginning to end, and it pushes the "hard R" rating just about as hard as you'll want to see it pushed. But the weird thing is, you can't stop watching it. Set in L.A., the film lovingly embraces that city's two most famous exports: hedonism and the movies.

Craig Wasson falls in love with a woman he's been spying on with a telescope. He witnesses an awful murder (look away), and the delightful, scantily clad Melanie Griffith appears to hold the answers to the mystery. She's a hoot as the punked-out porn queen who is as naive as she is raunchy. Nice trick if you can pull it off, and she does. DePalma borrows freely from *Vertigo* and *Rear Window,* but he puts his own stamp on the often disturbing material with his obvious love of, and talent for, handling color and energy.

If you're in the mood for edge-of-your-seat excitement, lots of sex, and truckloads of intricately choreographed violence, you should check this one out. Those with low tolerances for directors who go ballistic are advised to check with the analyst first, though.

★ 1984, 109 minutes, color, R.

★ With: Craig Wasson, Melanie Griffith, Gregg Henry. Director: Brian DePalma.

★ *Who is Melanie Griffith's mother?* (Answer on page 190.)

"I get $2,000. I do not do animal acts. I do not do S&M or any variations of that bent."
—Griffith lays down the rules.

For a great double feature, rent it with
Rear Window.

Seen it but in the mood for something similar? Try
Dressed to Kill.

Answer to page 178 trivia question:
Hamlet; great swordfights, huh?

Suspense

The most brilliant dim bulb of them all.

"I'd like to learn how to talk good."

—Judy Holliday, who's about to learn that a little knowledge is a dangerous thing

For a great double feature, rent it with

The Seven Year Itch.

Seen it but in the mood for something similar? Try

Educating Rita.

Answer to page 213 trivia question:

The Blob.

The breezy, polished finish on Judy Holliday's Oscar-winning comic turn in *Born Yesterday* didn't just happen by accident. For the three years before she began work on the film, Holliday had been playing the role of Billie Dawn on Broadway. So she had a head start. Dawn is a kept woman who matches wits, kind of, with her corrupt, powerful millionaire lover (Broderick Crawford). William Holden plays the handsome tutor Crawford hires to bring his occasionally slow mistress a touch of class.

Although Holliday's work here launched a thousand dumb-blond stereotypes, the movie is not a one-note symphony by any stretch of the imagination. Holliday's Billie Dawn is a woman who learns, grows, and matures before our eyes. (Yes, you guessed it: she dumps Crawford for Holden. It's a tougher call than it looks.) Holliday, who learns some hard-won lessons about the consequences of taking the easy way out, delivers a sparkling, unforgettable performance. And she plays a mean, if occasionally irritating, game of gin rummy. Garson Kanin wrote the supple, funny, and insightful script.

★ 1950, 103 minutes, B&W, not rated.

★ With: Judy Holliday, Broderick Crawford, William Holden. Director: George Cukor.

★ *Who starred in the 1993 remake?* (Answer on page 122.)

Comedy

Bound for Glory

Riding the rails.

Although these days he seems to be condemned to relive his work on the 1970s television series "Kung Fu," David Carradine can't really complain that he never got the chance to showcase his uniquely understated acting style on the big screen. At least this time he doesn't have to pretend to be Asian. Carradine gives the performance of a lifetime as the legendary folk singer Woody Guthrie in this perfectly executed adaptation of Guthrie's autobiography. Director Hal Ashby uses Carradine's laconic, inscrutable wanderer as the departure point for a series of thoughtful portraits of Depression-era America.

The picture seems to know full well how much it owes to John Ford's superb direction in *The Grapes of Wrath*; it's comfortable enough to admit the debt, and it assumes you won't have any problem with it, either. You won't. There's not much of a plot here, only a series of marginally connected incidents drawn from Guthrie's period of hard traveling, but the picture has been assembled with such love, and with such superior craft, that it all hangs together quite nicely. Let's give Carradine some credit for handling all the singing duties himself—and with enough feeling to carry the day.

★ 1976, 147 minutes, color, PG.

★ With: David Carradine, Ronny Cox, Melinda Dillon, Randy Quaid. Director: Hal Ashby.

★ *What action with regard to Woody Guthrie did Robert Kennedy promise to take if he were elected president?* (Answer on page 93.)

"I hate a song that makes you think you're just born to lose, bound to lose, no good to nobody, no good for nothing."
—David Carradine holding forth on the power of positive thinking

For a great double feature, rent it with *Alice's Restaurant.*

Seen it but in the mood for something similar? Try *The Grapes of Wrath.*

Answer to page 248 trivia question: *Drugstore Cowboy.*

Drama

Brain Donors

Make a new Marx Brothers movie?
Now that's the most ridiculous thing I've ever heard.

"You didn't want me to keep seeing her in those cheap hotels, did you? For God's sake, man, she was your wife."

—Shyster lawyer John Turturro's logically unassailable rationale for doubling an alimony obligation

For a great double feature, rent it with
A Night at the Opera.

Seen it but in the mood for something similar? Try
Duck Soup.

Answer to page 148 trivia question:
Rhinestone.

You know that feeling you get after you watch a classic Marx Brothers comedy and you say to yourself, "My God, why can't they make movies as loopy as that nowadays?" Well, they did. Mainstream critics were split on this more-often-than-not-hilarious tribute to the Groucho, Chico, and Harpo school of comic excess. Words like *uneven* and *intermittent* came up a lot, but if you compare it to the originals that inspired it, you realize that it's got quite a bit *less* filler between its 50-megaton routines than the classics of the thirties did.

Brain Donors is familiar in all the places it ought to be familiar and relentlessly original where it needs to be original. All three updated Marxes are marvelous, but John Turturro, as the fast-talking lawyer who bears more than a passing resemblance to Groucho, is worthy of special note here. He's gunning second gear pretty much throughout the picture; you hope he never tries the decaf.

A movie like this one is very special indeed: it resurrects an old act and yet does something sparklingly new with it at the same time. *Brain Donors* is delightful; bless Turturro and company for taking the risky project on in the first place and bless 'wem for delivering the goods.

★ 1992, 80 minutes, color, PG.

★ With: John Turturro, Bob Nelson, Mel Smith. Director: Dennis Dugan.

★ *In what film did Turturro play a New York playwright who finds the transition to Hollywood a little rocky in spots?* (Answer on page 194.)

Comedy

Breathing Lessons

Love is a many-splendored thing . . . sometimes it just gets on your nerves.

Nobody can drive you nuts faster than the person you love the most. James Garner and Joanne Woodward shine in this delightful study of a quirky middle-aged couple whose marriage is strained when they find things falling apart around them; fortunately they have the good sense to forgive each other after their squabbles.

It's hard to imagine better casting for this adaptation of Anne Tyler's Pulitzer Prize–winning novel. The two pros in the lead roles clearly take delight in their well-written characters, and both exhibit their usual consummate skill.

Breathing Lessons is an homage to the work that goes into monogamy; it knows all about the many small efforts that make for a good marriage, and it shows compassion for the titanic challenges that face a bad one.

Tyler's observant story doesn't (or, at any rate, shouldn't) make for a "women's movie"; this parade of family crises and glorious eccentricities is a masterful vindication for members of both sexes. It celebrates the welcome notion that with a little work you can spend thirty satisfying years with the same person and still be your own cantankerous self.

★ 1994, 100 minutes, color, not rated.

★ With: Joanne Woodward, James Garner, Paul Winfield. Director: John Erman.

★ *In what romance did James Garner star with Sally Field?* (Answer on page 259.)

"Life has been like a long weekend. When it's coming up, you think it will go on forever, and then it's gone, and you've done nothing."

—Joanne Woodward gets a poignant observation on the passage of time from an old friend.

For a great double feature, rent it with
Barbarians at the Gate.

Seen it but in the mood for something similar? Try
Adam's Rib.

Answer to page 184 trivia question:
"The Addams Family." He played Uncle Fester.

Comedy

*Talk about a
fly-by-night operation.*

*"You must have faced
a crisis like this at the
Stork Club when the
waiter brought you the
wrong wine."*
—James Cagney, making light
of Bette Davis's complete
inability to "rough it"

**For a great double
feature, rent it with**

Footlight Parade.

**Seen it but in the mood
for something similar?
Try**

*It Happened One
Night.*

**Answer to page 219
trivia question:**

Dirty Harry.

Nothing like a good old-fashioned abduction when it comes to getting out of a financial dilemma, huh? James Cagney owes money that has to be paid back quick, or he's going to lose both his airplane and his small air freight company. Lucky for him, he learns that rich society girl Bette Davis is about to run off to Vegas for a quickie marriage to a big-band leader, a man Davis's father does not approve of. Cagney agrees to kidnap the would-be bride and bring her home to Papa. For a price. He tells Davis's father that he will have to charge him by weight. Davis's weight, that is.

Sure, it's silly, but the banter is clever and fast-paced, and the two stars are at the top of their form. A charming example of how Hollywood studio moviemaking can deliver an hour and a half of gentle, delightful, unapologetic escapism. Nothing wrong with that at the end of a long day, right? Watch for the bop on the head Cagney lays on Davis. It's almost as good as pushing a grapefruit in a dame's face.

★ 1941, 92 minutes, B&W, not rated.

★ With: James Cagney, Bette Davis, Jack Carson. Director: William Keighley.

★ *Name Bette Davis's two Oscar-winning performances as a lead actress.* (Answer on page 331.)

Comedy

Bride of Frankenstein

Oh, sure, you can put her body together from spare parts, but couldn't you have done something with her hair?

You'd think people would have learned something from the last time. This whole building-a-monster thing just doesn't work out. The villagers will put up with only so much before they ask you to leave town. This superb sequel to the 1931 horror classic may not be exactly what Mary Shelley had in mind, but it does have an intriguing, evocative fairy-tale quality that you won't forget. Not that it is, by any stretch of the imagination, to be considered a film for young children, but there is something soft and magical going on here—that is, when people aren't building brides out of dead bodies.

This one is even better than the first Frankenstein flick, and it's certainly less bloody than the remake by Kenneth Branagh, which had its moments but played the nausea card a little too enthusiastically for some viewers' tastes. This version may well be the most mesmerizingly fun to watch of all the "give-my-creature-*life*" entries.

★ 1935, 75 minutes, B&W, not rated.

★ With: Boris Karloff, Elsa Lanchester, Colin Clive.
Director: James Whale.

★ *In what film did Elsa Lanchester play Miss Jessica Marbles?* (Answer on page 345.)

"But this isn't science—it's more like black magic!"
—Colin Clive has his doubts about the whole, er, undertaking. He, unlike everyone else on the set, remembers the last movie.

For a great double feature, rent it with
Frankenstein (1931).

Seen it but in the mood for something similar? Try
Dracula (1931).

Answer to page 255 trivia question:
The King of Comedy.

Bright Eyes

Quintessential Shirley.

"You mean my mother cracked up too?"
—Once again, Shirley finds herself orphaned.

For a great double feature, rent it with
3 Men and a Baby.

Seen it but in the mood for something similar? Try
Curly Top.

Answer to page 162 trivia question:
Sophie's Choice.

The first Shirley Temple film created especially for her, *Bright Eyes* gives us a lovable little tyke who adores flying and spends all her time hanging out at the airport with the pilots. Of course, she's so charming, none of them can think of anything better to do than trade witticisms with a five-year-old girl. (Hey, it was the Depression, OK?)

After Shirley's mother is—sob—killed while rushing across a busy street bearing Shirley's Christmas cake, our little star is left an orphan. And wouldn't you know it—*everyone* wants to adopt her . . . but no one more than the aptly named Loop, her pilot godfather. I won't spoil the ending for you, but rest assured everything works out OK. This is also the one where Shirley sings her first big hit, "On the Good Ship *Lollipop*."

★ 1934, B&W, 83 minutes, not rated.

★ With: Shirley Temple, James Dunn, Jane Withers. Director: David Butler.

★ *What is the good ship* Lollipop, *anyway?* (Answer on page 265.)

Bring Me the Head of Alfredo Garcia

OK.
And then what?

Nothing like a Peckinpah picture to cheer up an evening, eh? But if you're in the mood for gritty realism, taut, action-packed violence, and the occasional exquisitely choreographed blood ballet, there's no one who can sell it like Sam. This is the story of a determined bounty hunter and his unlikely, um, companion. Warren Oates plays a hard-drinking, road-weary loser whose desperation is surpassed only by his greed. Amazingly, Peckinpah somehow coaxes us into sympathizing with this character. We want him to succeed in returning the severed head to the drug lord so he can collect his bounty. What's even weirder, we understand the relationship between Oates and "Al" (the burlap-bound head of the title). The odd pair are both oppressed by the same man; both loved the same woman; both are down on their luck in a big way.

If there's ever been a weirder buddy movie, I'm not sure I want to see it. Isela Vega is hauntingly beautiful as a woman who has been loved too often and by the wrong men. And just when you're wondering for the second or third time what on earth Gig Young and Robert Webber are doing in this picture, Peckinpah convinces you that the casting is perfect. Grab on and hold tight.

★ 1974, 112 minutes, color, R.

★ With: Warren Oates, Isela Vega, Gig Young, Robert Webber. Director: Sam Peckinpah.

★ *Can you name the actor playing the would-be rapist biker?* (Answer on page 353.)

"I've got a chance, a ticket, and we're gonna take it."
—A desperate Oates explains why he's trying to get . . . well . . . ahead.

For a great double feature, rent it with
El Mariachi.

Seen it but in the mood for something similar? Try
Badlands.

Answer to page 197 trivia question:
Riff Raff.

Drama

Buck Privates

Three words:
Patti, Maxine, Laverne.

"We're lucky fellas, Mr. Smith."
—The Andrews Sisters convince you that being drafted is actually a heck of a lot of fun.

For a great double feature, rent it with
Private Benjamin.

Seen it but in the mood for something similar? Try
Stage Door Canteen.

Answer to page 233 trivia question:
It was the only Oscar ever awarded to a film that had not been nominated in its category; academy members wrote in enough votes to secure the statue for cinematographer Hal Mohr.

And let's not forget Bud and Lou! This rollicking, pre–Pearl Harbor piece of forties pro-draft propaganda was the first film created especially to showcase the ample comedic talents of Bud Abbott and Lou Costello. It's a gleaming, innocent, and frequently hilarious piece of work that was a massive hit at the box office.

The picture moves like lightning and showcases reams of thoroughly engaging vaudeville material from Bud and Lou's years on the burlesque circuit. When things threaten to slow down (which isn't often), the Andrews Sisters materialize and blow the roof off the joint with "Boogie Woogie Bugle Boy." What are they doing hanging out at boot camp? Who cares? Don't worry about the plot. There isn't one.

Check your political correctness meter at the door, and you'll have a great time. Every once in a while a line makes you blush red, white, and blue, but that's OK—those colors look good on you.

★ 1941, 84 minutes, B&W, not rated.

★ With: Bud Abbott, Lou Costello, the Andrews Sisters. Director: Arthur Lubin.

★ *What sequel did the stars of the film team up for in 1947?* (Answer on page 335.)

Family

Butterflies Are Free

More than meets the eye.

This movie may look like a bit of a period piece at first glance, but there's more to it than that groovy facade would suggest. Edward Albert plays a young blind man struggling to establish a sense of independence despite well-meaning incursions from his loopy neighbor (Goldie Hawn) and his loving but hypercontrolling mother (Eileen Heckart, who is superb). Even though this may sound like your typical late-sixties, early-seventies youthquake story line, the acting is quite strong, and the script even springs a few surprises. Not everyone over 30 is bad, and not everyone under 30 has a boundless potential for love.

Hawn does the ditzy-blond routine again, but she manages to impart some depth to the role of the next-door neighbor who takes Albert under her wing, gives him confidence, and helps him see himself anew. A surprisingly powerful film that covers a large emotional landscape with a small story.

★ 1972, 109 minutes, color, PG.

★ With: Goldie Hawn, Eileen Heckart, Edward Albert. Director: Milton Katselas.

★ *For what film did Goldie Hawn win an Oscar?* (Answer on page 266.)

" . . . and so are we."
—Edward Albert realizes he has more options than Mother might like.

For a great double feature, rent it with *$ (Dollars).*

Seen it but in the mood for something similar? Try *Cactus Flower.*

Answer to page 271 trivia question: The unions were on strike in New York at the time, so shooting moved to San Francisco.

Cabin in the Sky

Ignore the script; it's a time-honored tradition to do so for Vincente Minnelli pictures.

"Shall we make a wager?"

—The angels and imps debate: Can Eddie Anderson be saved?

For a great double feature, rent it with

Orchestra Wives.

Seen it but in the mood for something similar? Try

Stormy Weather.

Answer to page 1 trivia question:

True; he provided part of the vocal track on Michael Jackson's "Thriller."

This, the first feature-length film directed by Vincente Minnelli, is an all-black musical, an unforgettable collection of (regrettable) racist stereotypes and blow-the-doors-down showstoppers from legendary artists. All-black films were nothing new in 1943; there had been all-black westerns, melodramas, and gangster films. But never before had a feature-length black film been treated to such loving care and high polish as this one. Its ample budget allowed it to reach a wider audience than any other film of the genre.

The script is embarrassing, but you hardly notice, because when the stars are allowed to show their stuff, there's very little Hollywood has offered that competes. Highlights include Lena Horne singing "Honey in the Honeycomb" and Ethel Waters testifying that "Happiness Is Just a Thing Called Joe." Louis Armstrong and Duke Ellington show up, too. Get the idea? By the way, does that tornado look familiar? It's the very same one that wreaked havoc in *The Wizard of Oz.*

★ 1943, 100 minutes, B&W, not rated.

★ With: Eddie Anderson, Ethel Waters, Lena Horne, Duke Ellington, Louis Armstrong. Director: Vincente Minnelli.

★ *What character did Eddie Anderson make immortal on television and radio?* (Answer on page 198.)

Cactus Flower

Ingrid meets Goldie, and no prizes for guessing which one plays the ditzy blond.

Irritable dentist Walter Matthau has to choose between two lovers: Ingrid Bergman and Goldie Hawn. OK, so there's a certain amount of willing suspension of disbelief here, but this snappy little comedy, adapted from Abe Burrows's Broadway hit, plays some intriguing games with timeless questions of love, commitment, and the consequences of infidelity . . . even if that infidelity is sometimes a little hard to define.

To keep Hawn from getting serious, Matthau has told her that he's married. Which he isn't. That's the first mistake in a likable comedy of romantic errors. Whenever things threaten to quiet down, Hawn materializes and makes you forget the occasional limitations of the material.

This isn't the most intellectually challenging film you're going to see this year, but hey, if you've read this far you already know you're not exactly in James Joyce territory. Between Hawn's breathless scene stealing and Matthau's periodic bursts of brilliance as a latter-day W. C. Fields, *Cactus Flower* delivers the goods. Hawn won a well-deserved Oscar as Best Supporting Actress for her work in the film.

★ 1969, 103 minutes, color, PG.

★ With: Walter Matthau, Goldie Hawn, Ingrid Bergman. Director: Gene Saks.

★ *What's the name of the dance Bergman invents on the dance floor?* (Answer on page 356.)

"It's a play in which the actors wear clothes . . . the public isn't ready for it."

—Ingrid Bergman is more than a little befuddled at a young playwright's descripton of a new avant-garde play.

For a great double feature, rent it with
The Dentist (with W. C. Fields).

Seen it but in the mood for something similar? Try
Butterflies Are Free.

Answer to page 35 trivia question:
The Long, Hot Summer.

The Candidate

Can Robert Redford be in the system, but not of it? Naaah.

Robert Redford is the rebellious son of an esteemed former California governor; politico Peter Boyle wants the young activist to make a run for a seat in the U.S. Senate. Redford, believing he hasn't a chance to win, reluctantly agrees—on two conditions: he can campaign for what he believes in, and his father (Melvyn Douglas) will have nothing to do with the campaign. Before too long the golden boy learns that he has an instinct for surface-oriented, good-looks politicking. He also learns that the road of his campaign is paved with compromises every bit as damning as those he'd held his father accountable for.

Redford's standards drop as his campaigning skills develop, but the film never hits you over the head with the progression; the movie wins points for treating you as though you're smart enough to draw your own conclusions about its enigmatic central character. Boyle is excellent as the campaign manager; keep an eye out for Natalie Wood as herself in a pleasantly surprising cameo. If you're looking for evidence that this classic is a product of the too-hip-for-words seventies, check out the sideburns on Redford at the beginning; they're big enough to scare off Dirty Harry.

★ 1972, 109 minutes, color, PG.

★ With: Robert Redford, Peter Boyle, Melvyn Douglas. Director: Michael Ritchie.

★ True or false: *One of the leads in the film starred in a successful adaptation of a Mary Shelley novel.* (Answer on page 144.)

Drama

If this doesn't buckle your swashes, nothing will.

A 25-year-old Errol Flynn plays Dr. Peter Blood, who has been imprisoned for treason on trumped-up charges and sent to the Caribbean to work as a plantation slave. He is promptly bought at auction by the beautiful Olivia de Havilland, who hopes to save him from being sold off to another, more ruthless bidder. Later she tells him how lucky he was to have been purchased by such a benevolent master; Flynn plants a big kiss on her, at which point she slaps him and reminds Flynn that he had better not forget his place. She owns him, not the other way around. Sexual tension mounts. Flynn takes on the duties of plantation doctor and eventually escapes, taking most of his fellow slaves along with him onto a stolen ship. Every man aboard pirate Flynn's vessel will get his fair share—and perhaps more, depending on which body part he lost in the previous battle.

The band swears never knowingly to attack an English ship and never to treat a woman unchivalrously . . . unless, of course, she wants it bad. When de Havilland is captured, Flynn returns her earlier favor by buying her freedom from the treacherous Basil Rathbone and nonchalantly reminds her that the tables have turned. Exciting, romantic fun from beginning to end.

★ 1935, 119 minutes, B&W, not rated.

★ With Errol Flynn, Olivia de Havilland, Basil Rathbone. Director: Michael Curtiz.

★ *How old was Olivia de Havilland at the time* Captain Blood *was filmed?* (Answer on page 270.)

"All right, my hearties, follow me!"

—Errol Flynn leads his scurvy but lovable band into battle as only he can.

For a great double feature, rent it with
The Adventures of Robin Hood.

Seen it but in the mood for something similar? Try
The Sea Hawk.

Answer to page 103 trivia question:
Steven Spielberg.

Action

Dames at sea.

Gregory Peck has crosses to bear. First of all, he's the captain of one of Her Majesty's warships, about to embark on a very dangerous mission to get munitions to the Crown's allies. Second, he's a no-nonsense, by-the-book kind of leader who must instill discipline in the crew in a tough situation. Third, he's named Hornblower. (Yeah, like they aren't making fun of *that* name behind his back.) As if all that weren't enough to worry about, he has to deal with the unexpected appearance of Virginia Mayo aboard his ship. See, Peck is not what you'd call a ladies' man, and Mayo is not exactly the swooning, delicate-flower type. Peck can run a ship filled with a couple of hundred men, but when he catches sight of Mayo, he more or less wants to find a corner to hide in.

Mayo is a joy to watch; she never intended to find herself at war on the high-seas, but now that she's there, she has no intention of sitting quietly in her cabin. She's not afraid to raise a few eyebrows, get her hands dirty, or tell Hornblower to blow off if the occasion arises—which, as it happens, it does. They fall in love, of course. *Captain Horatio Hornblower* is a satisfyingly lush Technicolor sea extravaganza that's lovely to look at and unfolds a delightful, sentimental romance.

★ 1951, 117 minutes, color, not rated.

★ With: Gregory Peck, Virginia Mayo, Denis O'Dea. Director: Raoul Walsh.

★ *Can you name another high-sea adventure Virginia Mayo starred in?* (Answer on page 219.)

Drama

Careful, He Might Hear You

Family affair.

You can go through a lot by the time you're six. This unforgettable Australian picture tells the Depression-era story of a young boy (Nicholas Gledhill) named, evocatively enough, P.S. His mom passed on shortly after he was born, and his father, having never seen his son, left town to dig for gold. The lad grows up happily enough in a lower-middle-class section of Sydney with his loving aunt and uncle, but when he's six a custody battle erupts. It seems Dad has signed a court order entitling another aunt, and a very wealthy one at that, to the boy's weekdays. Severe familial and cultural dislocation ensues.

This is a carefully crafted, child's-eye view of some difficult issues: class, forgiveness, and adaptation to change. It features magnificent performances from young Gledhill and Wendy Hughes (who plays the rich aunt). *Careful, He Might Hear You* was named Best Film of the Year by the Australian Film Institute.

★ 1983, 116 minutes, color, PG.

★ With: Nicholas Gledhill, Wendy Hughes. Director: Carl Schultz.

★ *Wendy Hughes appeared with Judy Davis in what breakthrough Australian film?* (Answer on page 206.)

"To the pure in heart, all things are pure."
—Soothing words that may benefit young Nicholas Gledhill, who is the object of a bitter custody dispute

For a great double feature, rent it with *Housekeeping.*

Seen it but in the mood for something similar? Try *My Life as a Dog.*

Answer to page 261 trivia question: *Rollerball.*

Drama

Casualties of War

Fox made some Oscar-caliber movies—but no one noticed.

"This is kidnapping, ain't it, Sarge?"
—Michael J. Fox is hoping Sean Penn's going to tell him things aren't as bad as they look.

For a great double feature, rent it with
Twelve Angry Men.

Seen it but in the mood for something similar? Try
Full Metal Jacket.

Answer to page 318 trivia question:
To a child; it's a shortened form of *whippersnapper.*

Bankable big-name comic actors usually get at least one shot at making a Serious Film. Steve Martin's was the memorable *Pennies from Heaven*, which bombed; Bill Murray's was the less-than-memorable *The Razor's Edge*, which bombed; and Michael J. Fox's was *Casualties of War*, which, although it, too, bombed, must stand as one of the highlights of his career. Michael J. Fox, as the only man in the squad who displays anything resembling a conscience after a Vietnamese woman is brutally raped and murdered, gives a performance to be remembered—or would have been the performance to be remembered had anyone bothered to see the film. Some stereotypes are tough to break, as Sean Penn, who also gives an amazing performance in this movie, would probably attest. Penn's two most notable attempts to escape his bad-boy image were the comedies *Shanghai Surprise*, which bombed, and *We're No Angels*, which bombed. Penn's efforts to chart new ground deserve to be forgotten; Fox's does not.

★ 1989, 113 minutes, color, R.

★ With: Michael J. Fox, Sean Penn, Don Harvey. Director: Brian DePalma.

★ *Can you name the actress Michael J. Fox married—and where the two met?* (Answer on page 349.)

Drama

"Queen of the outlaws . . . Her Highness, Cat Ballou."

This parody of western melodramas earned Lee Marvin an Oscar; he plays both the drunken good guy out to save the day and the despicable bad guy. The bad guy wears a metal nose (his real one was shot off), and the good guy can't walk very well for most of the picture. That gives you a pretty good idea of how seriously director Elliot Silverstein takes the task at hand: not at all, and you wouldn't want it any other way.

The film tweaks the classic plot lines of a dime-store novel. Jane Fonda returns from finishing school, where she's been trained to be a schoolmarm, but her father's ranch is about to be stolen out from under them. When the hired-gun hero of her beloved pulp novels turns out to be a dud in real life, she decides to take matters into her own hands.

In one of the more stunningly incongruous features of any western ever filmed, Nat King Cole and Stubby Kaye materialize from time to time to provide running musical commentary. It's a strange choice, but it does keep this deliciously weird film humming along at the right pace. Fonda, who's just charming and vacuous enough here to get the job done, would turn in some Oscar-winning work of her own a few years hence in *Klute*.

★ 1965, 96 minutes, color, not rated.

★ With: Lee Marvin, Jane Fonda, Michael Callan. Director: Elliot Silverstein.

★ *This was the last film appearance for one of the stars of this film. Name the performer.* (Answer on page 274.)

"The first time I ask you to do one little thing, like rob a train, you won't do it."
—Jane Fonda does the Laura Petrie thing to get her way. It works.

For a great double feature, rent it with
Klute.

Seen it but in the mood for something similar? Try
A Big Hand for the Little Lady.

Answer to page 339 trivia question:
All the President's Men.

Comedy

Cat People (1942)

Nice kitty . . . nice kitty . . .

"*Sister.*"
—Simone Simon finds her soulmate.

For a great double feature, rent it with

The Curse of the Cat People. (This 1944 sequel is a surprisingly gentle fantasy, entirely suitable for children.)

Seen it but in the mood for something similar? Try

Island of Lost Souls.

Answer to page 292 trivia question:

The Private Life of Henry VIII.

When the dashing Kent Smith sees Simone Simon sketching the big cats at the zoo, he's immediately taken with her. There's something unique about this girl: maybe it's the way she curls up on the couch; maybe it's the way she eats fish; maybe it's the way she chases that little ball all around the house. OK, OK, she doesn't really do any of those things, but she is strangely, intriguingly feline, and Smith wants to get to know her better. He arrives at her door the next day with a kitten as a present. But the kitten can't stand to be around her; Simon explains that she's never cared for *domesticated* cats. So he buys her a bird instead. Tweety dies after Simon plays a little too rough—but Smith, like most lead characters in a horror movie, has no idea he's in one and insists on getting married.

You have to tip your hat to director Jacques Tourneur and producer Val Lewton for taking an idea this outlandish and making something truly compelling out of it. The conceit that Simon can turn into a murderous feline works both as silly monster-movie yarnspinning and as uneasy Freudian fantasy. Top-notch direction and a masterly visual style put this horror film several notches above your average B movie; it's what we *don't* see that's truly scary.

★ 1942, 73 minutes, B&W, not rated.

★ With: Simone Simon, Kent Smith, Tom Conway. Director: Jacques Tourneur.

★ *Who starred in the grisly, forgettable 1982 remake?*
(Answer on page 224.)

Horror

66

Charade

*Even when you're being chased by ruthless killers,
you have to look good.*

Poor Audrey Hepburn. Her husband's just died, and now all of his mourners seem to want to kill her. Lucky for her, there's Cary Grant to turn to, so no matter how bad things get, it will probably all be worth it. It seems Hepburn's husband pulled off a very big heist just before he was thrown from a moving train; now the loot is missing, and there are some very angry accomplices who would like to have a talk with his widow. When it was released, this picture was criticized for being too violent; today's audiences probably won't have any problem enjoying this smart, funny suspense movie that does in fact get truly scary in spots.

Hepburn is a major flagbearer for Givenchy in this picture; she looks—and acts—*fabulous*. And Cary Grant is, well, Cary Grant; he shows up just in the nick of time to help Hepburn—unless, of course, he's out to kill her, too. Hey, just because he's handsome doesn't make him trustworthy.

★ 1963, 114 minutes, color, not rated.

★ With: Cary Grant, Audrey Hepburn, James Coburn, Walter Matthau. Director: Stanley Donen.

★ Charade *was a departure from form for director Stanley Donen; what types of films was he better known for?* (Answer on page 202.)

"How do you shave in there?"

—Hepburn, on the cleft in Grant's chin.

For a great double feature, rent it with
Notorious.

Seen it but in the mood for something similar? Try
Wait Until Dark.

Answer to page 327 trivia question:

Blanche Dubois in *A Streetcar Named Desire.*

Suspense

Choose Me

What happens when your shrink is a basket case?

Check out how prim and proper talk-show therapist Genevieve Bujold looks at the beginning of this film. She's poised, she's in control, she's confident—and she's barely keeping the lid on her libido. In that regard she's a step ahead of the rest of the principal characters in this round-robin affair fest, but it's an advantage she may not retain.

Choose Me is a thoughtful extended meditation on the risks of acting on that Big Rumble Down Below; since it's the early eighties, everyone more or less gives in, everyone more or less sells everyone else out, and the price to be paid is hefty but manageable. (This is back when heterosexuals still thought there wasn't much to worry about on the AIDS front.) This unpredictable series of overlapping affairs carries an unintentionally prophetic sense of sexual menace and foreboding; it's as if choosing the wrong person will send you rocketing off the satin sheets and over a cliff.

Fine performances from top to bottom, especially Keith Carradine's pathological liar—who turns out to be the only one capable of any meaningful self-assessment.

★ 1984, 106 minutes, color, R.

★ With: Lesley Ann Warren, Keith Carradine, Genevieve Bujold. Director: Alan Rudolph.

★ *What career-highlight TV role did Bujold turn down at the last minute in the 1990s?* (Answer on page 97.)

Chuck Berry Hail! Hail! Rock 'n' Roll!

Chuck, be good tonight—
and he is.

At some point an irony about Chuck Berry struck Rolling Stones guitar hero Keith Richards. Although Berry was a living legend, the Great Duckwalker had a disconcerting habit of playing poorly rehearsed sessions in crammed, ill-lit dives, backed by third-rate pickup bands with whom he had literally never rehearsed.

This film chronicles Richards's tribute concert celebrating Berry's 60th birthday. Berry himself was the main attraction of the evening. Keith puts up with a lot here, which is part of the fun. Who else on the face of the earth but Berry could get away with telling the guy who played lead guitar on "Sympathy for the Devil" that he's botched an opening lick? And who but Keith could laugh with good humor when Chuck pulls a power play and tries to change keys midtune during the performance?

Berry comes off as a true American original: fiercely individualistic, resolutely uncompromising, and still, at 60, capable of leaving 'em jumping in the aisles. Along the way, there are inspired appearances by Julian Lennon, Eric Clapton, and Linda Ronstadt. One of the best films about rock and roll ever made.

★ 1987, 120 minutes, color, PG.

★ With: Chuck Berry, Keith Richards, Bo Diddley, Little Richard. Director: Taylor Hackford.

★ *What Chuck Berry single caused an uproar in the 1970s, thanks to its supposedly lascivious lyrics?*
(Answer on page 60.)

"Keep the home fires burning."
—Berry's advice for mixing life and rock 'n' roll

For a great double feature, rent it with
Rust Never Sleeps.

Seen it but in the mood for something similar? Try
That Was Rock.

Answer to page 287 trivia question:
Peter De Vries.

Documentary

Cinema Paradiso

No smooching!

"Twenty years I've gone to movies, and I've never seen a kiss!"
—A local can't believe how much he's been missing, thanks to the local priest who's been screening every film shown in town.

For a great double feature, rent it with
The Purple Rose of Cairo.

Seen it but in the mood for something similar? Try
The Last Picture Show.

Answer to page 322 trivia question:
Nineteen Eighty-Four.

In a small Sicilian village shortly after World War II, the whole town has fallen in love with the local movie house. A little boy named Toto strikes up a friendship with the town projectionist—then finds himself in charge of showing the films that are the center of the town's social life.

Giuseppe Tornatore's nostalgic love letter to movies, youth, and adolescence won an Oscar for best foreign film; some of its most memorable moments arise out of the unceasing attempts of the local church authorities to excise anything even vaguely sensual from the films the townspeople see. A priest sits alone and previews each film; he rings an annoying bell anytime something amorous threatens to grace the silver screen, thereby signaling the projectionist to cut the scene. How long can such prudishness hold sway? Don't bet on the guy with the bell; the real place of worship in the little village isn't the church; it's the movie house. *Cinema Paradiso* is an unforgettable study of innocence and growth told through one boy's lifelong passion for film.

★ 1988, 123 minutes, color, PG.

★ With: Philippe Noiret, Jacques Perrin, Salvatore Cascio. Director: Giuseppe Tornatore.

★ *Where did Toto's father die?* (Answer on page 89.)

Foreign

Citizen Cohn

How to succeed in business by making everyone, but everyone, hate you.

James Woods turns in a spellbinding performance as onetime Joseph McCarthy aide Roy Cohn, an anti-Semitic Jew and homophobic homosexual. Let's just say there are some self-esteem issues to deal with here. Cohn, a pathologically ambitious manipulator, managed to carve out a position of considerable power over a period of decades while convincing everyone with whom he came in contact that he was downright hateful. It was pretty easy; he was. But fun at a party . . .

The film uses an intriguing combination of AIDS-ward hallucinations, newsreel footage, and straight-ahead reenactments of historical events to bring us into Cohn's world; he uses circular logic, sheer guts, and good old-fashioned intimidation to get around anything and anyone in his way. File this intense, supremely watchable biopic under "Don't let this happen to your soul."

★ 1992, 115 minutes, color, not rated.

★ With: James Woods, Joe Don Baker, Joseph Bologna, Lee Grant. Director: Frank Pierson.

★ *Can you name the oddball horror adventure that starred James Woods and Deborah Harry?* (Answer on page 119.)

"I mean it's a free country—so far."
—Dashiell Hammett's withering response to Cohn's threats

For a great double feature, rent it with
The Front.

Seen it but in the mood for something similar? Try
Bugsy.

Answer to page 343 trivia question:
Tomorrow.

*Meet blond; get in fight; do hard time. Sounds like
a Cagney picture to me.*

*"Tomorrow the birds
will sing. Be brave!"*
—If anybody knows how to
talk to a guy who's about to
drown himself, it's Charlie
Chaplin.

**For a great double
feature, rent it with**
The Kid.

**Seen it but in the mood
for something similar?
Try**
Modern Times.

**Answer to page 149
trivia question:**
His Girl Friday. The
name, Archie Leach.

There's some neat backstage gossip about this Depression-era Charles Chaplin classic, in which the Little Tramp encounters a drunken millionaire and a blind flower girl. Having cast the lovely, but inexperienced, Virginia Cherrill as his leading lady, Chaplin had to renegotiate with her halfway through the nightmarishly long, script-optional shooting schedule; she decided she wanted more money for what she was putting up with, and she threatened to walk if she didn't get it. Faced with the choice of scrapping thousands of feet of film or coughing up more dough, Chaplin coughed up the dough. It's a testament to his abilities that the worshipful reverence the Tramp shows toward the beautiful blind girl never slips or seems forced; in real life, Chaplin wanted to throttle her.

Friends and studio executives begged Charlie not to make this one, warning him that the public was tired of silent pictures; he shot his masterpiece anyway and got the last laugh when critics and audiences alike fell in love with it. This gentle, sentimental story of anonymous love is widely considered his greatest achievement. I dare you not to cry at the fade-out.

★ 1931, 86 minutes, B&W, not rated.

★ With: Charlie Chaplin, Virginia Cherrill, Hank Mann. Director: Charles Chaplin.

★ *What 1947 picture is generally considered Chaplin's last masterpiece?* (Answer on page 187.)

Clean and Sober

A bad case of the sniffles.

Michael Keaton wakes up, talks on the phone for a while, does a couple of sizable lines of coke, and then notices that the girl lying in bed next to him has stopped breathing. Oops. This is not a man who is overly concerned with other people; why should he be? He's slick, smarter than anyone else, and pretty much convinced that everyone is out to make his life miserable. But he's not an addict; he can stop anytime he wants. (Uh-huh.)

This film takes an interesting approach to the stereotypical man-on-the-way-down story: Keaton signs himself into the detox center because he hears that, while he's in there, no one can contact him, not even the police. (The cops have shown considerable interest in him since the overdose of his girlfriend.) Keaton knows he can con his way into, or out of, just about anything; he has the place all figured out—until he meets Morgan Freeman, who isn't about to waste time on a con man. The two are worthy adversaries, and the sparks that fly keep you watching this intriguing, well-written film. Although it has its down moments, *Clean and Sober* offers undeniable proof of Keaton's top-drawer credentials as an actor.

★ 1988, 125 minutes, color, R.

★ With: Michael Keaton, Morgan Freeman, M. Emmet Walsh. Director: Glenn Gordon Caron.

★ *On what public television children's show did Keaton once have a recurring role?* (Answer on page 212.)

"Richard, your life is no longer manageable."
—Morgan Freeman has Michael Keaton's number.

For a great double feature, rent it with
Postcards from the Edge.

Seen it but in the mood for something similar? Try
The Man with the Golden Arm.

Answer to page 185 trivia question:
Tommy.

Drama

Coma

I'll just stay out here
in the waiting room, thanks.

"What's the status?"
"Greeley? Complete
squash rot. She's a
total Gomer."

— An intern's pungent assessment of a patient who's in bad shape. But I'm sure hospital people would never talk about *you* that way.

For a great double feature, rent it with

Invasion of the Body Snatchers (1956).

Seen it but in the mood for something similar? Try

Jagged Edge.

Answer to page 220 trivia question:

Gaslight (1944).

Patients seem to be dropping like flies at Boston's Memorial Hospital—dropping into comas, that is. The cases of unexplained coma resulting in death are not so high as to attract the attention of the authorities, but when one of the fatalities is Genevieve Bujold's best friend, the young surgeon decides to investigate. No one, not even Bujold's handsome, ambitious boyfriend, Michael Douglas, will believe her when she says something at the hospital is very, very wrong. The thinking seems to be that even an accomplished woman surgeon is still a woman and therefore prone to hysterics. Bujold, of course, is right; there are sinister doings afoot.

This fast-paced hospital thriller, based on Robin Cook's bestseller, makes the most of its intimidating surroundings. Let's face it: even without sinister doings afoot, and even if you're healthy, hospitals are pretty scary places, what with all those narrow hallways leading to God knows where, where doctors are up to God knows what.

Director Michael Crichton (didn't he write a thriller or two himself?) does a creditable job of giving you the creeps as he weaves his way through Memorial Hospital. His movie not only scares the pants off you; it reinforces the fundamental wisdom of asking for a second opinion.

★ 1978, 113 minutes, color, PG.

★ With: Genevieve Bujold, Michael Douglas, Rip Torn. Director: Michael Crichton.

★ *What actor who played a corpse in this movie went on to stardom?* (Answer on page 251.)

The Compleat Beatles

Do you suppose this band has any staying power?

More than three decades after they first attracted notice, and two and a half after their last release as a foursome, the Beatles remain the most adored act in rock and roll. (Name another band that could put out a historical retrospective of poorly recorded, much-bootlegged mono tapes from the early 1960s and watch it go multiple platinum.)

This superior documentary, released two years after John Lennon's death, is a responsible overview of the group's genesis, working style, and impact on popular culture. In addition to the great music you'd expect, *The Compleat Beatles* is crammed with insider's-view film clips and interviews with various principals; producer George Martin's remembrances of the glory days are of particular interest.

Go out of your way to find this one—and steer clear of the recycled concert tapes, which usually feature uneven (at best) production values. Until the powers that be see fit to remedy the mysterious series of events that led to *Let It Be* going out of print on video, *The Compleat Beatles* was the best real-life look at the group that changed everything.

★ 1982, 120 minutes, color, not rated.

★ With: The Beatles, Malcolm McDowell. Director: Patrick Montgomery.

★ *Who was the oldest Beatle?* (Answer on page 279.)

"The act you've known for all these years."
—Paul McCartney's lyrical assessment of the Lonely Hearts Club Band

For a great double feature, rent it with *Yellow Submarine.*

Seen it but in the mood for something similar? Try *A Hard Day's Night.*

Answer to page 256 trivia question: Steppenwolf.

Documentary

Compromising Positions

Remember to see your dentist every six months.
Even if he is a sex maniac.

"A dentist. God, I'd love to kill a dentist."
—Hey, who wouldn't? But Susan Sarandon's got a case to solve.

For a great double feature, rent it with
American Dreamer.

Seen it but in the mood for something similar? Try
The Morning After.

Answer to page 159 trivia question:
Hamlet (1948).

Susan Sarandon was a journalist. Then she became a housewife. She loves her husband and her children. She is completely fulfilled. Almost. When her dentist is murdered and several of her close friends are considered suspects, she sharpens her pencil and starts asking some questions. Her husband wishes she would get back to her housework. Handsome Raul Julia, the detective on the case, wishes pretty much the same thing, not because she's in the way, but because she's solving the case faster than he is. He's also finding himself attracted to her, and not just to her body but also to her mind. Now what woman can resist that?

The movie boasts a great roster of quirky suspects, any one of whom would be a plausible enough murderer: the dentist seems to have been having affairs with all his women clients except Sarandon (one of those developments that make you feel glad you weren't involved but at the same time get you wondering whether there's anything wrong with you; from the looks of things he wasn't very picky). A funny, smart little mystery that gets the most out of its two accomplished leads.

★ 1985, 98 minutes, color, R.

★ With: Susan Sarandon, Raul Julia, Edward Herrmann. Director: Frank Perry.

★ *What nineties film did Sarandon appear in, if ever so briefly, with her husband, Tim Robbins?* (Answer on page 328.)

Suspense

76

Conrack

Culture shock.

An inspiring true story of a teacher (Jon Voight as Pat Conroy) who sets out to share the joy of learning with a bunch of illiterate African-American kids in rural (and I do mean rural) South Carolina. These youngsters have never seen the white lines on a paved street before; they're about a century behind even the most disadvantaged inner-city students. Voight's self-appointed mission is to get them to believe in themselves and, at the same time, get ready to overcome the seemingly insurmountable social goals they'll face growing up. Hume Cronyn is the crusty old-school Representative of an Order That No Longer Works If Indeed It Ever Did.

The picture's anti-Establishment posturing seems a little too easy now, but it's not the main attraction. That honor goes to Voight's fine work as the earnest, inventive instructor who puts the kids first and everything else second. Based on Conroy's book *The Water Is Wide*.

★ 1974, 107 minutes, color, PG.

★ With: Jon Voight, Paul Winfield, Hume Cronyn. Director: Martin Ritt.

★ *What landmark spy thriller starring Richard Burton did Martin Ritt direct?* (Answer on page 339.)

"Teachers lie all the time."

—One of the many unconventional lessons Jon Voight shares with his pupils

For a great double feature, rent it with *Dead Poets Society.*

Seen it but in the mood for something similar? Try *Up the Down Staircase.*

Answer to page 194 trivia question:

Marilyn Monroe's; she claimed during a press conference to wear only Chanel No. 5.

Drama

The Conversation

Who said I'm paranoid?

"I am not afraid of death. I am afraid of murder."
—Gene Hackman draws the line.

For a great double feature, rent it with
Rear Window.

Seen it but in the mood for something similar? Try
Blow Out.

Answer to page 230 trivia question:
Queen.

A crew of undercover men surreptitiously records the conversation of a young couple walking through a crowded park. After the surveillance agents combine their recordings, they ask audio man Gene Hackman if he can make any sense out of what the man and woman were talking about. Once he's spliced the tapes together, he finds that what he has sounds like a plan for murder. What's an alienated anti-hero to do?

This is one of Hackman's best performances. His character has enough skill to know when something nasty is going to happen and enough experience to know that if he acts he runs the risk of becoming trapped.

The Conversation offers a world where privacy is the most deadly illusion of all, and the life the soundman has made for himself in that world is terrifyingly barren. He inhabits a desolate little apartment with no phone; other than the saxophone that he plays long into the night, there's little evidence of human life. The film's supremely isolated hero would like to reach out to another person—a friend, a confessor, a woman, or a stranger in peril—but he knows this kind of thing carries awful risks. Someone could be listening.

★ 1974, 113 minutes, color, PG.

★ With: Gene Hackman, John Cazale, Allen Garfield. Director: Francis Ford Coppola.

★ *Cindy Williams and Harrison Ford have supporting roles here; in what 1973 film did these two also appear?* (Answer on page 254.)

The Count of Monte Cristo

When bad things happen to bad people.

A udiences stood up and cheered in the aisles when the bad guys got their just desserts in this rousing adventure picture. It may well be the most satisfying adventure movie ever made. This version of the much-filmed classic Dumas tale is not only the handsomest to look at; it's also got the strongest cast by a long shot. Hey, Richard Chamberlain is OK, but he's no Robert Donat.

Donat plays a young seaman on his way to marry the girl of his dreams; before he can meet her, he is kidnapped and placed in a prison by a mysterious rival, where he is promptly forgotten. Through the help of a fellow prisoner who has dug his way into his cell, he devises an escape. Soon he'll have a buried treasure—and the key to seek revenge on those who ruined his life. Unless, of course, he has a sudden change of heart and realizes that violence only begets more violence. Naaaaaaah. Read the book. I hear it's pretty good, too.

★ 1934, 119 minutes, B&W, not rated.

★ With: Robert Donat, Elissa Landi, Irene Hervey. Director: Rowland V. Lee.

★ *Why did Donat leave Hollywood and never return?* (Answer on page 256.)

"The world is mine!"
—Robert Donat has a feeling payback time has come around at last.

For a great double feature, rent it with
The Shawshank Redemption.

Seen it but in the mood for something similar? Try
The Man in the Iron Mask.

Answer to page 268 trivia question:
Dead Poets Society.

The Court Jester

Disorder in the court.

"Get it?" "Got it." "Good."
—Kaye makes sure there are no misunderstandings.

For a great double feature, rent it with
Captain Blood.

Seen it but in the mood for something similar? Try
Knock on Wood.

Answer to page 168 trivia question:
All of them.

He wants to be the heroic adventurer known as the Black Fox, but someone already has the gig, so he can't. He's Danny Kaye, and when he's put in charge of the royal heir, who has a royal birthmark on his royal backside, all heck breaks loose. This unremittingly silly movie refuses to let a scene go by without some inspired shtick, some double talk, or a combination of the two. It includes several now-classic Kaye routines—the tongue-defying "pellet with the poison" skit, the zero-to-hero finger-snapping hypnosis scene, and a great deal of memorable miscommunication that only seems to get Kaye in deeper trouble.

The supporting cast is quite strong: Glynis Johns has never been more fetching, and Basil Rathbone has great fun parodying his own most celebrated movie roles. Then there's a shockingly young Angela Lansbury; after you see her in her bombshell phase in this film, you'll never think of the matronly mystery writer of Cabot Cove in the same way again.

★ 1956, 101 minutes, color, not rated.

★ With: Danny Kaye, Basil Rathbone, Glynis Johns, Angela Lansbury. Directors: Norman Panama, Melvin Frank.

★ *What is the Purple Pimpernel?* (Answer on page 216.)

Comedy

Creature from the Black Lagoon

Have fun looking for the zipper.

This film supports my theory that women who wear white bathing suits in movies are just asking for trouble (see also *Suddenly, Last Summer*). Everyone knows this movie, but has anyone really *watched* it? It's great fun and a particularly good rental choice if you're planning to have a gang of friends over. There are lots of underwater scenes with no dialogue, leaving you plenty time to chat about the movie without losing sight of the plot. (As if.)

This is the classic story of a beautiful girl in the Amazon and the sea creature who loves her. Alas, our hero (the Creature) has some tough competition. First there's the scientist with big dreams about making the world a better place. Then there's the other scientist who just wants the fame and fortune that will surely be his if he can bag the big fish; I mean our hero. These two guys may be more conventionally handsome, but they don't have that *je ne sais quoi* that amphibian boy does.

Warning: Julie Adams screams at the drop of a hat. She then falls helplessly to the ground, leaving the menfolk to fight the battles. (And she goes swimming with total disregard for the buddy system, but that's another story.) Still, you have to admire a girl who thinks to pack so many fetching ensembles to travel upriver with, don't you?

★ 1954, 79 minutes, B&W, not rated.

★ With: Richard Carlson, Julie Adams, Richard Denning. Director: Jack Arnold.

★ *What gimmick was part of the picture's original release?* (Answer on page 191.)

"My brother was dragged down into the water . . . by a demon."
—One crew member's explanation of what lurks below

For a great double feature, rent it with
King Kong (1933).

Seen it but in the mood for something similar? Try
The Creature Walks Among Us.

Answer to page 202 trivia question:
Asta.

Horror

Crimes of the Heart

Can you say "family therapy"?

Nice to see someone get a little comic mileage out of unexpected horse electrocution, attempted murder, parents who are about to kick the bucket, and other staples of deep-South domesticity, isn't it? This offbeat film is a skillfully managed adaptation of Beth Henley's bizarre Pulitzer Prize–winning comedy about three Mississippi sisters who have a series of really bad days. It retains the kooky but somehow life-affirming complexity of the original play.

The movie is part birthday party, part crisis management session, and part support group; it's also an excuse for Sissy Spacek to show off some of her best moves. When she's "on," she's just about unbelievable—and she's "on" for most of the movie. Jessica Lange and Diane Keaton shine, too, in equally strong roles.

You'll come to know the strange ways of the tiny town of Hazlehurst, Mississippi, intimately after you have watched this one. Where you go from there is up to you.

★ 1986, 105 minutes, color, PG-13.

★ With: Sissy Spacek, Diane Keaton, Jessica Lange. Director: Bruce Beresford.

★ *What Henley screenplay poked fun at a small-time beauty pageant?* (Answer on page 123.)

Crossing Delancey

The distance may be shorter than you think.

Amy Irving manages a bohemian bookstore, organizes readings of new and exciting authors, and enjoys attending literary salons in which the elite participants duel to outrank one another intellectually. In short, she enjoys living on New York's Upper West Side. But if you ask her grandmother (or even if you don't), she'll tell you Amy lives alone like a dog, with bars on the window.

The grandmother, played by Reizl Bozyk with great charm, takes matters into her own hands; she hires a matchmaker for her granddaughter. When Irving realizes what's happened, she's furious; when she learns that her perfect match appears to be a pickle seller from the Lower East Side (Peter Riegert), she's mortified. She loves her grandmother enough to meet with Riegert, planning to give him the brush-off immediately afterward. But suprise, surprise: the pickle guy is more captivating than she'd anticipated. Will Irving hold to the plan and find a way to get rid of Riegert, or will she loosen up and learn to enjoy life a little?

A gentle, entirely satisfying romantic comedy that showcases Irving at her best and gives the underrated Riegert the chance to strut his stuff as an improbable romantic lead.

★ 1988, 97 minutes, color, PG.

★ With: Amy Irving, Peter Riegert, Reizl Bozyk. Director: Joan Micklin Silver.

★ *For what animated character did Amy Irving deliver a knockout musical number?* (Answer on page 94.)

"You should try a new hat sometime, Isabel. It might look good on you."
—Peter Riegert suggests a new look for Amy Irving.

For a great double feature, rent it with *Moonstruck.*

Seen it but in the mood for something similar? Try *Hester Street.*

Answer to page 276 trivia question: *Arthur.*

Romance

Cyrano de Bergerac (1990)

Say, this sure looks a lot like Roxanne. *I wonder if Steve Martin got royalties out of it.*

"Je touche!"
— Gerard Depardieu nose what's up with the whole fencing thing.

For a great double feature, rent it with *Roxanne.*

Seen it but in the mood for something similar? Try *The Adventures of Robin Hood.*

Answer to page 175 trivia question:
Jimmy Durante.

How do you suppose this story would have ended if there'd been decent plastic surgery back then? This is a delicious film interpretation of Rostand's classic romantic play, with Gerard Depardieu perfectly cast (what with him being both French and the possessor of a rather pronounced schnoz). The ungainly cavalier composes lines for his beloved that he must watch another deliver; he's got the body of a clown and the heart of a poet.

As movie adaptations of stage dramas go, this one fares far better than most, in part because the exotic settings of Rostand's drama change frequently. In other words, this ain't no piece of one-set kitchen-sink realism that screenwriters have to struggle to "open up." In a wise move, considering the literary merits of the source material, Anthony Burgess (of *A Clockwork Orange* fame) oversaw the translation of the English subtitles.

You may, in your travels, run into the creditable 1950 black-and-white production that earned Jose Ferrer an Oscar, but the supporting cast here is far stronger. A joy from start to finish; Depardieu's Cyrano is the definitive nose for our time.

★ 1990, 138 minutes, color, PG.

★ With: Gerard Depardieu, Anne Brochet, Vincent Perez. Director: Jean-Paul Rappeneau.

★ *What drama set in the French countryside featured Depardieu as a hunchbacked farmer?*
(Answer on page 195.)

That's Irish for "Dad," not Russian for "yes."

Martin Sheen plays a successful playwright who learns, just before the opening of his new Broadway show, that his father has died. He skips the opening and returns to Dublin for the funeral. In his childhood home Sheen begins to relive the past in a style reminiscent of Charles Dickens's *A Christmas Carol:* as he replays his childhood, he finds himself reviewing the events that separated him from his father, played masterfully by Barnard Hughes. Offered the opportunity to see his own past with 20/20 vision, Sheen comes to realize that his recently deceased father always loved him . . . even if he did drive him crazy at the time. Now, if Sheen can only get rid of his father's ghost, he'll be all set.

This funny, endearing tale of intergenerational reconciliation won a shelf full of Tony Awards during its run as a play on Broadway; it's hard to figure why the movie didn't make more of a splash. No car chases, I guess. The picture features some of Sheen's best acting work, and that's saying something.

★ 1988, 102 minutes, color, PG.

★ With: Barnard Hughes, Martin Sheen, William Hickey. Director: Mat Clark.

★ Da *boasts one of the shortest movie titles on record— but what Costa-Gavras film features a title that's even shorter?* (Answer on page 260.)

"What was it like?"
"What?" "Dying."
"I didn't care for it."
—Martin Sheen and Barnard Hughes resolve any lingering questions you may have about the hereafter.

For a great double feature, rent it with
The Trip to Bountiful.

Seen it but in the mood for something similar? Try
Housekeeping.

Answer to page 208 trivia question:
"Don't Stand So Close to Me."

Drama

She's long in the legs; he's long in the tooth.

"I can manage the box step."

—Astaire's reply to a debutante who's unsure about his ability to keep up on the dance floor

For a great double feature, rent it with

Gigi.

Seen it but in the mood for something similar? Try

Good News.

Answer to page 244 trivia question:

Sir Alec Guinness and Maggie Smith.

Leslie Caron plays a spunky French orphan who charms debonair millionaire Fred Astaire. In a sweetly platonic way, of course. After he realizes that adopting an 18-year-old French girl may be a little awkward, Astaire decides to become Caron's guardian. He promises never to make his identity known to her and to see to her every need. Astaire then sends her to a posh New England college and promptly forgets all about her—until his secretary, Thelma Ritter, who has been reading every letter from the lonely orphan, decides she can take no more.

Ritter persuades Astaire to read two years' worth of neglected letters, and Astaire is charmed all over again, as only Leslie Caron can charm someone all over again. Under the guise of visiting a niece, Astaire visits Caron at college. Now she's 21 and charming in a new, not-quite-so-sweetly-platonic way, and things get complicated.

A lovely fairy tale of a musical (the standout numbers are "Something's Got to Give," "History of the Beat," and the jitterbuggy "Slue Foot"), *Daddy Long Legs* features a graceful performance from Caron that presages her memorable turn as a nubile young courtesan who'd rather not be a courtesan in *Gigi*.

★ 1955, 126 minutes, color, not rated.

★ With: Fred Astaire, Leslie Caron, Thelma Ritter. Director: Jean Negulesco.

★ *Can you name the star who played Julie in the original 1919 version?* (Answer on page 332.)

Musical

Thank God. Timothy Hutton does *have* an evil twin after all.

The book that this film is based on was Stephen King's answer to the inevitable question "Where *do* you get those scary ideas?" In this case the inspiration comes from another part of the writer. A living, breathing part. An author, Timothy Hutton, has decided to stop writing pseudonymous horror books; he wants to set aside the grotesque world that has made him rich and famous. He's written another book, a real work of real art, but there's a problem: Hutton's other half doesn't feel like retiring. People start dying gruesome deaths; curiously, they're all the people who encouraged Hutton to expand his writing horizons. Even more curiously, Hutton's fingerprints seem to be all over every crime scene. Although the writer has an airtight alibi for his locations at the time of each murder, the local sheriff has begun wondering. Amy Madigan, as Hutton's wife, has the biggest problem: she has to worry which half of Hutton is going to show up for dinner.

Thanks to director George A. Romero, of *Night of the Living Dead* fame, this one's a fascinating, well-crafted gross-out session with some haunting special effects. Be honest, now; every so often that's just what you're in the mood for.

★ 1993, 115 minutes, color, R.

★ With: Timothy Hutton, Amy Madigan, Julie Harris. Director: George A. Romero.

★ *Can you name two other Stephen King movies that take place in the fictional town of Castle Rock, Maine?*
(Answer on page 346.)

"Will it be your ending or mine?"
—Timothy Hutton learns that things can get ugly when your muse decides to take matters into his own hands.

For a great double feature, rent it with
The Birds.

Seen it but in the mood for something similar? Try
The Dead Zone.

Answer to page 282 trivia question:
Dersu Uzala.

Horror

The Day the Earth Stood Still

*Weirdos with whom we seem to have nothing in common
take over Washington—so what else is new?*

"Klaatu barada nikto."
—It may be Greek to you, but these are the words one particular heavy metal fan has been longing to hear.

For a great double feature, rent it with
Close Encounters of the Third Kind.

Seen it but in the mood for something similar? Try
When Worlds Collide.

Answer to page 2 trivia question:
Cornet, electric guitar, and piano.

Have you ever noticed how most movies about aliens feature landing sequences that take place in remote cornfields or deserted plains? If the idea is to get in touch with humankind, why don't they drop down in, say, the middle of Washington, D.C.? Well, the answer may be contained in this film: that's exactly what the space voyagers do, and they get nothing but trouble for their efforts.

You can look at this landmark science fiction film two ways. Either the aliens represent the creeping Communist threat, or Klaatu is a Christ figure. (Notice the name on the laundry tag inside his coat: "Mr. Carpenter." Hmm.) This influential, much-imitated thriller has suffered because it inspired so many lousy movies. In fact the sets and general production values are quite strong, the script is palatable and even, dare I say it, engaging here and there, and the cast, headed by Patricia Neal as the earth mother/enigmatic love interest, is superb. Michael Rennie, as Klaatu, comes off as more "humane" than nearly anyone else in the movie.

★ 1951, 93 minutes, B&W, not rated.

★ With: Michael Rennie, Patricia Neal, Hugh Marlowe. Director: Robert Wise.

★ *For what later television role is the actor who played little Bobby better known?* (Answer on page 303.)

The Dead

James Joyce, pretty much word for word— and it's painless!

John Huston's final film is a masterwork. In *The Dead* he offers up a wise, intimate, and quietly powerful tribute to Ireland, James Joyce, and the painful lessons of life lived at a remove from others. What's it about? Well, this may be hard to believe, but back in the long-lost days before electronic entertainment, people used to gather together with their friends over a good dinner and entertain each other. Hard to imagine, I know, but apparently it was quite popular. In any event, *The Dead* chronicles one such evening in a 1904 upper-middle-class Dublin household.

That's about as much of a plot summary as you're likely to get from this luminous, unforgettable motion picture, but it's really all you need. Plot is not the point; what we have here is a series of poignant, powerful meditations on the transitory nature of human experience. Sounds highfalutin and academic, but Huston, who seems to use the film to come to terms with his own detachment from his family's homeland, is the man to make Joyce's material work on a cinematic level. Work it does—stand back when Anjelica Huston makes her way into the unforgettable monologue to her husband near the end of the film.

★ 1987, 83 minutes, color, PG.

★ With: Anjelica Huston, Donal McCann, Ingrid Craigie. Director: John Huston.

★ *What other member of the Huston family contributed to the making of* The Dead *besides Angelica and John?*
(Answer on page 114.)

"Snow is falling through the universe, and faintly falling, like the descent of their last end upon all the living and the dead."
—Donal McCann learns how it all comes down in the end.

For a great double feature, rent it with *Hear My Song.*

Seen it but in the mood for something similar?
Rent it again. There's no other movie quite like this one.

Answer to page 70 trivia question:
The Russian front.

Drama

The Dead Zone

I think I must have overslept.

"You're in the possession of a very new human ability—or a very old one."

—Well, *that* certainly narrows things down for Christopher Walken.

For a great double feature, rent it with

Eyes of Laura Mars.

Seen it but in the mood for something similar? Try

The Shining.

Answer to page 36 trivia question:

Cat Ballou (1965).

Christopher Walken has had an up-and-down career since his Academy Award–winning performance in *The Deer Hunter*; here he's the beneficiary of a role that looks for all the world as though it were written especially for him. Actually, though, this picture is one of only a handful of capable adaptations of Stephen King chillers.

Walken plays a man who emerges from a five-year-long coma to find that he has the power to see the future of those objects and people he touches. It's a gift that would probably come in handy at the racetrack, but it's Walken's fate to learn the truth about impending disasters, serial murders, and even the fate of the world. Sometimes people believe him; sometimes they don't; sometimes he takes matters into his own hands. When Walken *is* able to take action and avert disaster, he's left with the difficult task of explaining why he has transgressed social boundaries to prevent an event that everyone knows didn't take place.

The Dead Zone features acting work from Walken that is every bit as compelling as his justly praised work in *The Deer Hunter*; it's a taut, well-put-together supernatural thriller that makes the most of its star's abilities and its promising central idea.

★ 1983, 103 minutes, color, R.

★ With: Christopher Walken, Brooke Adams, Tom Skerritt, Martin Sheen. Director: David Cronenberg.

★ *What baseball team does Stephen King root for?*
(Answer on page 354.)

Deep Cover

He's gone so deep he may never get back.

Local beat cop Larry Fishburne has doubts about taking on the undercover role of a low-level street dealer. To build credibility, he has to sell drugs to kids, pregnant women, and anyone else who asks—all with the blessing of the DEA. Fishburne does a nice job of trying to retain a shred of honor in a morally bankrupt environment, but the odds are against him. Eventually he meets Jeff Goldblum, who is Fishburne's key to entering the world of big-time narcotics.

Goldblum, an actor who's built a career out of playing vaguely likable eccentrics, crosses the line in this film and becomes one very scary individual. He has connections that can lead Fishburne to a new designer drug that will not only get you high but is (for the time being, at least) also completely legal. Can Goldblum get the money he needs before he gets himself killed? Can Fishburne bag the bad guys before he becomes one himself? *Deep Cover*, which may look, as you scan the boxes on the wall, like your standard B-level shoot-'em-up, is a whole lot more. It's a piercing examination of the dire consequences of selling your soul for the organization.

★ 1992, 112 minutes, color, R.

★ With: Larry Fishburne, Jeff Goldblum, Victoria Dillard. Director: Bill Duke.

★ *In what film did Fishburne play the father of a troubled L.A. teenager?* (Answer on page 267.)

"Undercover, all your faults will become virtues. You'll be a star there."
—Larry Fishburne gets the lowdown on the pluses and minuses of his new job.

For a great double feature, rent it with
True Romance.

Seen it but in the mood for something similar? Try
Pulp Fiction.

Answer to page 104 trivia question:
The Outsiders.

Drama

Dersu Uzala

It's Siberian for "Where the hell are we?"

"Dersu!"
—When in doubt, shout your guide's name at the top of your lungs through the vast Siberian wilderness. That's Yuri Solomine's technique.

For a great double feature, rent it with
Lawrence of Arabia.

Seen it but in the mood for something similar? Try
Ran.

Answer to page 15 trivia question:
Dyan Cannon.

Next time you get lost on a rural back road during a vacation trip, use this picture to remind yourself that it could be worse; you could be trekking through a vast, forbidding Siberian plain, getting ready to starve to death. Somehow, stopping at that poky little filling station to ask for directions doesn't seem like such a tragedy now, does it?

An old hunter, serving as a guide for a surveyor on expedition in Siberia, befriends him—and summons spiritual resources to deal with the forbidding natural world they face. The legendary Japanese director Akira Kurosawa shot this 1975 masterwork of human survival that won an Oscar for Best Foreign Film. If a more beautiful outdoor epic has ever been filmed, I've never seen it—and yes, I've seen *Lawrence of Arabia.*

This one is a must-see, but do yourself a favor and rent it when you have access to a big-screen television; the visuals are so exquisite that it would be a crime to watch them on a postage-stamp size screen.

★ 1975, 140 minutes, color, not rated.

★ With: Maxim Munzuk, Yuri Solomine. Director: Akira Kurosawa.

★ *What Kurosawa film adapted Shakespeare's* King Lear?
(Answer on page 199.)

Desk Set

Future shock.

One of the most satisfying of the Katharine Hepburn/Spencer Tracy pairings, this one features Hepburn as a librarian who does research work for a television network and Tracy as the "efficiency expert" (nowadays, we'd say "consultant") out to computerize everything and perhaps take away her job. It's loads of fun, in part because of the inimitable sparks that fly between the two stars and in part because of the wary attitude the film takes toward technology.

These days, there's a rumor going around that whole societies used to operate without on-line keyword file searches, bar codes, and ATM machines; this perfectly executed comedy seems to indicate that such may in fact have been the case. Its blinking lights and churning, room-sized computer notwithstanding, *Desk Set* hums along like a good little laptop, crunching its way through a crisp, funny plot with nary an error.

Great chemistry between the principals; too bad they couldn't have gotten together offscreen. (Oops. Never mind.) Gig Young and Joan Blondell turn in great supporting work, too. They don't make 'em like this anymore. It's too hard to get the vacuum tubes.

★ 1957, 103 minutes, color, not rated.

★ With: Spencer Tracy, Katharine Hepburn, Joan Blondell. Director: Walter Lang.

★ *In what musical did Joan Blondell star with James Cagney?* (Answer on page 358.)

"If she becomes frustrated, her magnetic circuit is likely to go off." "Something like that happens to me."
—Maybe Katharine Hepburn has more in common with the computer than meets the eye.

For a great double feature, rent it with:
Adam's Rib.

Seen it but in the mood for something similar? Try
Woman of the Year.

Answer to page 49 trivia question:
He promised to introduce legislation making "This Land Is Your Land" the national anthem.

Comedy

*Cary Grant gets wet,
looks buff.*

"We gotta take it; we can't win if we can't take it."

—Cary Grant reminds his men that they are not cruising the bottom of the Pacific for their health.

For a great double feature, rent it with

Operation Petticoat.

Seen it but in the mood for something similar? Try

Das Boot.

Answer to page 83 trivia question:

Jessica Rabbit in *Who Framed Roger Rabbit;* Kathleen Turner provided the dialogue, but Irving sang.

A single sub on a secret mission against the entire Japanese fleet courses silently into deadly enemy waters. But with a plucky all-American crew that features Cary Grant at the helm, you know that no matter how dicey things get, our boys will see the job through. Sure, they miss their sweethearts, their hamburgers, and their homemade applejack (not necessarily in that order), but, hey, there are orders to follow and enemy boats to sink.

All right, this is a shameless propaganda film, and it's not exactly what would pass for politically correct these days. But it's a slick, well-put-together vehicle that knows exactly where it's going—not at all unlike the craft the story is set in. The depth-charge sequence alone, during which crew members put on studiously brave faces while rivets pop out of the hull left and right, is worth the price of admission.

★ 1943, 135 minutes, B&W, not rated.

★ With: Cary Grant, John Garfield, Alan Hale. Director: Delmer Daves.

★ *What was Cary Grant's last film?* (Answer on page 153.)

Action

Destry Rides Again (1939)

Talk about your odd couple.

Adorable, low-key Jimmy Stewart teamed up with European femme fatale Marlene Dietrich—in a western, no less. It worked, and *Destry Rides Again* became the cowboy movie Hollywood imitated for decades to come.

Stewart sets out to uphold the law in just the way you'd imagine he would: no guns, just straight talk, cool thinking, and a good sense of humor. That's usually all Jimmy needs to change the average bad guy's mind. Of course, if the bad guy turns out to be *worse* than average, Stewart can outshoot anybody in town; he'd just rather not. His father, Destry, wore guns and ended up getting shot in the back; Jimmy's not eager to have that happen to him. Neither, as it turns out, is Dietrich, who plays the chanteuse at the local saloon. (She's called Frenchy. Don't ask.) The two hate each other the moment they meet, which can only mean true love.

Dietrich's musical numbers add a kick to one of the most engaging westerns the studio system ever produced. You may spot an inferior 1954 remake, starring Audie Murphy, on the late show. Turn the set off immediately.

★ 1939, 94 minutes, B&W, not rated.

★ With: James Stewart, Marlene Dietrich, Brian Donlevy. Director: George Marshall.

★ *What part of Jimmy Stewart's costume looks worse with every western he made, and why?* (Answer on page 271.)

"If you shoot it out with 'em, it makes 'em heroes. Put 'em behind bars, and they look little and cheap."

—A laid-back James Stewart explains why he never carries a gun.

For a great double feature, rent it with *Blazing Saddles.*

Seen it but in the mood for something similar? Try *The Oklahoma Kid.*

Answer to page 118 trivia question: *The Far Pavilions.*

Everybody's coming to dinner.

"I was reading a book the other day . . . It's about civilization, something. Do you know what the guy said? Machinery is going to take the place of every profession." "Oh, dear, that's something you will never have to worry about."

—Marie Dressler reads Jean Harlow like a book.

For a great double feature, rent it with

Red Dust.

Seen it but in the mood for something similar? Try

Grand Hotel.

Answer to page 34 trivia question:

The Adventures of Buckaroo Banzai Across the Eighth Dimension.

Drama

Everyone has a different reason for coming to Billie Burke's dinner party, and nobody's interested in the food. (And, no, since this movie was shot six years before *The Wizard of Oz*, the guests aren't out to ask Burke how to get to the Emerald City.) This is a gathering that features second chances, financial windfalls, torrid affairs, and, last but not least, a supremely oblivious hostess. In short, *Dinner at Eight* is a happy excuse to watch well-dressed people take themselves way too seriously.

This sophisticated 1933 glitzfest may represent the high-water mark of Depression-era glamour films; not only the surroundings but nearly all the characters who glide by are impossibly, dangerously stylish. The surrealistically witty script, adapted from George S. Kaufman and Edna Ferber's Broadway hit, revels in the spectacle of old money facing off against new money at a time when hardly anyone had *any* money. It still plays like gangbusters.

Jean Harlow is wonderful here, having learned at long last, in *Red Dust*, how to act. Toss in John Barrymore, Wallace Beery, and Glinda, er, Billie Burke, and you've got a classic.

★ 1933, 113 minutes, B&W, not rated.

★ With: Marie Dressler, Jean Harlow, John Barrymore, Wallace Beery, Billie Burke. Director: George Cukor.

★ *Can you name Jean Harlow's last picture?*
(Answer on page 220.)

Divorce—Italian Style

What a guy.

Quite scandalous at the time of its release, but capable of being seen simply as a great comedy now, this fast-paced spoof of predatory male sexuality lets Marcello Mastroianni stake his claim as a landmark cinema male chauvinist pig. He plays a rich, philandering husband who's grown tired of his wife (Daniela Rocca). Divorce in Italy is, alas, impossible at this time, so he sets about planning the best way to murder her. If he can pull it off, he reasons, he'll be able to run away with that nubile teenager he's been seeing quite a lot of.

The movie's farcical kick comes from Mastroianni's scheming to take advantage of a (genuine!) Italian law of the period that allowed a husband to do away with his wife if he learned that she was involved in an adulterous relationship. Pretty convenient, huh? All Mastroianni has to do is figure out a way to get his honor convincingly besmirched, and he can knock off his wife and claim he was only avenging himself—legally. Mastroianni's exquisite comic performance earned him an Oscar nomination for Best Actor.

★ 1962, 104 minutes, B&W, not rated.

★ With: Marcello Mastroianni, Daniela Rocca, Stefania Sandrelli. Director: Pietro Germi.

★ *In what film did Mastroianni team up with Jack Lemmon?* (Answer on page 207.)

"The memory of those nights—or, rather, of one night."
—Marcello Mastroianni, reflecting on the events that led to a fateful encounter

For a great double feature, rent it with
La Dolce Vita.

Seen it but in the mood for something similar? Try
A Slightly Pregnant Man.

Answer to page 68 trivia question:
Captain Kathryn Janeway in "Star Trek: Voyager"; Kate Mulgrew took the role.

Foreign

Don't Look Now

*Control freaks beware: this film knows
there's no way to be in charge.*

*"Don't worry, I've
found the real world.
It's right down here."*
—Julie Christie's found the
way out of one maze.

**For a great double
feature, rent it with**

*Invasion of the Body
Snatchers* (1978).

**Seen it but in the mood
for something similar?
Try**

*The Railway Station
Man.*

**Answer to page 102
trivia question:**

Time Bandits.

John and Laura Baxter (Donald Sutherland and Julie Christie), trying to adjust to the accidental drowning of their daughter, head for Venice. They find themselves thrust into a completely unfamiliar world in which perspective is impossible and omens are everywhere. John Baxter, for instance, vividly envisions his own death. Recurring apparitions of a young girl in red, reminiscent of the Baxters' dead daughter, plague the couple—as do memories of drowning rats.

Some of the clues deliver a knockout punch. Others don't add up to anything. The triumph of *Don't Look Now* is that it involves its audience—and then some—while it keeps us wondering what the heck is happening. Director Roeg succeeds in summoning up not confusion but the terrifying unpredictability of the future . . . and the equally terrifying inscrutability of the past.

★ 1973, 110 minutes, color, R.

★ With: Donald Sutherland, Julie Christie. Director: Nicolas Roeg.

★ *For what film did Julie Christie win the Oscar for Best Actress?* (Answer on page 350.)

Horror

Jeremiah Johnson straps on the boards.

Beyond being dashing with a touch of icy recklessness, Robert Redford has basically no personality in this film; in between the predictable encounters with snowbabes, he simply lives to *schuss*.

Downhill Racer explores the intense, highly focused world of Olympic speed skiing; it includes some of the most exciting downhill racing footage ever shot. There's more to Gene Hackman's top-notch performance as the coach than meets the eye; without him the movie would lose its balance (and most of its dialogue). The American team arrives in Europe with all the jocular charm you'd expect, but their taut, relentless competitive drive never lets up for a moment. Redford, the top racer, is the win-at-all-costs philosophy personified. Everything he does is for the sake of a challenge, either spoken or unspoken, and life without some form of victory seems never to occur to him.

Much to Redford's credit, he keeps us interested in a character who seldom speaks, is fairly shallow emotionally, and is not, when you come right down to it, very likable. The star, however, like the scenery, is never less than riveting to watch.

★ 1969, 102 minutes, color, PG.

★ With: Robert Redford, Gene Hackman, Camilla Sparv. Director: Michael Ritchie.

★ *What member of the team went on to star in* War Games? (Answer on page 275.)

"You never had any real education, did you? All you ever had were your skis, and that's not enough."
—Gene Hackman's got the goods on Robert Redford.

For a great double feature, rent it with

Personal Best.

Seen it but in the mood for something similar? Try

This Sporting Life.

Answer to page 138 trivia question:

Sunset Boulevard.

Drama

Dracula

"The Strangest Love Story of All"

"I never drink . . . wine."

—Bela Lugosi politely refuses a drink . . . for now.

For a great double feature, rent it with:

Nosferatu (1922).

Seen it but in the mood for something similar? Try

The Mummy (1932).

Answer to page 288 trivia question:

It wasn't live. They were terrified he would say something nasty, so they put the show on a seven-second delay.

Audience members actually fainted in the aisles when this film premiered in 1931. Is it that scary today? Well, no, but *Dracula* does retain an eerie charm and an ethereal romanticism that most contemporary horror films regrettably miss.

Bela Lugosi makes up for what he lacks in sex appeal with an oddly disconcerting self-assurance in the role of the count. Sixty years later, Francis Ford Coppola offered in Lugosi's place Gary Oldman, who, while he may have had the sought-after sexual charge, had less than a tenth of Lugosi's hypnotically dominating style.

Coppola's film is a full-color, high-gore, erotically explicit treatment of the story; this version leaves you wondering about what takes place off-screen. Its understated, even naive approach, without wave after wave of superfluous special effects, is far more satisfying. Although there have been tremendous technical advances in moviemaking in the six decades between the two films, the original *Dracula* still has more, um, bite, than virtually anything else in the genre. Lugosi is impossible not to watch, which is more than you can say for most (all?) horror leads these days.

★ 1931, 75 minutes, B&W, not rated.

★ With: Bela Lugosi, Dwight Frye, Helen Chandler. Director: Tod Browning.

★ *What was Bela Lugosi's last film appearance?* (Answer on page 225.)

Horror

Dragon: The Bruce Lee Story

Enter the biopic.

What if Bruce Lee had made a film that had a talented director, a convincing script, and none of the bad dubbing? Unfortunately, the legendary martial arts star died before that film could be made, but Jason Scott Lee (no relation) is an entirely convincing substitute in this high-octane biopic. Director Rob Cohen cannily uses images from old Bruce Lee films as starting points for reenacting some of the situations in the celebrated star's all-too-brief life.

Dragon will captivate people who don't usually like martial arts films. It provides a portrait of a gifted, driven man who makes his way to America to confront obstacles such as debilitating injury, racism, and some sinister forces seemingly beyond the control of any human.

This well-constructed biography, which mixes fact with fantasy, has the good sense to keep certain elements of its story unresolved, and its image of Lee, a man caught between two cultures, is memorable. Released before the death of Bruce Lee's son, Brandon Lee, *Dragon* contains some eerie, unintended foreshadowing of that tragic event.

★ 1993, 119 minutes, color, PG-13.

★ With: Jason Scott Lee, Lauren Holly, Nancy Kwan. Director: Rob Cohen.

★ *In what musical did Nancy Kwan star?* (Answer on page 203.)

"EeeeeewwWOAHA!"
—Jason Scott Lee gets in the mood.

For a great double feature, rent it with
Enter the Dragon.

Seen it but in the mood for something similar? Try
Bird.

Answer to page 323 trivia question:
The Krays.

Biography

Dragonslayer

Nice work if you can get it.

It is long ago, in the dim, dark time situated between a pagan world of dragons and a Christian world that has no room for mythical creatures. And a dragon—the last dragon, in fact, on the face of the earth—is extorting the kingdom. If the people don't give up a virgin to the dragon every so often, she (the dragon) will destroy the kingdom. Not that high a price to pay if you're the king. The villagers, however, have had enough, so they send a couple of lads out to get a sorcerer. Ralph Richardson is sweet—and hilarious—in the role of the bumbling magician whose young apprentice (Peter MacNicol) must set out to face the dragon on his own, as earnest young men in fairy tales are wont to do.

A warning is in order. This movie, though executed elegantly and laced with exquisite special effects, is *not* for children. The dragon, by virtue of its expensive, realistic look, is very scary; the real reason the dragon is terrorizing the town is very scary; the scenes of virgins about to be eaten are very scary, especially if you happen to be one when you're watching it. If, however, you are old enough to handle the suspense yet young enough to believe in things like dragons and the innocence of first love, then this is a great rent.

★ 1981, 108 minutes, color, PG.

★ With: Peter MacNicol, Ralph Richardson, Caitlin Clarke. Director: Matthew Robbins.

★ *In what film did Ralph Richardson play the Supreme Being?* (Answer on page 98.)

Dreamscape

The president's been having nightmares.

ere's the premise: Max von Sydow has gathered some of the world's most accomplished psychics to test out his new method for eliminating sleep disorders caused by severe nightmares. The psychics are supposed to enter the patients' nightmares and help guide them out of their psychoses. Say . . . what if that method were to be used not for good but for evil? Who *knows* what could go haywire? Well, I don't think I'll be giving much away by saying that von Sydow's method does in fact fall into the Wrong Hands, but watching how it happens, and what unfolds as a result of its happening, is great fun.

Top-notch performances from von Sydow and Christopher Plummer, naturally; you should also keep an eye out for a very young Dennis Quaid, who turns in some nice work that hints at good things to come in the future. This picture features some masterful special effects and dream sequences that rival those in *The Manchurian Candidate*. All this, and Kate Capshaw, too.

★ 1984, 99 minutes, color, PG-13.

★ With: Dennis Quaid, Max von Sydow, Christopher Plummer, Kate Capshaw. Director: Joseph Ruben.

★ *Who is Kate Capshaw's husband?* (Answer on page 61.)

"In this world you're nothing, Alex, and I'm God."
—Talk about a head trip for Dennis Quaid. . . .

For a great double feature, rent it with *Brainstorm*.

Seen it but in the mood for something similar? Try *Altered States*.

Answer to page 312 trivia question: W. C. Fields; he wanted more money than MGM was willing to pay him.

Sci-Fi

Drugstore Cowboy

*William Burroughs as a drugged-out priest.
I can buy that.*

I'll admit that it doesn't *sound* like a comedy: a band of small-time thieves rob drugstores so they can supply their pill-popping habit. Sounds depressing, but their story is told here with such imagination that the picture never stops being fascinating in a strangely peppy way. Not unlike the protagonist when on speed.

Matt Dillon is the leader of the gang; he's all of 26, and he's really tired of being a druggie. But he's got responsibilities; there are other people's highs to think of besides his own. Dillon is one very short step ahead of the law; he wants to do the right thing, and if he had a clue, he probably could. His confessor, the defrocked priest who introduced him to drugs in the first place (played by writer William Burroughs!), isn't much help. Edgy, brave, and guiltily funny. If you're not sure whether it's OK to laugh, don't worry, it is.

★ 1989, 100 minutes, color, R.

★ With: Matt Dillon, Kelly Lynch, James Remar, William S. Burroughs. Director: Gus Van Sant.

★ *In what 1983 movie did Matt Dillon star with seemingly every promising young male actor of the day?*
(Answer on page 91.)

Duel

You'll never look at an 18-wheeler the same way again.

This remarkable *pas de deux* between a harried motorist and a menacing, faceless truck driver was the first sign of the great things to come from a young director named Steven Spielberg.

Dennis Weaver stars as the driver who gets a little more than he bargained for after what seems like a fairly routine incidence of highway rudeness; we never actually see the knight of the road who terrorizes him, but we sure get to know the guy. There in the shadows of his immense rig, he's relentless, unstoppable, and more than a little intimidating—just like the movie we're watching. Spielberg makes this film more than an exercise in mindless cruelty by convincing us that Weaver is doing everything a rational person *should* do in response to his "partner's" bizarre provocations. But because neither he nor we live in a rational world, his struggles only intensify the more he thinks them through. Weaver has simply been selected, seemingly at random, to take part in a conflict he never imagined he'd be sucked into.

Unlike the landmark *French Connection* (released at roughly the same time), *Duel* sticks with a single extended, lethal chase from beginning to end. This unforgettable film is proof that a movie consisting solely of car chases can be intellectually rigorous.

★ 1971, 90 minutes, color, PG.

★ With: Dennis Weaver, Tim Herbert, Charles Perl. Director: Steven Spielberg.

★ *What was the name of the character Dennis Weaver played on TV's "Gunsmoke"?* (Answer on page 120.)

"I'm in no mood to play games."
—Dennis Weaver has had enough of being mister nice guy.

For a great double feature, rent it with
The Sugarland Express.

Seen it but in the mood for something similar? Try
Speed.

Answer to page 300 trivia question:
Shirley Temple.

Suspense

A likely story.

Rita is not the real name of Julie Walters's character; she changed it after reading *Rubyfruit Jungle* by Rita Mae Brown. Have ya read it? Well, Walters has, and now she's ready to grow and change, no matter what (or whom) she has to leave behind. After all, once you've made the decision to improve yourself there's no going back. Or is there? Walters has signed up for classes at the university; her tutor is Michael Caine. He *doesn't* particularly want to grow. In fact he doesn't want to do much but drink and slowly ruin both his career and his life.

Walters has the advantage of not being a regular student. She's been around the track once or twice, and she doesn't treat Caine as an academic icon, like the awestruck kids he usually works with do. She knows she has a lot to learn, but she's got a direction . . . and she knows Caine has lost his. Would Rita Mae Brown speak up? Sure she would.

★ 1983, 110 minutes, color, PG 13.

★ With: Michael Caine, Julie Walters, Michael Williams. Director: Lewis Gilbert.

★ *What starring role launched Michael Caine's career as a lead actor?* (Answer on page 188.)

84 Charing Cross Road

One for the books.

Anthony Hopkins and Anne Bancroft propel this engaging study of how a life-affirming friendship takes root and blossoms. The film is based on the real-life experiences of playwright Helene Hanff, who struck up a correspondence beginning in 1949 with the staff of an English bookstore that specialized in rare books. Initially Bancroft's notes are chatty but restrained; the ones she receives back are formal, compliant, and signed by someone called F. P. D. Bancroft. Thrilled at being able to get the books she needs, Bancroft continues to write ever more spontaneous and ever more entertaining letters. Soon the mysterious F. P. D. reveals himself as Mr. Frank Doel (Hopkins) and finally simply as Frank. Bancroft soon becomes pen pals with the entire staff, and the letters she writes and receives give rise to an extended family of sorts. This is fortuitous, since Helen has no real family of her own.

84 Charing Cross Road is a love story, but the love that develops is the deep love of friends and the abiding love of the written word that they all share. A delightful little film.

★ 1987, 99 minutes, color, PG.

★ With: Anne Bancroft, Anthony Hopkins, Judi Dench. Director: David Jones.

★ *What film is Bancroft watching when she's alone in the cinema?* (Answer on page 213.)

"What kind of trip is it, business or pleasure?" "Unfinished business."

—The stranger in the next seat unwittingly poses the film's central question to Anne Bancroft.

For a great double feature, rent it with
Brief Encounter.

Seen it but in the mood for something similar? Try
The Efficiency Expert.

Answer to page 357 trivia question:
The banjo.

Drama

El Mariachi

Have guitar, will travel.

"That morning started like any other. No love. No luck. No ride."

—At the end of the day, Gallardo will have more—and less—than what he started with.

For a great double feature, rent it with

She's Gotta Have It, another impressive low-budget debut.

Seen it but in the mood for something similar? Try

Desperado.

Answer to page 295 trivia question:

The Conqueror.

It's amazing. You can take a couple of bazillion dollars and make *Last Action Hero,* or you can take seven grand and make *El Mariachi,* an imaginative action film far more memorable than the above-mentioned Arnold, Incorporated, mess. Robert Rodriguez's entry is predictably rough around the edges, and it looks as though it may have been shot with one camera, but it does what a good action flick has to do: it grabs your attention and doesn't let go until the end.

Now a word of warning is in order. This tale of mistaken identity among drug dealers is a very violent movie. But it's never gratuitous; the story is told with an almost poetic shooting style that at times appears to be an open homage to Peckinpah's blood-spattered classic *Bring Me the Head of Alfredo Garcia.* Yet Rodriguez, unlike Peckinpah, never goes over the line for the sheer thrill of doing so. Amazingly, all the characters in *El Mariachi* are quite intelligent. They actually think before they shoot. Talk about a change of pace.

★ 1992, 80 minutes, color, R.

★ With: Carlos Gallardo, Consuelo Gomez, Jamie de Hoyos. Director: Robert Rodriguez.

★ *Why is Carlos Gallardo targeted to die?* (Answer on page 252.)

Foreign

Elvis: One Night with You

Post–Ed Sullivan, pre–huge jumpsuit. Thankyuhverymuch.

What Eric Clapton succeeded in doing with his *Unplugged* album, the King did first—and, arguably, better. In 1968, after a 10-year hiatus from public performing, Elvis shot a comeback TV special. It put him back on the map. The highlight of the special was the impromptu, no-net-in-sight live sessions with a pared-down acoustic combo.

This is the uncut version of the live portion of the show, complete with false starts and chat between songs. It's a fascinating piece of music history and proof positive that the King could still rock, which was what he had set out to demonstrate.

In a crisp, informal set, Elvis punches his way through inspired versions of "That's All Right, Mama," "Heartbreak Hotel," "Hound Dog," and all the rest. This unedited session features some vintage (and often very funny) Elvis mumbling, and the music can't be topped.

★ 1986, 53 minutes, color, not rated.

★ With: Elvis Presley. Director: Steve Binder.

★ *Spot the woman in the audience with the biggest hair.* (Answer on page 280.)

"I just work here."
—Elvis, apologizing for having to end the set.

For a great double feature, rent it with *King Creole.*

Seen it but in the mood for something similar? Try *Chuck Berry Hail! Hail! Rock 'n' Roll!*

Answer to page 330 trivia question: Donald Sutherland.

Musical

The Emerald Forest

Don't you hate it when your teenager is more together than you are?

"When dreams become flesh, trouble is not far behind."

—Charley Boorman gets a warning from his adoptive father.

For a great double feature, rent it with

Sorcerer.

Seen it but in the mood for something similar? Try

The Last of the Mohicans (1992).

Answer to page 351 trivia question:

Blanco.

Relax. This is *not* the story of how modern man is destroying the rain forest and with it the very planet on which he lives. Nor is it a meditation on how man has lost touch with his mother, the earth, and, simultaneously, his deepest spiritual self. Nope, none of that tree hugging stuff here. This is an adventure story, pure and simple.

OK, I'm fibbing a little; there is a good deal of pontificating about the state of the equatorial jungles and just what repercussions we can expect from man's tireless destruction of the rain forest. But it doesn't last long, and I didn't want any of that stuff to deter you from this exciting tale of a man's search for his son, who was appropriated by a tribe called the Invisible People 10 years before the main action of the story. When the father finally tracks his boy down, he's not a boy anymore; he's a young man of 17. (Buff, too, but I digress.) The lad has become a brave, noble warrior who loves his tribal father deeply—as well as the man called Dadee he sees in his dreams. *The Emerald Forest* is a relationship movie, a morality tale, and a grand adventure. Most amazing of all, it's a true story. A keeper.

★ 1985, 113 minutes, color, R.

★ With: Powers Boothe, Meg Foster, Charley Boorman. Director: John Boorman.

★ *Where did director John Boorman find his young star?*
(Answer on page 329.)

The Enchanted Cottage

You look marvelous.

There are love stories and there are love stories; this one's a *love story*. Robert Young plays a pilot who left for World War II suave, carefree, and charming, but comes back a physically—and emotionally—scarred man. He returns, alone, to the cottage that was to be his honeymoon retreat (his fiancée has walked out on him because he's become such a jerk). There he meets the housekeeper, Dorothy McGuire, for the second time. He doesn't remember the first time because McGuire comes off as, um, pretty plain in this movie. Back when Young was handsome and dashing, lots of plain girls passed his radar screen unnoticed.

The cottage the two spend so much time in has a mysterious history: some people say it's haunted; others say it's enchanted. Whatever—something wonderful happens when these two unhappy people find each other within its walls. I won't tell you what it is, but I will let you in on my own opinion: I think it's magic. This is a wonderful romantic film that will leave you believing that love may just conquer all.

★ 1945, 91 minutes, B&W, not rated.

★ With: Robert Young, Dorothy McGuire, Herbert Marshall. Director: John Cromwell.

★ *In what World War II film did Robert Young costar with Margaret O'Brien?* (Answer on page 340.)

"You've both been touched by a power beyond this world."
—Herbert Marshall tries to explain the inexplicable.

For a great double feature, rent it with
Now, Voyager.

Seen it but in the mood for something similar? Try
The Ghost and Mrs. Muir.

Answer to page 307 trivia question:
Jason and the Argonauts.

Romance

The Endless Summer

*Wax your stick and
get stoked.*

"You guys really
missed it. You should
have been here
yesterday."

—The classic response to
today's surfing, no matter
how great it was today

**For a great double
feature, rent it with**

*The Endless Summer
II.*

**Seen it but in the mood
for something similar?
Try**

On Any Sunday.

**Answer to page 163
trivia question:**

Both will probably
have to wait until hell
freezes over to be
voted another Oscar.

Documentary

If you want to enjoy this fully, rent the sequel, the recent, unimaginatively titled *Endless Summer II*, at the same time. The first film treats the whole sixties surfing scene as an emerging cultural phenomenon; the second registers higher on the awe-inspiring moves scale because both the waves and the camera work are a lot better than they were the first time out. Between the two films, you'll get the skinny on the whole bitchin', tube-scarfing world of surfing, a sport that's really more a way of life than a form of recreation.

The first picture shows us two guys who believe that to live in search of the perfect wave is completely fulfilling; the sequel demonstrates how, a couple of decades down the pike, that pursuit is still the name of the game . . . even if the young men are now highly paid sports professionals rather than anti-Establishment loafers.

Now, I don't want to mislead you; we're not talking about *Waiting for Godot* here. The surfers in each film are boys who can be distracted from a bikini only by a great wave. Not only is there no subtext; there's no *text* to speak of: the principals aren't allowed to talk. But the world they live in is so spectacular, you won't care. Way gnarly.

★ 1966, 95 minutes, color, not rated.

★ With: Mike Hynson, Robert August. Director: Bruce Brown.

★ *Who introduced surfing to the mainland?* (Answer on page 261.)

Enemies, a Love Story

It's not a love triangle; it's a love quadrangle!

Adventures in bigamy. Ron Silver, Anjelica Huston, and Lena Olin star in this unforgettable adaptation of Isaac Bashevis Singer's story. A Jewish intellectual, having evaded death at the hands of the Nazis during World War II, makes his way to Coney Island only to find himself married to three women at the same time. Despite what you may be thinking, Silver *isn't* an utter schmuck; it really wasn't his fault . . . completely. Things get complicated during wartime, OK? Cut the guy a little slack.

Powerhouse performances from Silver, Huston, and Olin mark this distinguished entry, which plays like a farce on the surface but features, in the Silver-Olin pairing, a story of love between guilt-ridden survivors that you will not soon forget. Paul Mazursky directed and, in an inspired piece of casting, allowed comic Alan King to demonstrate his ability to handle serious material. Nice touch.

★ 1989, 119 minutes, color, R.

★ With: Ron Silver, Anjelica Huston, Lena Olin, Alan King. Director: Paul Mazursky.

★ *Name the film for which Anjelica Huston won an Oscar as Best Supporting Actress.* (Answer on page 257.)

"If men had their way, a woman would lie down a prostitute and get up a virgin."
—Anjelica Huston, outlining a fundamental truth

For a great double feature, rent it with
Hester Street.

Seen it but in the mood for something similar? Try
Crossing Delancey.

Answer to page 362 trivia question:
1993's *Faraway, So Close!*

Drama

The Entertainer

*I know you're out there, folks. I can
hear you breathing.*

Irony of ironies: what is arguably Laurence Olivier's greatest performance comes in the role of a lousy actor. The beautiful thing is, you buy it completely— and you keep watching.

Laurence Olivier plays a washed-up song-and-dance man of distinctly mediocre ability who pulls his famous father out of retirement to mount one last try at the big time. It takes a hell of a lot of talent to make an audience care about someone as awful as Olivier's Archie Rice; his fading vaudevillian is heart-wrenchingly convincing both on his own pathetic terms and as a metaphor for an England that has seen much, much better days. (The story unfolds during the Suez Canal fiasco.)

This unforgettable film, which shows off its leading man at the height of his powers, boasts an extraordinary supporting cast: Alan Bates, Albert Finney, and Joan Plowright (who would later marry Olivier) in their screen debuts. They're great, but they all know when to get out of the big guy's way.

★ 1960, 97 minutes, B&W, not rated.

★ With: Laurence Olivier, Joan Plowright, Albert Finney. Director: Tony Richardson.

★ *What film did Greta Garbo fire Laurence Olivier from?*
(Answer on page 165.)

Drama

Escape from New York

Although I hear some parts of the Village are still nice.

I n the not-too-distant future, New York City has been turned into a giant penal colony.

Kurt Russell stars in this thriller, which centers around his effort to rescue the president of the United States from a band of really scary dudes in nightmarish midtown. How tough is Russell? Well, he's got a snake tattoo that starts on his belly and heads . . . um, south. This is a fast-paced, violent, very funny action picture that scores some serious points by parodying current New York traditions against the backdrop of a decaying Big Apple run entirely by corrupt crooks. In addition to Russell's fine work, there are some nice comic turns from some unlikely sources: Ernest Borgnine (no, really, he's great) and Isaac Hayes, who has a lot of fun with his leader-of-the-pack role.

★ 1981, 99 minutes, color, R.

★ With: Kurt Russell, Ernest Borgnine, Isaac Hayes. Director: John Carpenter.

★ *Who played the female lead in Carpenter's* Halloween? (Answer on page 217.)

"Call me Snake."
—Kurt Russell prefers to keep things informal.

For a great double feature, rent it with
The Thing (1982).

Seen it but in the mood for something similar? Try
No Escape (1982).

Answer to page 317 trivia question:
Joan Fontaine.

Action

Europa, Europa

Lost in the masquerade.

"Is it hard to play someone else?" "It is much easier than playing yourself."
—Marco Hofschneider has an identity crisis.

For a great double feature, rent it with
Empire of the Sun.

Seen it but in the mood for something similar? Try
Au Revoir, Les Enfants.

Answer to page 338 trivia question:
"Windmills of Your Mind."

This spellbinding film, based on the true-life story of Solomon Perel, charts the journey of a teenage Jewish boy who will do anything, and become anyone, to survive the horrors of the Second World War. Many of the outrageous subterfuges the lad gets away with (artfully avoiding physical examinations as he pretends to be a member of the German infantry, for instance, or joining a chapter of the Hitler Youth) turn on simple luck, but the movie comes across as far more than a series of extraordinary coincidences. Paradoxically enough, the young Jew on the run finds himself happy, for a brief moment, in a world that can't possibly accept him: praised by an instructor as the possessor of a classically Aryan face, he learns his first lesson about love from a fiercely anti-Semitic German girl.

The price of acceptance is high for most of us who manage to make it through adolescence; for Perel it's a series of steadily more impossible soul-shattering choices. His remarkable journey, which affords an eerie true-to-life view of both sides of the Holocaust, is reminiscent of Chauncey Gardiner's travels in the Peter Sellers classic *Being There* . . . but Perel's story is all the more remarkable because it really happened. Not to be missed.

★ 1991, 115 minutes, color, R.

★ With: Marco Hofschneider, Julie Delpy, Piotr Kozlowski. Director: Agnieszka Holland.

★ *What popular family film did Holland later direct?*
(Answer on page 192.)

Everything You Always Wanted to Know About Sex (but Were Afraid to Ask)

Baaa.

Having struck comic gold with one unlikely film-rights purchase (see the entry for *What's Up, Tiger Lily?*), Woody Allen tossed the dice again and laid down the modest cash required to purchase the right to make a movie out of Dr. David Reuben's landmark sex-ed book. It had been a huge bestseller, of course, but people must have wondered exactly what *kind* of picture Allen had in mind when word got out about the sale.

Well, it's not a cinematic sex manual; it's a loosely connected evening of deft sketches dealing with various absurd obsessions having to do with the most popular topic on earth. Each of the skits has the good sense to stop when the laughs stop coming.

High points: Allen as a spermatazoan; Allen being pursued by a giant breast through the countryside; and Gene Wilder head-over-heels in love with a sheep.

Lots of pleasant, talented, and familiar faces in the cast. Adult-oriented humor, to be sure, but the film is not explicit. It's about as risque as an episode of "The Benny Hill Show" but with a measurable IQ.

★ 1972, 87 minutes, color, R.

★ With: Woody Allen, Louise Lasser, Lynn Redgrave, Gene Wilder. Director: Woody Allen.

★ *What member of the cast was a former wife of Allen's?*
(Answer on page 124.)

"I must think of something quickly, because before you know it the Renaissance will be here and we'll all be painting."
—Woody Allen makes a remarkably prescient medieval jester.

For a great double feature, rent it with *Night on Earth.*

Seen it but in the mood for something similar? Try *What's Up, Tiger Lily?*

Answer to page 3 trivia question: Horse.

Experience Preferred . . . but Not Essential

A sex comedy that will let you respect yourself in the morning.

"A girl who hasn't, a boy who thinks he can't—this to me doesn't sound like a happy combination."

—Elizabeth Edmonds dismisses a male friend who keeps asking her pointedly about the movie *Tea and Sympathy.*

For a great double feature, rent it with

Circle of Friends.

Seen it but in the mood for something similar? Try

Gregory's Girl.

Answer to page 37 trivia question:

Bill & Ted Go to Hell.

This gentle coming-of-age comedy follows a young waitress (Elizabeth Edmonds) at a Welsh seaside resort hotel through the summer of 1962. She's the only virgin on the boisterous staff, and it shows. Will she sleep with the charming cook? OK, then, when and how?

Hollywood would turn this simple premise into a series of excuses to get the waitresses to take their blouses off. Thankfully, this well-crafted English effort resists the temptation. It's a subtly rendered account of one young woman's journey to adulthood that boasts a generous supply of lovable eccentrics (expertly portrayed by an obscure but quite talented ensemble cast).

This is not another foray into adolescent voyeurism but a wise, consistently funny exercise in slice-of-life moviemaking that will keep you thinking from beginning to end. Its moral, never shoved in your face, is contained in the apt title, which is a good deal more profound than it may seem at first glance.

★ 1983, 80 minutes, color, PG.

★ With: Elizabeth Edmonds, Sue Wallace, Geraldine Griffith. Director: Peter Duffell.

★ *What interracial romance did Peter Duffell direct?*
(Answer on page 95.)

Comedy

Eye of the Needle

*He'd be a great catch if he weren't
a merciless fascist spy.*

The unexpectedly sexy Donald Sutherland plays the Needle, a German spy who makes his way into the arms of a lonely British housewife (Kate Nelligan) in 1944. Sutherland got the nickname because of his skill with a switchblade, but the moniker might just as well refer to his piercing intelligence and his ability to vanish in an instant.

Sutherland knows where and when the D-Day invasion is to take place, and the British authorities know he knows, and he knows the British authorities know he knows. Unfortunately, Nelligan doesn't know a thing—and if she doesn't stop Sutherland from getting the word to Hitler, the war will end with the bad guys on top. In one of his most impressive performances, Sutherland comes across as both ruthless and essentially human; his affair with Nelligan summons up the best in both of them . . . for a while.

This taut, sexy thriller, based on the Ken Follett novel, keeps you hooked from beginning to end. Its most memorable scenes are not the macho displays of espionage and derring-do but the Needle's attempts to get Nelligan to open up emotionally.

★ 1981, 112 minutes, color, R.

★ With: Donald Sutherland, Kate Nelligan, Christopher Cazenove. Director: Richard Marquand.

★ *In what film does Donald Sutherland expose his bare posterior for the greater glory of art?* (Answer on page 196.)

"You don't despise me, do you?"
—Donald Sutherland is looking for a woman who'll understand that beneath his Nazi exterior, there's a nice guy waiting to be discovered.

For a great double feature, rent it with
The Fourth Protocol.

Seen it but in the mood for something similar? Try
The Railway Station Man.

Answer to page 71 trivia question:
Videodrome.

Suspense

A Face in the Crowd

Andy Griffith as the heavy?
You bet.

"Rednecks, house-wives, shut-ins, pea pickers . . . everybody's got to jump when somebody else blows the whistle."

—Andy Griffith explains that everyone has to answer to somebody . . . eventually.

For a great double feature, rent it with

Quiz Show.

Seen it but in the mood for something similar? Try

Network.

Answer to page 105 trivia question:

Chester Goode.

By 1957 television was already being used to elect presidents, sell soap, and generally corrupt the populace. (Ah, the more things change. . . .) As *A Face in the Crowd* opens, Andy Griffith would seem the least likely person to put the new medium to its most ominous uses; he's a nondescript drifter in jail for loitering. Patricia Neal, whose father owns a radio station, interviews the earthy Griffith, a guitar-picking everyman who calls himself Lonesome Rhodes. After hearing Griffith speak out on the plight of the little people, Neal suspects she's stumbled onto something she can sell in the new media-driven world she's determined to master. She's right.

On radio and TV, Griffith begins to accumulate unexpected power and the ability to generate truckloads of money, but he also has big-time political ambitions. What happens when a media-savvy but fundamentally irresponsible man wins the whole country's ear? Neal starts to wonder about that herself and about the consequences of what she has created. Should she pull the plug? By the time she decides, it may be a little too late.

Griffith, who has been imprisoned in his Andy Taylor persona since 1964 or so, proves here that he is capable of a truly great performance that puts a grim twist on that seductive, down-home likability of his.

★ 1957, 125 minutes, B&W, not rated.

★ With: Andy Griffith, Patricia Neal, Lee Remick. Director: Elia Kazan.

★ *Name the three A-list actors who made their movie debuts in this film.* (Answer on page 262.)

Drama

Fantastic Voyage

All right, who dropped the scissors?

Say there's this really important scientist, right? And he's got this blood clot on his brain, OK? And say the only way to treat it is to shrink down Raquel Welch and a bunch of other medical specialists and inject them right *into* the guy. Wouldn't that be cool? Well, it is.

Even though the awe-inspiring-at-the-time special effects are still a hoot to watch, the real focus here is on the characters, particularly Donald Pleasance's creepily atheistic saboteur. (Was it ever easier to spot a bad guy at the beginning of a movie?) At a time when the nation was fixating on the exploration of outer space, *Fantastic Voyage* summoned up a technologically inspiring image of the inner recesses of the human body. (Nothing you couldn't watch with the kids, of course, but you may come away with a case of indigestion if you munch too heavily on that popcorn.)

Even with all the razzle-dazzle process shots of the aorta and such like, the visual high point has to be the sight of a microscopic Raquel Welch having invading antibodies plucked away from, um, various parts of her form-fitting wet suit. Don't worry; they're all doctors.

★ 1966, 100 minutes, color, not rated.

★ With: Raquel Welch, Edmond O'Brien, Donald Pleasance. Director: Richard Fleischer.

★ *In what film did Pleasance star as a good guy who goes blind at just the wrong time?* (Answer on page 333.)

"A woman has no place on a mission like this."

—Raquel Welch gets static, as all women in pre-1965 science fiction movies must, just for being there. Maybe the wet suit won them over.

For a great double feature, rent it with

Journey to the Center of the Earth.

Seen it but in the mood for something similar? Try

Innerspace.

Answer to page 14 trivia question:

The Last Detail.

Sci-Fi

The Field

A great plot.

"*I'll not meet my mother in heaven and tell her I've lost that land.*"

—Good old Irish guilt— there's a motivation for Richard Harris to hold onto that field.

For a great double feature, rent it with

Far and Away.

Seen it but in the mood for something similar? Try

King Lear (1984).

Answer to page 48 trivia question:

Melanie Griffith, Don Johnson, and John Goodman.

asily Richard Harris's best work; he fought hard to get the lead role, going so far as to travel to Ireland for character study work *before he was awarded the part.* It's a lucky thing for both him and us that he got it.

The story is that of a family that chooses to stay in Ireland during the great potato famine because Harris loves the land more than anything else—and he pays a dear price for that love. Harris, who is determined to pass the family farm on to his son, tends a small piece of land cleared by hand by his forebears and lovingly nurtured for generations. The field is the most important thing in Harris's life, and he works it like a demon, but starvation looms. When an American (Tom Berenger) threatens to assume control of the field, a lot more than the deed to a modest stretch of land is at stake.

A powerful piece of work that features John Hurt as a considerably more moving fool than he played in *King Lear* (1984).

★ 1990, 107 minutes, color, PG-13.

★ With: Richard Harris, Tom Berenger, John Hurt. Director: Jim Sheridan.

★ *The actor portraying the son played the role of the evil nemesis in what Tom Clancy movie?* (Answer on page 347.)

Drama

Five Easy Pieces

Hold the chicken . . .

This breakthrough Jack Nicholson film comes at you from several odd angles at once. Just when you think you've got a bead on the uneasy relationship between oil-field worker Nicholson and his waitress wife (Karen Black), the movie throws you the first of its many curveballs. It turns out that Nicholson pursues his hardscrabble lifestyle not out of economic necessity but as the result of his refusal to conform to the standards of others; his estranged family is quite well-to-do, and Nicholson himself is an accomplished classical pianist.

That's the earliest, but by no means the last, indication of the mystery lurking about the heart of Nicholson's character, who personifies both the restless individuality of the era and its skepticism of established social norms. Nicholson chooses to hang out with people who have stopped growing emotionally—but why?

The film poses more questions than it answers, but it hangs together wonderfully. The justly memorable diner scene between a waitress who knows the rules and Nicholson, who has no interest in them, has, sadly, been reduced to a much-quoted sound bite with the passage of the years. The whole movie deserves a good look from beginning to end.

★ 1970, 90 minutes, color, R.

★ With: Jack Nicholson, Karen Black, Sally Struthers. Director: Bob Rafelson.

★ *In what film did Jack Nicholson first showcase his distinctive talents as a singer?* (Answer on page 336.)

"Do you see that sign, sir?" "Do you see this sign?"
—Jack Nicholson bucks the system.

For a great double feature, rent it with *Paris, Texas.*

Seen it but in the mood for something similar? Try *The Four Hundred Blows.*

Answer to page 82 trivia question: *Miss Firecracker.*

Drama

The 5,000 Fingers of Dr. T.

Boy in a beanie gets chased by meanies.

"When the plumber Zabladowski has installed the last sink, I want him disintegrated!"
—Piano-dictator Hans Conreid goes on yet another power trip.

For a great double feature, rent it with *Yellow Submarine.*

Seen it but in the mood for something similar? Try *Willie Wonka and the Chocolate Factory.*

Answer to page 117 trivia question: Louise Lasser.

"Practice makes perfect!" That's the oft-repeated slogan of Dr. T. (Hans Conreid), a cryptofascist piano instructor whose aim is to enslave 500 kids and imprison them in a kind of anti-Disneyland where five-finger exercises never end. An unflappable young lad (Tommy Rettig) prefers baseball and sets about foiling the evil doctor's scheme.

Along the way there's a pair of bewhiskered, roller-skating Siamese twins, acres of masterful visual puns, and a hilarious extended dance sequence. (Picture the Cat in the Hat directing the fantasy ballet from *An American in Paris*.) It's hard to say why this enchanting, inventive movie took four decades to find an audience. But who cares? It's a must-rent, and it's a lot of fun.

★ 1953, 89 minutes, color, not rated.

★ With: Peter Lind Hayes, Hans Conreid, Tommy Rettig. Director: Roy Rowland.

★ *What does the* T *in "Dr. T." stand for?* (Answer on page 355.)

Forbidden Planet

Leslie Nielsen shows up in this one; for current moviegoers, it's hard to take a word he says seriously.

Considered by many to be the finest science fiction film of the 1950s, this is, no kidding, a loose adaptation of Shakespeare's *The Tempest*. (It was also an important early influence on Gene Roddenberry's "Star Trek" series.) The special effects—state of the art at the time—aren't exactly earth-shattering now, but the story and direction are strong enough to keep you hooked.

It's the year 2200; on the planet Altair-4, a band of earthlings encounters a lone doctor (Walter Pidgeon, who's kind of like Prospero) with a beautiful young daughter (Anne Francis, who's kind of like Miranda). They're the only ones left from a failed attempt at colonization. What strange, invisible force is at work on the surface of the alien world, which boasts two moons and a green sky? And what's the deal with the friendly robot Robbie, who does everything Pidgeon tells him to (kind of like Ariel)? Stay tuned—and no peeking at those old notebooks from English class.

★ 1956, 98 minutes, color, not rated.

★ With: Leslie Nielsen, Walter Pidgeon, Anne Francis. Director: Fred McLeod Wilcox.

★ *Name the film in which Anne Francis appeared with Spencer Tracy and Lee Marvin.* (Answer on page 133.)

"Why don't you kiss me, like everyone else does?"

—Anne Francis can't figure out what's up with Leslie Nielsen.

For a great double feature, rent it with
The Day the Earth Stood Still.

Seen it but in the mood for something similar? Try
Voyage to the Moon.

Answer to page 141 trivia question:
Annie Leibovitz.

42nd Street

A testament to the tremendous healing power of clichés.

"You're going out a youngster—but you've got to come back a star."
—Ruby Keeler gets the big speech. No pressure, though.

For a great double feature, rent it with
Pennies from Heaven.

Seen it but in the mood for something similar? Try
Footlight Parade.

Answer to page 179 trivia question:
The dress Davis wears is really jet-black; because it's the only pure black object in the scene, it's the most dominant element.

Forget the brief excerpts in anthology shows and retrospectives; forget the Broadway musical inspired by the film decades after its release; forget the endless parodies and one-liners this archetypal backstage musical has spun off. Forget . . . well, I forget. But that's the point of the whole undertaking, isn't it?

It's the Depression; the producers of a splashy Broadway musical are out to get people to forget the breadlines. By the time they're done, they've even made us forget that last-minute replacement Ruby Keeler can't really dance very well. Or act. But, boy, is she spunky! By the time the movie moves into the home stretch, you're convinced she's the hottest thing since the electric refrigerator.

The picture fairly radiates energy from its first frame to its last, and the inventive visual numbers still pack quite a punch. Casting Ruby Keeler could have been either a disaster or a masterstroke; thanks to Busby Berkeley's unforgettable choreography and some expert direction from Lloyd Bacon, her lack of ability somehow comes across as fresh-faced earnestness, so let's call it a masterstroke.

★ 1933, 89 minutes, B&W, not rated.

★ With: Dick Powell, Ruby Keeler, Ginger Rogers. Director: Lloyd Bacon.

★ *Who directed the Broadway stage play based on the film?* (Answer on page 268.)

The Fountainhead

Edifice complex.

The image: Gary Cooper standing with rolled-up sleeves, sweaty, holding a pneumatic drill. Could this tableau be intended symbolically? Could be. What girl could resist Coop? Not Patricia Neal, here playing the classic ice queen.

Ayn Rand's bestselling story of a perfectionist architect is just as stylized as Cooper's skyscrapers. His steadfast refusal to change his designs mirrors Rand's own approach to her work. She insisted on writing the screenplay here, a decision that led many critics to find fault with the picture's occasionally stilted dialogue.

Personally, I've always thought of the picture as a vast, big-budget comic book with themes big enough to hold up under a little inspired artificiality. Individualism is all-important; power corrupts. And if you ask Gary Cooper to come around to fix your fireplace, you better be ready to admit that you need the heat.

★ 1949, 114 minutes, B&W, not rated.

★ With: Gary Cooper, Patricia Neal, Raymond Massey. Director: King Vidor.

★ *Patricia Neal was married to what well-known author of children's books?* (Answer on page 200.)

"A building has integrity—just like a man, and just as seldom."

—Gary Cooper has a point. But can you take a building out dancing?

For a great double feature, rent it with
A Face in the Crowd.

Seen it but in the mood for something similar? Try
Love Letters (1945).

Answer to page 214 trivia question:
Revenge.

Drama

127

The Four Feathers (1939)

Not to be confused with
The Three Caballeros.

"There's no place in England for a coward."
—The reluctant John Clements is on the receiving end of this declaration from his very stodgy, very English father.

For a great double feature, rent it with
Zulu.

Seen it but in the mood for something similar? Try
Gunga Din.

Answer to page 249 trivia question:
Ishtar.

A young man from a prominent family (John Clements) has been raised on tales of war and death. He comes from a long line of military heroes and is expected to follow in their footsteps, but his father is worried: he caught him reading a book of poems (Shelley, no less). Clements understands his family obligations—but he feels that war is a terrible waste and is certain that if men would put their energies elsewhere the world would be a better place.

Fifteen years pass, and just before his regiment leaves for battle, Clements's father dies. This frees him to resign his commission and live the life he chooses; after his regimental buddies hear of this, they send him a package containing three white feathers attached to their calling cards. When his girlfriend tells him that he has made a mistake, that he was honor bound to go to battle, Clements takes a white feather from her fan and adds it to his collection. But is he a coward?

Filmed with miles of impressive footage of the North African landscape (much of it shows up in several other movies), *The Four Feathers* is a poised, accomplished, very British examination of what constitutes real manhood. It's aged well over the years.

★ 1939, 115 minutes, color, not rated.

★ With: John Clements, Ralph Richardson, June Duprez. Director: Zoltan Korda.

★ *Can you name Clements's regiment?* (Answer on page 359.)

The Four Hundred Blows

Look out, kid,
it's somethin' you did . . .

François Truffaut's masterful portrait of a young boy in conflict with the world is honest and moving in a way that few motion pictures ever manage to be. With infinite compassion and subtlety, the film follows the onset of one human being's quest to find a place where he belongs; it's a quest that starts at home and one beset with tragic obstacles.

Films that place the central weight of a story on the shoulders of a single child actor, yet don't depend on easy laughs or cute shtick, usually collapse in a titanic fireball. Here's one exception to the rule.

Jean-Pierre Leaud turns in a stunning, informed performance as the disaffected youngster; the work he does in this film will stay with you for a long, long time. Part of the picture's remarkable effect arises out of the sheer wonder of watching someone so young act with such obvious depth and understanding of the role. The film, which features groundbreaking (for the time) New Wave editing and shooting techniques, was Truffaut's directorial debut.

★ 1959, 99 minutes, B&W, not rated.

★ With: Jean-Pierre Leaud, Claire Maurier, Albert Remy. Director: François Truffaut.

★ *What Truffaut film parodied the art of moviemaking?*
(Answer on page 163.)

"Take out the garbage."
—Jean-Pierre Leaud gets all the dirty work.

For a great double feature, rent it with *The Bicycle Thief.*

Seen it but in the mood for something similar? Try *Small Change.*

Answer to page 150 trivia question: *Big Business.*

Foreign

Emily Post will be of no help here.

"They tell me you are the star of the illegals' directorate. You'll need to be."

—Clearly, Pierce Brosnan's got his work cut out for him.

For a great double feature, rent it with

The Ipcress File.

Seen it but in the mood for something similar? Try

Eye of the Needle.

Answer to page 186 trivia question:

Sun Records.

If ever an actor was born to play a spy, it was Michael Caine. He brings to the role a savvy, street-smart sensibility that combines perfectly with a healthy (and often very funny) disrespect for authority. As in *The Ipcress File,* Caine here finds himself up against a crowd of boorish bureaucrats who care more for their positions than for the fate of the free world. Pierce Brosnan, having been passed over for the role of James Bond in favor of Timothy Dalton, seems to have defected as a result; here he plays a Russian spy whose mission is to build an atomic bomb on an American air base in England in order to destroy NATO.

Brosnan is just as clever as Caine; he brings something very special to a part that could easily have been played as an emotionless Marxist robot. Instead Brosnan is reluctant, hesitating slightly before every kill; but as time ticks away, so does his conscience, until all that is left is a killer who has gone too far to turn back now. The two exceptional performances of the principals make this a must-rent.

★ 1987, 119 minutes, color, R.

★ With: Michael Caine, Pierce Brosnan, Joanna Cassidy. Director: John Mackenzie.

★ *In what film was Michael Caine the only person to appear?* (Answer on page 272.)

Freebie and the Bean

Have you ever noticed that nobody obeys the speed limit in San Francisco?

How many quadrillion dollars has Hollywood made from the odd-couple police buddy picture? You've got to figure in all three *Lethal Weapon* pictures, *48 Hours*, *Red Heat*, *Stakeout*, and, yes, even *K-9* and *Turner and Hooch*. James Caan and Alan Arkin team up here for a memorable contribution to the genre that may well have been the genesis of the whole thing.

Caan's the hothead; Arkin's the eccentric. They're hot on the trail of a big-time gangster, and they don't mind tearing the city of San Francisco apart to find him. At least Caan doesn't. Arkin isn't too keen on having any more nervous breakdowns per day than are absolutely necessary, but then again, he's having a rough week. His wife (Valerie Harper, who shines here when given the chance to display deeper-than-sitcom acting ability) may be cheating on him.

This picture's a heck of a lot more fun than most of the very similar entries that followed it. The chemistry between the two leads is so good you wish they'd succumbed to the urge to make a sequel, like everyone else.

★ 1974, 113 minutes, color, R.

★ With: Alan Arkin, James Caan, Valerie Harper. Director: Richard Rush.

★ *In what chilly, offbeat network comedy did Alan Arkin's son Adam win notice?* (Answer on page 222.)

"We've had a little . . . at 618 Elm St. Could you send a tow truck please? It's the third floor, apartment 304."
—James Caan makes a difficult call.

For a great double feature, rent it with
Midnight Run.

Seen it but in the mood for something similar? Try
Stakeout.

Answer to page 222 trivia question:
Only two months, marking what had to be a stateside land speed record for sequels.

Action

131

The Freshman (1925)

*Roll call of silent comic geniuses: Chaplin and Keaton . . .
and Lloyd, the third man.*

"Alla-ga-zink! Alla-ga-zink! Boola bink! Wow!"

—Harold Lloyd practices a catchy little cheer in preparation for his first day on campus

For a great double feature, rent it with
The General.

Seen it but in the mood for something similar? Try
Safety Last.

Answer to page 257 trivia question:
Ragtime.

One of silent comic master Harold Lloyd's most exhilarating efforts. (You remember—he's the guy in glasses hanging from the clock hand in that famous poster print.) Lloyd plays an earnest newcomer to college who will do anything, but anything, to win popularity on campus and has no idea that virtually the entire student body is making fun of him behind his back. He steadfastly works his way up from punching bag to football hero.

The Big Game sequence, seemingly obligatory for any comedy set in a college town, is one of the funniest ever put on film. Together Lloyd, Charlie Chaplin, and Buster Keaton formed the reigning comic triumvirate of the silent era; even in our current period of high-tech, industrial-magic blockbuster filmmaking, Lloyd's unparalleled physical comedy is sensational to watch. Did all his own stunts, too.

If you've never seen his stuff, you're in for a pleasant surprise. *The Freshman* is one of his very best; if you like it, and you will, you may want to look around for *Safety Last*, which is not quite as strong but does contain the famous clock-face-of-the-skyscraper sequence.

★ 1925, 70 minutes, B&W, not rated.

★ With: Harold Lloyd, Jobyna Ralston, Brooks Benedict. Directors: Sam Taylor and Fred Newmeyer.

★ *What happened to comic daredevil Lloyd's film career after a freak on-the-set accident blew off most of one of his hands?* (Answer on page 208.)

Silent

The Freshman (1990)

Featuring a strangely familiar "importer" with an Italian accent who's awfully hard to refuse.

Matthew Broderick shines as a film student who gets mixed up with endangered species, mob deals, and Bert Parks. It sounds dangerous, folks, and it is.

This deliciously weird little comedy benefits more from its young star's endearing, fresh-faced innocence than it does from its eccentric plot; Broderick has a plucky, naive comic persona that is quietly reminiscent of Harold Lloyd. (Note the film's title, which echoes that of a Lloyd classic.)

The tributes to film legends don't stop there: Marlon Brando's magical (and brave) parody of his own legendary Mafia don from *The Godfather* must be seen to be believed. He single-handedly pushes the movie into overdrive. The old pro and the eager newcomer work together very well; watch Brando's gentle, fatherly dismissal of Broderick's sudden alarm when the youngster spots a reverently positioned portrait of Mussolini in the mob boss's "social club."

Having attained cinema icon status with his unforgettable performance as Don Vito Corleone in 1972, Brando comes close to it again by playing the same character for laughs. He and Broderick are very funny indeed here.

★ 1990, 102 minutes, color, PG.

★ With: Matthew Broderick, Marlon Brando, Bruno Kirby. Director: Andrew Bergman.

★ *What picture marked Brando's screen debut?* (Answer on page 288.)

"Every word I say is, by definition, a promise."

—This doesn't seem to comfort Matthew Broderick as much as Marlon Brando means it to.

For a great double feature, rent it with
The Godfather.

Seen it but in the mood for something similiar? Try
Ferris Bueller's Day Off.

Answer to page 125 trivia question:
Bad Day at Black Rock.

Comedy

Friendly Persuasion

Sometimes being a pacifist can make you really want to smack someone.

Gary Cooper stars in this fine adaptation of Jessamyn West's novel about a pacifist Quaker family's struggles to come to terms with the realities of the Civil War. It's tough to continue arguing in favor of a nonviolent lifestyle when Confederate raiders keep hammering away at you. Cooper's son, Anthony Perkins, decides he's had enough and resolves to take up arms against the Rebs.

Fine performances from the leads and superb direction, as usual, from William Wyler. The relationship between Perkins and his adolescent sister (Phyllis Love) is particularly well rendered.

★ 1956, 140 minutes, color, not rated.

★ With: Gary Cooper, Dorothy McGuire, Anthony Perkins. Director: William Wyler.

★ *What film, directed by Wyler, set a record for the most Academy Awards won by a single picture?* (Answer on page 351.)

The Front

Are you now, or have you ever been, a talentless fraud?

The script for this 1976 drama about the despicable blacklisting of writers during the McCarthy period was strong enough for Woody Allen to do something he very rarely does: act in somebody else's movie. Allen plays the no-talent bookie paid to turn in scripts under his own name; in actuality they're the product of writers accused of having ties to leftist organizations. The practice was a common one among writers whose careers came to a standstill because they had attended the wrong social gatherings 10 or 15 years earlier.

A witty, intelligent examination of a very dark time indeed in American history, the film features strong performances from Allen and Zero Mostel. Allen's appearance before an investigating committee really sparkles; his political awakening provides the necessary comic counterpoint to the sober main story. Mostel's entrance to, and exit from, a rented hotel room will stay with you for a long, long time.

★ 1976, 94 minutes, color, PG.

★ With: Woody Allen, Zero Mostel, Andrea Marcovicci, Joshua Shelley. Director: Martin Ritt.

★ *In what adaptation of a Shakespearean tragedy did Allen appear?* (Answer on page 276.)

"I am blacklisted."
"Yeah, but other than that, you're OK?"
—Woody Allen gets in a little deeper than he'd intended during a conversation with a friend.

For a great double feature, rent it with
Citizen Cohn.

Seen it but in the mood for something similar? Try
Broadway Danny Rose.

Answer to page 191 trivia question:
Powaqqatsi.

Drama

The Funeral

Trust me, it's a comedy—and a damned good one.

"Say 'Your presents would have pleased the deceased greatly.'"

—Video instructor on funereal etiquette.

For a great double feature, rent it with

The Big Chill.

Seen it but in the mood for something similar? Try

A Taxing Woman.

Answer to page 227 trivia question:

25.

This inspired Japanese ensemble piece is by turns hilarious and poignant; the older and younger generations of the family whose patriarch has passed away are equally befuddled by the question of how to deal with his sudden departure, but they're befuddled in fundamentally different ways. The four-day gathering at which the family members mark his passing provides ample opportunity for personal reflection, amorous activity in the woods, and quality control work on many bottles of sake.

The standout performance comes from Nobuko Miyamoto, who plays the deceased's daughter with compassion, intelligence, and transcendent beauty. She's the good daughter, the good wife, and the good mother—the center of the ritual and perhaps the only member of the group who comes away having experienced a measure of personal growth.

Beyond being an exquisite, moving piece of comedy, *The Funeral* is a painlessly effective introduction to the motivations behind the Japanese fascination with ritual and order. At the same time it tackles a universal human topic: our uneasiness with our shared mortality and our sometimes halting attempts to say and do the right thing in the face of that mortality.

★ 1984, 124 minutes, color, not rated.

★ With: Nobuko Miyamoto, Tsutomu Yamazaki, Kin Sugai. Director: Juzo Itami.

★ *What other film did Miyamoto, Yamazaki, and Itami make about an income tax collector?* (Answer on page 226.)

Gas Food Lodging

*Everything a restless teenage girl could ask for.
Not.*

I know, I know: another picture about women who are left holding the bag when the man of the house evaporates. But this one is something very special. In the middle of a godforsaken patch of New Mexico, single mom Brooke Adams holds down a job as a waitress and tries to bring a measure of order and stability to the lives of her two daughters. Every once in a while she succeeds. This well-executed three-way character study doesn't exactly have what you'd call high-budget production values, but boy, do you care about the three principals.

The film looks unflinchingly at the inevitable challenges of growing up and becoming your own person; it's a coming-of-age picture in which the barrenness of the three women's surroundings and their lack of fulfilling options leads to difficult choices that carry painful ramifications—but the picture is, ultimately, one of hope and endurance.

This gem features strong performances from Adams, Ione Skye, and Fairuza Balk. Allison Anders both directed and adapted the screenplay from Richard Peck's novel.

★ 1992, 101 minutes, color, R.

★ With: Brooke Adams, Ione Skye, Fairuza Balk.
Director: Allison Anders.

★ *Name another film in which three women try to come to terms with the many and varied ramifications of life in a small town. (Hint: This one's adapted from a Pulitzer Prize–winning play by Beth Henley.)*
(Answer on page 204.)

"I think you just hate men."
—Ione Skye to her waitress mom, who has seen her share of them

For a great double feature, rent it with
Mystic Pizza.

Seen it but in the mood for something similar? Try
The Snapper.

Answer to page 263 trivia question:
Anchors Aweigh.

Drama

The General

As Buster Keaton always said,

"   ."

"There were two great loves in Johnny Gray's life: his engine and his girl."

—Buster Keaton has a tough choice to make when it comes to dates on Saturday night.

For a great double feature, rent it with

Sherlock, Jr.

Seen it but in the mood for something similar? Try

Safety Last.

Answer to page 164 trivia question:

Swing Shift.

Here's one to badger your local video store into ordering. (Hey, what better place to stage a sit-in? There are plenty of movies to watch, and you may even get popcorn.)

This hilarious but now sadly neglected comic masterpiece represents Buster Keaton's finest hour; it serves as a relic of those long-lost days when the stars not only performed their own stunts but thought them up, too. *The General* is an inspired, extended ballet performed by the stone-faced Keaton and a stolen locomotive; appropriately, the train has the title role.

Keaton sees to it that the engine emerges as a character in its own right—and a metaphor for the movie itself, since the sublime visual gags come at you with delicious speed, just like the locomotive.

It's a clinic in minimalistic comic acting in the face of overwhelming physical spectacle. This film, which features some fantastic battle scenes, is based on an actual incident from the Civil War.

★ 1927, 74 minutes, B&W, not rated.

★ With: Buster Keaton, Marion Mack, the General. Director: Buster Keaton.

★ *In what Billy Wilder classic about an aging silent movie queen does Keaton have a cameo role?* (Answer on page 99.)

Silent

138

The Getaway (1972)

The movie that dares to ask, "How many cowboys can you fit into a convertible?"

If you're in the mood for dusty, gritty, desperate people on the run, bullets flying, and blood spewing, then director Sam Peckinpah is your man. Here Steve McQueen plays a professional bank robber who's behind bars and is ready to do anything to get out. With the help of his lovely wife, Ali MacGraw, he will, but the price is pulling another job with a bunch of scruffy characters who somehow seem less than trustworthy. Sure enough, our heroes soon find themselves on a mad dash for the Mexican border.

This film features the usual grueling Peckinpah bloodbaths; even if that's not usually your thing, you'll be immersed in the characters and the confident style, and you'll be hooked. Masterful intercuts abound—even the opening credits are spectacularly edited.

McQueen and MacGraw portray what are probably the most likable of all Peckinpah's characters (which isn't really saying much). McQueen is predictably strong; MacGraw is more successful than usual in camouflaging her fundamental inability to act. Just goes to show what you can get away with when you hook up with a great director. Sally Struthers shows up as one of the most memorable bimbos in film history.

★ 1972, 122 minutes, color, PG.

★ With: Steve McQueen, Ali MacGraw, Ben Johnson, Sally Struthers. Director: Sam Peckinpah.

★ *What married couple starred in the unfortunate 1994 remake?* (Answer on page 4.)

"Get to Banyon; tell him I'm for sale. His price. Do it now."
—Steve McQueen, who's had enough of hard time, is ready to make a deal.

For a great double feature, rent it with
$ (Dollars).

Seen it but in the mood for something similar? Try
Bonnie and Clyde.

Answer to page 198 trivia question:
His father was a ward boss in Maine in the early part of the century.

Action

*The perfect forties love story:
no physical contact.*

"Blast!"
—Rex Harrison, using
language that would make
a sailor blush.

**For a great double
feature, rent it with**
I Married a Witch.

**Seen it but in the mood
for something similar?
Try**
Heaven Can Wait
(1943).

**Answer to page 234
trivia question:**
Grand Canyon.

Drama

A destitute young British widow (Gene Tierney) comes to live in Gull Cottage, the home of a long-dead sea captain, with her young daughter (Natalie Wood). There they encounter Captain Gregg (Rex Harrison), who offers nearly everything the young family could want: he's outgoing, masculine, knowledgeable, and concerned for their welfare.

There's only one catch—he's also dead. Tierney and Harrison strike it off agreeably enough, though, and in time they're, well, living together. In a manner of speaking.

If the truest love is the one that is willing to step aside for what the beloved really wants, *The Ghost and Mrs. Muir* is a first-rank romance; no gore, no heebie-jeebies, no shock cuts. This is a gentle, tender story of two people who learn how to make love work in the long (very long) run; it's one of the better odd-couple pairings you're going to find in the video store. Not to be confused with the formulaic, predictable 1960s television situation comedy.

★ 1947, 104 minutes, B&W, not rated.

★ With: Gene Tierney, Rex Harrison, Natalie Wood, George Sanders. Director: Joseph L. Mankiewicz.

★ *What is the title of the book Mrs. Muir wrote with Captain Gregg?* (Answer on page 46.)

Gimme Shelter

Rock and roll—the devil's music? This movie may make you wonder.

The Hell's Angels in charge of security at a rock concert? Maybe not the best idea. This is a riveting documentary account of the Rolling Stones' ill-fated 1969 tour, which concluded tragically at the now-infamous anti-Woodstock that took place at the Altamont Speedway.

The Stones seem stunned by the violence; it's as if their own carefully cultivated bad-boy image has punched them in the solar plexus. As dark as the film's account of the events is, the main reason to rent *Gimme Shelter* is the music; in addition to vintage Stones renditions of such classics as "Brown Sugar" and "Satisfaction," there are memorable appearances by Jefferson Airplane and Ike and Tina Turner. In retrospect, Tina's spellbinding performance is more than a little eerie; we now know that, in addition to the thugs in the audience, there's one backing her up.

A raw, unpolished look at the dark side of rock, *Gimme Shelter* is a movie you won't be able to look away from, one that knows from bitter experience that mindless good vibes and peace signs don't always cut it.

★ 1970, 91 minutes, color, PG.

★ With: the Rolling Stones, Jefferson Airplane, Melvin Belli. Directors: David Maysles, Albert Maysles, Charlotte Zwerin.

★ *What* Rolling Stone *photographer traveled with the Stones in the early seventies?* (Answer on page 125.)

"Brothers and sisters, brothers and sisters. . . ."
—From the stage, Mick Jagger pleads to the crowd, hoping everyone will calm down. Nobody does.

For a great double feature, rent it with
Woodstock.

Seen it but in the mood for something similar? Try
The Kids Are Alright.

Answer to page 272 trivia question:
The Princess Bride.

Documentary

Give 'Em Hell, Harry!

I'm just wild about Harry.

James Whitmore's tour-de-force one-man tribute to Harry Truman translates surprisingly well to the small screen. Whitmore whizzes through time as he sees fit, offering up, in the blink of an eye, a former president who connives his wife into letting him skip mowing the lawn, a future president telling off the Missouri Ku Klux Klan at peril of his life, and an occupant of the Oval Office lambasting Joseph McCarthy despite the earnest pleadings of advisers to ignore the red-baiting demagogue.

Whitmore's exquisite diatribe against McCarthy is a particularly effective set piece: the man from Independence shows undisguised contempt for a popular figure who nevertheless deserves every drop of presidential venom reserved for him. (Apparently there was a time when politicians did not check each syllable against a focus group before taking a stand.)

The tight script contains many such exhilarating moments and enough references to the dangers of Nixonian manhandlings of the Constitution to remind you that the play first won acclaim shortly after the Watergate scandal erupted. But this is no period piece. It's a gem of a performance that still rings as true as its subject, which is no mean feat.

★ 1975, 102 minutes, color, PG.

★ With: James Whitmore. Director: Steve Binder.

★ *In what film adapted from a Stephen King novel did Whitmore play a long-term convict?* (Answer on page 173.)

Biography

The Glass Menagerie (1987)

Dream play, dream cast.

What *is* it with Joanne Woodward? Doesn't she know people hate a show-off? In yet another superb performance she brings Amanda Wingfield, one of the great Tennessee Williams roles, to life in a way no one else has managed. When you consider that the domineering, aging southern belle is one of the half dozen most popular female lead roles in American theater history, you realize Woodward's unique work here is quite an accomplishment.

Woodward's husband, Paul Newman, directed this notable entry, and you can tell he did it with love. Karen Allen shines as Laura; add the breathtaking John Malkovich in the role of Tom, and you've got yourself an evening.

An exquisite, deeply felt rendition of a now-classic piece of drama, this outing is far superior to the 1950 film version that starred Gertrude Lawrence and Kirk Douglas. Newman appears to have a better sense for the delicate, dreamlike currents of the script than director Irving Rapper (of *Marjorie Morningstar* fame) did.

★ 1987, 134 minutes, color, PG.

★ With: Joanne Woodward, John Malkovich, Karen Allen. Director: Paul Newman.

★ *How did Tennessee Williams rationalize to friends the dismissal of his psychotherapist?* (Answer on page 233.)

"I said I had pleurosis and you thought I said Blue Roses. So that's what you always called me after that."
—Karen Allen explains the history of her unusual nickname.

For a great double feature, rent it with
Mr. and Mrs. Bridge.

Seen it but in the mood for something similar? Try
Baby Doll.

Answer to page 26 trivia question:
"Holocaust."

Drama

In the mood?

For a great double feature, rent it with
Cabin in the Sky.

Seen it but in the mood for something similar? Try
The Five Pennies.

Answer to page 60 trivia question:
True. Boyle played the Monster in *Young Frankenstein.*

Jimmy Stewart and June Allyson head up the cast of this surprisingly strong musical biopic, and Gene Krupa and Louis Armstrong show up, too. Stewart, of course, plays the legendary bandleader Glenn Miller, who rose from obscure trombone player to national icon, then disappeared in a tragic airplane mishap during World War II.

Stewart's patented American-Everyman routine is particularly appropriate for Miller's rags-to-riches story, and Harry Morgan, later of "Dragnet" and "M*A*S*H" fame, does a better second banana than anyone in the business. Miller's toe-tapping music leaves little doubt as to this American master's status as a true genius.

This color extravaganza is a great example of Hollywood period filmmaking; the on-target costumes, sparkling el trains, and gleaming autos of Miller's era lend a feeling of abundant, high-budget authenticity to the proceedings.

★ 1953, 116 minutes, color, not rated.

★ With: James Stewart, June Allyson, Louis Armstrong. Director: Anthony Mann.

★ *Why did Miller never record a solo?* (Answer on page 161.)

Biography

Grand Hotel

If she wants to be alone so much, what the heck is Garbo doing in the lobby of a packed four-star hotel?

There's something about Greta Garbo's role in this film that seems to ring a little too true. Here she plays a weary ballerina who'd like nothing more than to walk away from it all. Hmm. Then there's a very young Joan Crawford, who's not above using her sexy wiles to become a star. Hmm. Then there's Wallace Beery, who plays the hard-drinking, overbearing tough guy. Hmm. Well, you go ahead and draw your own conclusions.

It's Berlin, 1932, and anything goes. The Grand Hotel is teeming with spicy stories from the chambermaids' carts to the penthouse suites. Who's doing what with whom—and who knows about it? Yes, this movie is the ultimate soap opera; the story is melodramatic, the acting is often, um, bad. But even if the sheer zingy glamour of this undertaking doesn't win you over, and it should, the few moments when the film rings shockingly true will. It's great fun to watch; rent it the next time you stay in a nice hotel, order room service, and just imagine all the sordid things that must be going on all around you.

★ 1932, 113 minutes, B&W, not rated.

★ With: Greta Garbo, John Barrymore, Joan Crawford, and everybody else. Director: Edmund Goulding.

★ *Can you name the actor Garbo literally left at the altar?* (Answer on page 281.)

"I want to be in the movies."

—A young Joan Crawford, confessing her true ambition

For a great double feature, rent it with
Camille (1937).

Seen it but in the mood for something similar? Try
Dinner at Eight.

Answer to page 204 trivia question:
I Was a Teen-age Werewolf.

Drama

Great Expectations (1946)

A Dickens of a movie.

"I realized that in becoming a gentleman, I had only succeeded in becoming a snob."

—John Mills realizes there's a problem somewhere.

For a great double feature, rent it with

Oliver!

Seen it but in the mood for something similar? Try

Nicholas Nickleby (1947).

Answer to page 240 trivia question:

Not a one. I tell ya, comics get no respect.

Not the Stuart Walker effort of 1934, though that one's fine, but a snazzy, altogether magnificent David Lean adaptation of the novel that far outshines any other version of this much-filmed classic. John Mills is flawless as Pip, the poverty-stricken orphan whose education is financed by an anonymous patron.

Lean's ability to manage the big canvas, later put to use in such epics as *Lawrence of Arabia* and *Doctor Zhivago*, is in evidence here; he fills the character- and incident-crammed story with nimble, masterful touches. Worthy of note among the many top-notch performances are those of Martita Hunt as the deranged Miss Havisham and Finlay Currie as Magwich.

Only in a career as storied as Lean's could a movie this good *not* end up as the movie the director would be remembered by. An extraordinary visual feast, the picture won richly deserved Oscars for Best Cinematography and Best Art Direction. Enjoy yourself.

★ 1946, 118 minutes, B&W, not rated.

★ With: John Mills, Alec Guinness, Valerie Hobson, Jean Simmons. Director: David Lean.

★ *What's the name of the catchy tune whistled in Lean's* Bridge on the River Kwai? (Answer on page 314.)

Drama

The Great White Hope

A knockout.

No joke: When African-American Jack Johnson used to successfully defend his heavyweight title, newspapers of the day would run pictures of the defeated Caucasian challenger rather than the victorious champ, analyzing the flaws in the white guy's style and praying for better luck next time. A little racial bias, you think?

This loose adaptation of Johnson's tumultuous life, adapted from the successful Broadway play about heavyweight champ "Jack Jefferson," features star turns by a pair of young whippersnappers: James Earl Jones and Jane Alexander. Jones, who has pulled a bit of an Orson Welles in recent years, is in very good shape physically here—he executes the role superbly on all levels.

The interracial theme raised almost as many eyebrows in 1970, when the film was released, as Johnson's real-life involvement with a white woman did in 1910. (Legend has it that billionaire recluse Howard Hughes went into conniption fits when he saw Alexander kiss Jones during a television broadcast of the film, but then he did that about a lot of things.) Rent it.

★ 1970, 101 minutes, color, PG.

★ With: James Earl Jones, Jane Alexander. Director: Martin Ritt.

★ *In what Disney animated feature was James Earl Jones the voice of the great father figure in the sky?*
(Answer on page 25.)

"I'm nothing to you but a black, ugly fist here."
—James Earl Jones knows he's not getting equal treatment, even if he is heavyweight champion of the world.

For a great double feature, rent it with *Raging Bull.*

Seen it but in the mood for something similar? Try *Jungle Fever.*

Answer to page 278 trivia question: *The Three Faces of Eve* (1957).

Drama

The Grey Fox

*The sexiest old guy to show up in a movie
this side of Paul Newman.*

"A professional always specializes."

—No matter what era he lands in, Richard Farnsworth is no amateur.

For a great double feature, rent it with

The Shootist.

Seen it but in the mood for something similar? Try

Comes a Horseman.

Answer to page 173 trivia question:

Gordon Jackson.

ool premise: what would happen if one of those old-time stagecoach robbers pulled a really long jail sentence back in the middle of the 19th century and then, after decades of hard time, had to figure out what to make of the 20th? Richard Farnsworth stars in the enthralling story of real-life Canadian bandit Bill Milner, who faced just such an adjustment.

The gentle, soft-spoken lead actor is hypnotic from beginning to end; he photographs magnificently, and cinematographer Frank Tidy lavishes almost as much attention on him as on the exquisite forest surroundings.

Jackie Burroughs is the suffragette Farnsworth makes eyes at; she makes 'em right back, and no viewer is going to blame her.

A supremely entertaining twist on standard western themes, *The Grey Fox* is the perfect movie to watch on birthdays ending with a zero. If Farnsworth can look this good and this undeniably old at the same time, there's hope for us all.

★ 1982, 92 minutes, color, PG

★ With: Richard Farnsworth, Jackie Burroughs, Ken Pogue. Director: Phillip Borsos.

★ *What film starring Dolly Parton and Sylvester Stallone does Richard Farnsworth probably wish he had never signed on for?* (Answer on page 50.)

Gunga Din

Wasn't there a poem about this that we all had to read in high school?

I t's obvious from the first few scenes of this film that the three stars are having the time of their lives. This is a dream assignment, and Cary Grant, Victor McLaglen, and Douglas Fairbanks, Jr., all know it. They happily tumble about the deserts of southern California—er, India—fighting the bad guys, slapping each other on the back, and anticipating that evening's margarita at the Beverly Hills Hotel.

Why shouldn't they relax and enjoy themselves? They know the movie has a great script (thanks to screenwriter Fred Guiol, who wrote for—get this—Laurel and Hardy) and a director who's willing to let them do pretty much anything they want. What's to get worked up about?

In this version of the Rudyard Kipling poem "Gunga Din" the loyal water bearer is almost secondary. Almost. Truth be told, Sam Jaffe as Gunga Din will probably have you crying at the end. But the three dashing soldiers who star in the film know they're what people are paying to see. So let's see now, you've got great stars, lots of fight scenes, plenty of poignant moments, and loads of laughs. Yep, it's a winner.

★ 1939, 117 minutes, B&W, not rated.

★ With: Cary Grant, Victor McLaglen, Douglas Fairbanks, Jr. Director: George Stevens.

★ *In what film did Cary Grant mention his real name?* (Answer on page 72.)

"You're all under arrest. Her Majesty is very touchy about having her subjects strangled."
—She's a pretty nice girl, too, but she doesn't have a lot to say to our three heroes during the course of the film.

For a great double feature, rent it with *Beau Geste.*

Seen it but in the mood for something similar? Try *The Man Who Would Be King.*

Answer to page 207 trivia question: *Jim Thorpe—All American.*

Action

Gypsy (1993)

Remember when a movie about strippers featured actors who kept all their clothes on?

"If I die, it won't be from sittin'—it'll be from fightin' to get out."

—A determined Bette Midler won't change her tune.

For a great double feature, rent it with

Annie, Get Your Gun.

Seen it but in the mood for something similar? Try

Auntie Mame.

Answer to page 243 trivia question:

Mel Brooks, with *Silent Movie.*

The 1962 film version of the Broadway hit cast Rosalind Russell as the domineering stage mother of stripper Gypsy Rose Lee. Roz was OK, but a little soft for my tastes; if you ask me, the role really requires a lady who's half Sherman tank and half Al Jolson. Now that Ethel Merman (who conquered the Great White Way in the lead role) has, alas, passed from the scene, does any contemporary entertainer spring to mind as a worthy successor to take up the part of Mama Rose? If you guessed Bette Midler, give yourself a gold star, head out to the video store, and rent this superlative adaptation of the Jule Styne–Stephen Sondheim–Arthur Laurents musical classic.

Midler gives a performance that must be seen to be believed; it's hard to imagine that she'll find any way to top this extraordinary tour de force, but then again, her career has had its fair share of jaw-dropping triumphs, hasn't it? Fans of the divine one will be transported to the heavens; others will, unless they are heavily sedated, become believers in short order.

★ 1993, 150 minutes, color, not rated.

★ With: Bette Midler, Edward Asner, Cynthia Gibb. Director: Emile Ardolino.

★ *In what film did Bette Midler play Lily Tomlin's "twin"?* (Answer on page 129.)

Musical

Hair

Turn it on, tune it in,
drop the remote.

When it came time to develop the screenplay for this counterculture-inspired Broadway smash of the sixties, the filmmakers had the good sense to retain the songs (which aged remarkably well) and deep-six the book (which didn't). The movie version takes a calculated risk in depicting the let-it-all-hang-out spirit of the times; it incorporates a plot. Fortunately, it works.

John Savage is the squaresville Oklahoma native who's about to enter the military; Treat Williams and company set out to raise his consciousness and save him from the evil clutches of the Establishment. Well, what else are you going to do with the songs?

The film barrels along, an unceasingly agreeable combination of practical jokes against authority figures, catchy free-associating show tunes, and exquisite Twyla Tharp choreography (Tharp even makes a cameo). As an excuse for having an unapologetic good time—which was at least *part* of what happened in the sixties—*Hair* is hard to beat, and it features appearances from a whole lot of people who went on to significant success a few years later. See if you can spot them all.

★ 1979, 121 minutes, color, PG.

★ With: Treat Williams, John Savage, Beverly D'Angelo. Director: Milos Forman.

★ *What Vietnam War picture won John Savage an Academy Award nomination?* (Answer on page 177.)

"Where you from?"
"Oklahoma."
"Listen, man, I know how it feels. I used to come from Kansas myself."

—Hayseed John Savage's newfound companions seem to know where he's coming from.

For a great double feature, rent it with
One Flew Over the Cuckoo's Nest.

Seen it but in the mood for something similar? Try
A Hard Day's Night.

Answer to page 281 trivia question:
Langston Hughes.

Musical

Hairspray

You'll understand completely just what happened to the ozone layer after this one.

Director John Waters once said he wanted to make a movie with as many "almost stars" as he possibly could. In *Hairspray* he comes close. I could list everyone who shows up in this film, but it would ruin about a dozen cool surprises.

Hairspray could well be the most tasteful movie of Waters's career. Not that that's saying much. He set out to parody the teen flicks of the early sixties, which is no easy task—once, the *Harvard Lampoon* tried to parody the *National Enquirer*. The project just came out looking like, well, the *National Enquirer*. The same thing could have happened here, but Waters wisely chose to take just one step further than the real thing.

The picture is set in 1962 in Baltimore; Ricki Lake plays the newest dancer on "The Corney Collins Show" (which bears a curious resemblance to "American Bandstand"). Her mother, played by the one, the only Divine (don't say I didn't warn you), loves her daughter and will support her at every turn, even when she risks all her newfound fame to fight for a group of African-American kids' right to dance on the show, too. Waters always manages to take us someplace new; it's just a question of whether we really wanted to go there in the first place. In this film he picks the right destination.

★ 1988, 96 minutes, color, PG.

★ With: Ricki Lake, Divine, Sonny Bono. Director: John Waters.

★ *What Waters "classic" distributed scratch-and-sniff cards with every ticket?* (Answer on page 302.)

The Harder They Come

Reefer madness.

This Jamaican gangster-scene musical follows a rural lad (Jimmy Cliff) as he makes his way to Kingston in search of success as a singer. He doesn't score a hit record until he commits himself to a life of crime.

The underworld-oriented plot has its grisly moments, but this exhilarating little movie boasts some surprisingly strong performances. It gets a lot of good work done on a shoestring budget, and it carries more real-life energy in any given minute than something like *The Cotton Club* delivers in two hours. The drug-culture milieu of the story isn't exactly in keeping with current mores, but you wanted a movie, not a social studies lecture, right?

Depending on your age and your level of devotion to reggae, the terrific music may or may not be considered sacred compositions—but you will, whatever your background, start rocking to the beat when the songs start. You stand forewarned: Even a single viewing of this film will leave you strongly predisposed to rush out and purchase the soundtrack album if you have not already done so. And maybe a big stash of ganja. But stick to the CD, bra.

★ 1973, 98 minutes, color, R.

★ With: Jimmy Cliff, Carl Bradshaw, Bobby Charlton. Director: Perry Henzell.

★ *What English punk rock group issued a scathing spoken diatribe against Jamaican mobsters on a landmark rock album of the late seventies?* (Answer on page 33.)

"*Johnny, you're too bad.*"
—Jimmy sure seems to be trying to be baaaaaaaad.

For a great double feature, rent it with
The Kids Are Alright.

Seen it but in the mood for something similar? Try
Scarface (1932).

Answer to page 94 trivia question:
Walk, Don't Run.

Musical

Do the hustle!

"We were born in
peacetime. We haven't
been where you've
been; we haven't seen
what you've seen."

—Maybe, just maybe, that
line will work for Adrian
Dunbar.

**For a great double
feature, rent it with**

The Playboys.

**Seen it but in the mood
for something similar?
Try**

Widow's Peak.

**Answer to page 337
trivia question:**

James Arness.

Adrian Dunbar (who helped write the screenplay) plays a small-time club owner who has a nasty habit of lying to, and hiding from, everyone in sight. He hires cheesy singers with names like Frank Cinatra; when his girlfriend tells him she loves him, his nervous reply ("Ditto") isn't exactly an invitation to deep emotional involvement.

Just about everyone has caught on to Dunbar's game, and the number of people who are willing to extend him the benefit of the doubt is dropping fast. But when the opportunity arises to book a bona fide, long-lost, truly legendary tenor (Ned Beatty), Dunbar smells redemption—and the chance to save his club from financial ruin. He sets out to find the guy and hops a plane for Ireland, where everything goes wrong in the most elaborately unexpected way imaginable.

This hilarious, fanciful tale of desperation hits every mark it sets out to; if you liked *Local Hero*, you'll like this one.

★ 1991, 104 minutes, color, R.

★ With: Ned Beatty, Adrian Dunbar, Shirley Anne Field, David McCallum. Director: Peter Chelsom.

★ *What TV role established McCallum as America's first defector sex symbol?* (Answer on page 318.)

Comedy

The Heartbreak Kid

"Meeting you has been the high point of my honeymoon."

A very young Charles Grodin finds the perfect vehicle for his talents in this offbeat Elaine May comedy about a guy who finds the woman of his dreams— on his honeymoon. Too bad it's not his wife. Too bad about the dreams, for that matter, since Grodin really should know better than to throw everything away for the gorgeous but emotionally empty Cybill Shepherd. Guys will be guys, I guess, and that's both very scary and very funny, as is the movie.

The klutzy new bride Grodin has second thoughts about is played by director Elaine May's real-life daughter, Jeannie Berlin. This sort of my-kid-can-do-it thing can backfire (remember *The Godfather, Part III*?), but Berlin is terrific. May exhibits a sure hand in rendering the tricky seriocomic script, a Neil Simon adaptation of a Bruce Jay Friedman short story.

The Heartbreak Kid is one of those rare movies where you worry that Eddie Albert may be about to explode in a supremely ugly way; he plays the father of the lovely young Shepherd, and he's none too thrilled about Grodin's attentions. Touchy, touchy.

★ 1972, 104 minutes, color, PG.

★ With: Charles Grodin, Cybill Shepherd, Eddie Albert, Jeannie Berlin. Director: Elaine May.

★ *What big-budget "road picture" comedy flopped for director Elaine May in 1987?* (Answer on page 290.)

"I don't hand out my daughter to newly-weds."

—Eddie Albert is none too thrilled with Charles Grodin.

For a great double feature, rent it with
Play it Again, Sam.

Seen it but in the mood for something similar? Try
Goodbye, Columbus.

Answer to page 313 trivia question:
Race car driving.

Comedy

Hearts of Darkness: A Filmmaker's Apocalypse

Hey, kids, let's head out to my uncle's place in the Philippines and put on a show!

"*Martin Sheen is not dead until I say he's dead.*"

—A frazzled Francis Coppola tries to maintain control.

For a great double feature, rent it with

Apocalypse Now.

Seen it but in the mood for something similar? Try

Gimme Shelter.

Answer to page 265 trivia question:

Buffy the Vampire Slayer.

You're Francis Ford Coppola. You've just won two Best Picture Oscars. You have all of Hollywood at your feet. Do you (a) play it safe by picking a nice, intimate little romantic comedy or (b) head into the wilds of the Philippines with half a script, several million dollars, an overweight Hollywood icon, and a leading man with some issues to work out?

If you picked b, get ready for a complete physical and nervous collapse, because that's what happened to Coppola. Coppola's wife, Eleanor, kept a faithul diary of the events of this excruciating production, which included a monsoon, Martin Sheen's near-fatal heart attack, civil uprisings, and way, way, way too much Marlon Brando, if you know what I mean.

This riveting documentary shows an artist simultaneously at his best (*Apocalypse Now* is considered a masterpiece by many critics) and at his worst (few directors in history have earned so much fear and hatred from their work on a single project). This movie may not be *better* than the film it documents, but it's probably *scarier*—because we're watching what looks for all the world like a gifted artist's real-world descent into madness.

★ 1991, 96 minutes, color, R.

★ With: Francis Ford Coppola, Marlon Brando, Martin Sheen. Directors: Fax Bahr, George Hickenlooper.

★ *How many days did Coppola spend in the Philippines on this shoot from hell?* (Answer on page 134.)

You say you like cowboys, eh, kid?

Ready for some fun? Jeff Bridges, aided by a strong supporting cast, stars in this valentine to the American wild-west movie. Bridges plays an aspiring writer who mistakes a cheesy correspondence school for a real-life campus that specializes in developing tomorrow's Zane Greys; he heads west in the hope of securing some face-to-face guidance and finds nothing but a PO box waiting for him. Not to fear: a series of improbable encounters launches the wanna-be novelist on the road to fame and fortune (maybe) as a movie cowboy.

A charming, inventive little story that showcases Bridges' bountiful comic talents, and also features fine work from Blythe Danner, Donald Pleasance, and Alan Arkin, who is unforgettable as the low-budget director of the lamentably bad western Bridges lands a part in. Also worthy of note: Andy Griffith playing the bad guy, a casting choice that adds a welcome, and disarming, feeling of tension to the proceedings. This one will charm the spurs off you. (The movie was also released under the title *Hollywood Cowboy*.)

★ 1975, 102 minutes, color, PG.

★ With: Jeff Bridges, Alan Arkin, Blythe Danner, Andy Griffith. Director: Howard Zieff.

★ *In what film with Patricia Neal did Andy Griffith play the heavy?* (Answer on page 42.)

"Wounds suffered in tropical climes can all too swiftly become nasty infections."
—Bridges's florid remark to the film crew that rescues him in the desert

For a great double feature, rent it with *Rustlers' Rhapsody.*

Seen it but in the mood for something similar? Try *Destry Rides Again.*

Answer to page 363 trivia question: *The Long, Long Trailer.* Desi was in it, too, of course.

Western

The Heiress

Always a bridesmaid . . .

If you're in the mood to watch some top-level forties moviemaking with extraordinary acting in every single frame, this magnificent period piece is the one to rent. Wealthy Olivia de Havilland is wooed by smooth Montgomery Clift, a fast talker with a bit of a bad reputation. Whom should de Havilland believe—her father, who claims that she can only be loved for her money, or Clift, who swears that for once in his life he has found the woman who can change him for the better?

Here de Havilland shows off her range (and snags a well-deserved Oscar for best actress) by turning in an unforgettable performance as a plain woman with a life-changing decision to make. When she loses her innocence, she doesn't need any lines to get the point across. The exquisite cinematography is seductive from beginning to end. Rent this picture if you want to convince someone of the folly of colorizing the classics.

★ 1949, 115 minutes, B&W, not rated.

★ With: Olivia de Havilland, Montgomery Clift, Ralph Richardson, Director: William Wyler.

★ *Who was Montgomery Clift's best female friend?*
  (Answer on page 12.)

Henry V (1945)

Vintage Olivier, with color and energy to spare.

Produced during World War II, Laurence Olivier's innovative adaptation of the most patriotic of Shakespeare's history plays is part comic book, part battlefield spectacle, and all audacity. Half the fun is watching the star—who also served as producer, director, and liberal rearranger and telescoper of the text—show off his unparalleled style. The other half has to do with poking fun at the French and finding innovative ways to dust them at Agincourt because God likes the British better. (Hey—sometimes you have to go with the script, right?)

Although Kenneth Branagh took a less battle-glorifying approach to the same material four decades later, Olivier's effort was the first film production to do full justice to the soaring poetry and rousing nationalism of the play. The central character is one of the few in Shakespeare drawn with something like the depth of the great tragic heroes who nevertheless *accomplishes everything he sets out to* and doesn't pretend otherwise. If Olivier swaggers a little bit now and then, well, it's in keeping with the spirit of the piece: Henry does, too.

★ 1945, 136 minutes, color, not rated.

★ With: Laurence Olivier, Robert Newton, Leslie Banks, Esmond Knight. Director: Laurence Olivier.

★ *For what film did Olivier win an Oscar as Best Actor?* (Answer on page 76.)

"All things are ready if our minds be so."
—Laurence Olivier has it all figured out, no matter how big the French army is.

For a great double feature, rent it with
Chimes at Midnight (an adaptation of the *Henry IV* plays).

Seen it but in the mood for something similar? Try
Henry V (1989).

Answer to page 365 trivia question:
Seven.

Drama

Hester Street

Welcome to America.
Now change your name.

"If you wanna be American, you gotta hurt."
—Carol Kane is on the receiving end of some tough marching orders.

For a great double feature, rent it with
Ragtime.

Seen it but in the mood for something similar? Try
Enemies, a Love Story.

Answer to page 305 trivia question:
Two for the Road.

Yet another example of a humble, low-budget movie that's 20 times more rewarding than the big-bucks, concept-by-committee stuff that crowds it off the top shelf at the video store. If you're tired of pictures that are more concerned with audience demographics than with acting values, make your way to the back of the store and look for this one.

Carol Kane stars in this quiet, unassuming picture about Jewish immigrants in New York's Lower East Side at the turn of the century. Her marriage is lousy; does one deal with such a situation differently in America than one would in the old country? Kane, as a painfully withdrawn Orthodox woman, delivers what may be her finest work in this gem; the dialogue, when she gets it, is good, but her performance is a reminder that top-drawer actors can get a whole lot accomplished without saying a word. Nicely executed all around.

★ 1975, 92 minutes, B&W, PG.

★ With: Carol Kane, Steven Keats, Mel Howard. Director: Joan Micklin Silver.

★ *In what film does Carol Kane beat the living daylights out of Bill Murray?* (Answer on page 181.)

Drama

Desk set.

Ding, ding, ding. That's the "comic masterpiece" bell you hear ringing—or is it the pleasant, nostalgic chiming of a hundred manual typewriters? Back in the twenties, Ben Hecht and Charles MacArthur crafted a brisk (and I do mean *brisk*), comedy about two veteran newspaper men who managed a loud love-hate relationship with each other and chased down an exclusive interview with an escaped convict. It was called *The Front Page*. It was a big hit on Broadway and then a pretty funny movie in 1931. Pretty funny. But not this funny.

His Girl Friday offers Cary Grant as the relentless managing editor and Rosalind Russell as the star reporter who used to be married to him—but now prefers Ralph Bellamy. Or, at any rate, thinks she does. The inspired gender switch adds sexual tension to the proceedings, and the result is one of the most hilarious battle-of-the-sexes comedies Hollywood ever produced. Makes sense, because the original play was a love story of sorts to begin with.

Director Howard Hawks' rat-a-tat-tat pace is perfectly sustained; the picture moves so fast, there's hardly time to make fun of Russell's outfits, which look like they're about to stage a mutiny. Easily Hawks's funniest film comedy.

★ 1940, 92 minutes, B&W, not rated.

★ With: Cary Grant, Rosalind Russell, Ralph Bellamy. Director: Howard Hawks.

★ *Who starred in the wobbly 1974 remake of* The Front Page*?* (Answer on page 310.)

"Oh, Walter, you're wonderful—in a loathsome sort of way."

—Rosalind Russell gives Cary Grant a compliment from the bottom of her heart.

For a great double feature, rent it with

Nothing Sacred.

Seen it but in the mood for something similar? Try

The Paper.

Answer to page 144 trivia question:

Early in his career Miller let Jack Teagarden try out his trombone. Once Miller heard Teagarden play, he never played solo again.

Comedy

Meryl's triumph.

"Jews have always been fair game. It's almost as if there's a moral precedent for punishing them."

—Michael Moriarty sleeps just fine at night, despite the hideous inhumanity of his job.

For a great double feature, keep watching it. It's long.

Seen it but in the mood for something similar? Try

Schindler's List.

Answer to page 360 trivia question:

He pulled this during the shooting of *Apocalypse Now.* The scene is included in the documentary *Hearts of Darkness: A Filmmaker's Apocalypse.*

Drama

P assing all the boxes on the store shelves, it's easy to fall into the trap of stereotyping *Holocaust* as the natural follow-up to *Roots* in the seventies' sprawling-miniseries sweepstakes. That's a shame, because this extraordinary multicassette rental represents some of the finest dramatic work ever produced by network television executives. (Maybe that's not saying much, but you get the idea.)

The story follows two families through the sudden perils, unexpected opportunities, and unspeakable horrors of the Third Reich. The remarkable cast is anchored by Michael Moriarty, James Woods, and Meryl Streep, each of them so good you'll find it tough to believe you're watching a made-for-television movie. The production values are top-notch, and the steadily grimmer story line never comes across as nihilistic or lacking in emotional appeal. Be warned, though, that the series pulls no punches, and several scenes are unsuitable for younger viewers.

★ 1978, 475 minutes, color, not rated.

★ With: Meryl Streep, Michael Moriarty, James Woods. Director: Marvin J. Chomsky.

★ *For what other Holocaust-related drama did Streep gain critical acclaim?* (Answer on page 54.)

The Hospital

*There's a doctor in the house, but he's busy
having a nervous breakdown.*

Those who enjoyed the lunatic goings-on at the Broadcasting System from Hell in *Network* will be similarly transfixed by this black-comedy satire about a chaotic big-city hospital. It's from the same legendary screenwriter (Paddy Chayefsky).

George C. Scott plays a head doctor struggling valiantly to avert a nervous breakdown despite rising levels of pandemonium in the corridors of his institution. Chayefsky uses the tumult of the hospital to mirror the generational and social conflicts of the day. The picture is a little like Altman's *M*A*S*H*, but Scott—who is great, as usual—has trouble finding an escape valve for the ever-mounting tension.

The strong documentarylike camera work lends an edge to the proceedings. Chayefsky won an Oscar for the screenplay.

★ 1971, 103 minutes, color, PG.

★ With: George C. Scott, Diana Rigg, Barnard Hughes. Director: Arthur Hiller.

★ *What do George C. Scott and Marlon Brando have in common?* (Answer on page 112.)

*"I never exercised
parental authority.
I'm no good at that."*
—George C. Scott would rather not play the father figure. Too bad he's in charge.

For a great double feature, rent it with
Network.

Seen it but in the mood for something similar? Try
Coma.

Answer to page 129 trivia question:
Day for Night.

Drama

Housekeeping

*Dysfunctional isn't always
a bad thing.*

*"Clearly, our aunt was
an unusual person."*

—Odd or not, Christine Lahti
may be just what the girls
need.

**For a great double
feature, rent it with**

*The Member of the
Wedding.*

**Seen it but in the mood
for something similar?
Try**

Fried Green Tomatoes.

**Answer to page 301
trivia question:**

Peter Gabriel's
"In Your Eyes."

This tale of the tricky side of individualism, set in the fifties, introduces us to sisters (played by Sara Walker and Andrea Burchill) who stay with their grandmother after their mother's suicide. While she was alive, Mom loved them, but in her own detached way. And that seems to be the key phrase for this line of oddballs: detachment.

The girls are left with many blanks in their lives, holes they would like to take care of—eventually. Wisely, they decide to cultivate the virtue of patience. When their grandmother dies, along comes a series of relatives to keep house and take care of the high school kids. The most interesting is Christine Lahti, their mother's sister, a woman they know very little about. There's something different about her. Either she's insane, in which case the two teenagers will have another responsibility on their hands, or she's not, which is somehow the more disturbing possibility. She lives by her own rules, not always a safe choice for women in the fifties.

★ 1987, 112 minutes, color, PG.

★ With: Christine Lahti, Andrea Burchill, Sara Walker. Director: Bill Forsyth.

★ *In what film did Lahti costar with Goldie Hawn?*
(Answer on page 138.)

Drama

Hud

The New West?

This beautifully filmed story of the Old West's struggle against the new boasts one of Paul Newman's very best performances. Melvyn Douglas plays the emotionally stifled father who wants to keep grazing cattle on his ranch. Newman, in the title role, plays his seething, sexually charged son, who sees change on the horizon and wants to turn the family ranch into an oilfield. When fate steps in, in the form of an epidemic of hoof-and-mouth disease that threatens the ranch's herd of cattle, Newman's frustration with his father's haughty nobility reaches its peak.

Patricia Neal is particularly strong as the seductive, raunchy earth-mother housekeeper. Her Texas twang can send a cowboy reeling. If Douglas is the embodiment of all that is noble and self-sufficient and honorable about the West, Newman is the iconoclastic boundary pusher. Both are essential parts of the American dream, but there's no prize for guessing which of the two is more fun to watch.

Newman radiates sexual charisma like nobody's business. Too bad he's such a jerk, but what can you expect with a name like Hud? Who would name a child that? Is it short for something? Were they trying to give the kid a complex? Well, it worked.

★ 1963, 112 minutes, B&W, not rated.

★ With: Paul Newman, Patricia Neal, Brandon de Wilde, Melvyn Douglas. Director: Martin Ritt.

★ *In what other classic western did Brandon de Wilde appear as a child?* (Answer on page 245.)

"Hell, I always say the law was meant to be interpreted in a lenient manner. And that's what I try to do. Sometimes I lean to one side of it, sometimes I lean to the other."

—Paul Newman's got no problem with legality. It has its place.

For a great double feature, rent it with *The Last Picture Show.*

Seen it but in the mood for something similar? Try *The Misfits.*

Answer to page 114 trivia question: *Queen Christina.*

Western

I Am a Fugitive from a Chain Gang

*So why the heck are you telling everyone about it?
That's what I'd like to know.*

"That's the only way you get outta here. Serve your time or die."

—Having been set straight on this point, Paul Muni has a feeling his time on the inside isn't going to be a picnic.

For a great double feature, rent it with

20,000 Years in Sing Sing.

Seen it but in the mood for something similar? Try

Scarface (1932).

Answer to page 356 trivia question:

The Road Warrior.

This picture, one of the highlights of Paul Muni's career, is the perfect movie to pop into the VCR when you've got a visitor over who thinks black-and-white pictures from the early thirties are all hiss and pop and no action.

Muni plays an innocent man who winds up at the mercy of the overseers of a horrific prison system. (The scenes of inmate abuse are powerful enough to shake up even moviegoers who made it through *Cool Hand Luke, Midnight Express,* or any number of other "guy stories.") Muni escapes and reinvents himself on the outside . . . but the long arm of the law can be just as ruthless in tracking down a falsely convicted man as it can be in finding a real-life bad guy. Muni is nothing short of extraordinary; Mervyn LeRoy's forceful direction makes this movie an unforgettable indictment of institutional inhumanity.

Keep an eye out for *The Man Who Broke 1,000 Chains,* the 1987 Val Kilmer TV movie based on the same material; it's no replacement for the original (nothing could be), but it's quite strong in its own right.

★ 1932, 93 minutes, B&W, not rated.

★ With: Paul Muni, Glenda Farrell, Helen Vinson. Director: Mervyn LeRoy.

★ *What happy accident made the final scene all the more dramatic?* (Answer on page 298.)

Drama

Iceman

*You should look this good after
30,000 years.*

Timothy Hutton stars in this fascinating story of an anthropologist who uncovers a frozen prehistoric man between 20,000 and 40,000 years old. Big surprise: he's still alive. I don't know why that kind of thing keeps happening in films, do you?

John Lone, as the iceman, gives a brilliant, completely believable performance as the ultimate fish out of water. Hutton and his colleague Lindsay Crouse do their best to understand and comfort the unlikely survivor, but there's always the risk that his value as an artifact will overshadow his status as a human being.

This picture is something special; it's not what you might expect, a depressing and predictable story of how a superior civilization (yours) always manages to destroy a less developed one. Instead the filmmakers chose to tell the gentler story of a man who loved, who had a family, who searched for spiritual truth in his life. Sound familar?

★ 1984, 99 minutes, color, PG.

★ With: Timothy Hutton, Lindsay Crouse, John Lone. Director: Fred Schepisi.

★ *Timothy Hutton's father played what TV detective?*
(Answer on page 322)

"He's a man. Not a specimen."
—Timothy Hutton wants to keep the priorities straight.

For a great double feature, rent it with
The Lost World
(1925).

Seen it but in the mood for something similar? Try
The Elephant Man.

Answer to page 296 trivia question:
Dirk McQuickley.

Sci-Fi

The Importance of Being Earnest

*Oh what a tangled web
we weave. . . .*

*"To lose one parent
may be regarded as
misfortune; to lose
both looks like
carelessness."*

—Maybe someone ought to
check behind the refrigerator
for Michael Redgrave's
forebears.

**For a great double
feature, rent it with**

*The Picture of Dorian
Gray.*

**Seen it but in the mood
for something similar?
Try**

Tom Jones.

**Answer to page 331
trivia question:**

Seven Beauties.

A superior, overpoweringly English cast brings Oscar Wilde's comic masterpiece to the screen with style and grace. Pay close attention; if you can catch the best lines, you might be able to recycle them at the next party you go to and come off as ever so witty.

This may well be the most perfectly constructed comedy ever written; its plot clicks along in an intricate, steady rhythm, marked off in 15-second intervals by more laugh lines per scene than any writer should be allowed to get away with. Love, gender roles, money, society, breeding—everything gets the once-over, and it all works.

The production here is a little on the stagy side, but who cares—it's deliriously funny from beginning to end, and Edith Evans's Lady Bracknell must be seen to be believed. This one will stick with you.

★ 1952, 95 minutes, color, not rated.

★ With: Michael Redgrave, Edith Evans, Joan Greenwood. Director: Anthony Asquith.

★ *Which of the actors above appeared in the stage version?* (Answer on page 80.)

Comedy

Impromptu

Who's going to wear the pants in this relationship?

Stand back; this one needs room. Judy Davis unleashes a swaggering, deliciously on-target performance as 19th-century cross-dressing author George Sand in this clever, historically inspired all-star literary romp. The object of her desire? The consumptive, painfully shy Frederic Chopin (Hugh Grant).

The movie quips, banters, and shouts its way through several delightful romantic intrigues, and Davis and Grant enjoy an embarrassingly strong roster of A-list actors in supporting roles. My favorite: Emma Thompson as the batty aristocrat, a wanna-be intellectual whose banana curls are as dingy as she is. You'll probably have your own nominee; there's a lot to choose from here.

One of the best period comedies to surface in quite some time; even if it weren't such a well-scripted, beautifully costumed undertaking, *Impromptu* would be fascinating. There's not a man or woman alive who can stalk through a door or chomp a cigar quite like Davis does here. She nearly scares the bejeezus out of the undernourished genius she's trying to bed.

★ 1991, 109 minutes, color, PG-13.

★ With: Judy Davis, Hugh Grant, Bernadette Peters, Emma Thompson, Mandy Patinkin. Director: James Lapine.

★ *In what picture did Judy Davis very nearly get an apple shot off her head?* (Answer on page 21.)

"I used to think I'd die of suffocation when I was married. Now it's my freedom that's killing me."

—Judy Davis concludes that the whole independence thing has its drawbacks.

For a great double feature, rent it with *The Big Chill.*

Seen it but in the mood for something similar? Try *The Importance of Being Earnest.*

Answer to page 352 trivia question:

She went on a nine-year hiatus—at the height of her popularity.

Comedy

Art imitates life.

**Answer to page 291
trivia question:**
Brazil.

**"I got you figured for a
natural-born killer."**
—Scott Wilson's got his
buddy Robert Blake pegged.

**For a great double
feature, rent it with**
The Onion Field.

**Seen it but in the mood
for something similar?
Try**
Badlands.

Truman Capote's breakthrough "nonfiction novel" told the chilling true-life story of two small-time hoods who committed a brutally pointless multiple murder in the heartland, then tried in vain to avoid the law. The book is a compulsively readable piece of work, and Richard Brooks's stark, powerful film adaptation pulls off the impossible by doing Capote's prose justice. Brooks walks a tightrope; the film *feels* like a documentary, yet you're aware throughout that you're in the presence of some great acting and truly inspired cinematography.

Look for the scene in which Robert Blake stares out a window into the storm and talks about his father; stylized reflections of raindrops—no, teardrops—course down his face. In an age of crimson bloodfests masquerading as crime thrillers, *In Cold Blood* serves as a reminder that more gore definitely *doesn't* mean more talent.

This supremely tense little black-and-white number from the sixties carries more real emotion and power, and gives you a worse case of the shudders, than anything Steven Seagal or Oliver Stone ever did. If you're into being screamed at and watching people get blown away, check out *Natural Born Killers.* If you want a chilling glimpse inside the tortured soul of a criminal, watch this one.

★ 1967, 134 minutes, B&W, not rated.

★ With: Robert Blake, Scott Wilson, John Forsyth.
Director: Richard Brooks.

★ *Whom did Capote interview in researching his book?*
(Answer on page 142.)

Into the West

*Once upon a time . . .
or maybe this morning . . .*

The best family films are the ones that keep the attention of the kiddies and give the grown-ups something to think about as well. Here's a timelessly charming one that manages both tasks expertly. You start out thinking this picture is going to be a long-ago-and-far-away fantasy; when you realize it takes place in the present day, the effect is both startling and oddly reassuring.

Into the West has all the elements of a classic fairy tale, but the problems that its young heroes face are believably modern ones. The father lives under a curse of sorts: alcoholism since the death of his wife. The boys, ragamuffins of the first order, live with their father in a low-income apartment: a large gray tower. As they beg for money on the streets, the older one urges his asthmatic younger brother to wheeze louder to boost their income. Sounds Grimm indeed.

Why does the beautiful white horse adopt the two boys? *Why* does it protect them? *Why* does it lead them to the grave of their mother, where neither boy has ever journeyed? Like many great fairy tales, *Into the West* keeps you hooked with big questions—and delivers redemption with its answers.

★ 1993, 97 minutes, color, PG.

★ With: Gabriel Byrne, Ellen Barkin, Ruaidrhi Conroy, Ciaran Fitzgerald. Director: Mike Newell.

★ *Name the retro-western in which Jeff Bridges plays an aspiring sagebrush novelist who finds himself up against a passel of real-life bad guys.* (Answer on page 294.)

*"Are you Travelers?"
"No, we're cowboys."*
—Young 'pokes set a stranger straight.

For a great double feature, rent it with
Darby O'Gill and the Little People.

Seen it but in the mood for something similar? Try
The Black Stallion.

Answer to page 326 trivia question:
Andy Warhol.

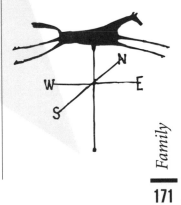

Family

171

Invasion of the Body Snatchers (1956)

This one will really get under your skin.

"*Love, desire, ambition, faith—without them life is so simple, believe me.*"

—Repeat as necessary until your soul disappears.

For a great double feature, rent it with

The Thing (from Another World) (1951).

Seen it but in the mood for something similar? Try

Invasion of the Body Snatchers (1978).

Answer to page 347 trivia question:

Edith Head—and she didn't even acknowledge Givenchy. Tsk, tsk.

Not unlike the supposed Creeping Red Menace everyone in the country was so worried about at the time, a passel of aliens is surreptitiously taking over a small town. They're sneaky, too; they wait until everyone in the little hamlet's asleep, quietly subdue their victims, then hatch docile look-alikes under the control of Someone Else. It goes to show you what happens when you let your guard down, even for a moment, doesn't it?

Today's moviegoers are probably more familiar with the fine 1978 remake starring Donald Sutherland, but the original white-knuckle entry, adapted from Jack Finney's *The Body Snatchers,* is a must-see classic, a superb cinematic reflection of the anti-Communist paranoia of the fifties. Quite scary.

★ 1956, 80 minutes, B&W, not rated.

★ With: Kevin McCarthy, Dana Wynter, Carolyn Jones. Director: Don Siegel.

★ *What future A-list director appears in a bit part as a meter reader?* (Answer on page 241.)

Horror

The Ipcress File

Harry Palmer: He cooks, he shops, he shoots to kill.

Not many superspies brew their own gourmet coffee, collect kitchen utensils, or shop for French mushrooms. But Harry Palmer is no ordinary spy. Bluejay (the bad guy) has kidnapped an important scientist code-named Raven. In a Bond movie 007's job would be to penetrate some high-tech lair, blow a lot of things up, and then escape with Raven and a bikini-clad young lady. Palmer, on the other hand, sets out only to *buy back* the scientist. When he does so, it turns out that Raven has been brainwashed. Palmer tries to get the money back but is himself kidnapped and subjected to torture and mind conditioning through exposure to psychedelic music (you knew there was a connection, didn't you?). What follows is exciting and incredibly complicated— but hey, that's what spy movies are supposed to be about, right? This is one of the best. *The Ipcress File* won the British Film Academy Award for Best Picture of the year.

★ 1965, 108 minutes, color, not rated.

★ With: Michael Caine, Nigel Greene, Sue Lloyd. Director: Sidney J. Furie.

★ *What cast member had a starring role in "Upstairs, Downstairs"?* (Answer on page 148.)

"Beefaroni— extraordinary."
—A withering assessment of supermarket fare from the upper echelons of the British intelligence establishment

For a great double feature, rent it with *Zulu.*

Seen it but in the mood for something similar? Try *The Spy Who Came in from the Cold.*

Answer to page 142 trivia question: *The Shawshank Redemption.*

Suspense

It Happens Every Spring

Maybe if the batters had x-ray eyes,
they'd be able to hit the ball.

"If a man is really serious, he doesn't have the right to say anything until he can be serious."

—Milland's crystal-clear explanation to Jean Peters of why he can't tell her what he's working on.

For a great double feature, rent it with

Bull Durham.

Seen it but in the mood for something similar? Try

The Absent Minded Professor.

Answer to page 215 trivia question:

François Truffaut; the others were Claude Rains and Robert Walker.

The "it" in *It Happens Every Spring* is baseball, of course, and during the spring in question it happens a little differently than people expect. That's because bumbling chemistry professor Ray Milland accidentally discovers a substance that, when applied to a baseball, will cause the leather sphere to leap and spin to avoid anything made of wood. (And you thought corking the bat was bad.) Needless to say, this development carries immense ramifications for serious students of the physics of the game, alters the time-honored balance between offense and defense, and results in an unlikely new pitching star who's no doubt piqued that he won't be able to file for free agency for another 35 years. Watch out for those new aluminum bats, though.

Lots of fun, without a pretentious bone in its body, *It Happens Every Spring* is a gentle, satisfying, family-oriented comedy that will probably appeal even to those in the family who wish something else would happen every spring.

★ 1949, 87 minutes, B&W, not rated.

★ With: Ray Milland, Jean Peters, Paul Douglas. Director: Lloyd Bacon.

★ *What picture earned Ray Milland an Oscar as Best Actor?* (Answer on page 38.)

Comedy

It's a Mad, Mad, Mad, Mad World

A portrait of man's inhumanity to man, 20th-century Western civilization, and Ethel Merman's inability to shut up.

Reminiscent, at key points, of early Bergman. Stanley Kramer's style, which utilizes Spencer Tracy as a slightly-too-obvious Christ figure, points toward rapid contrasts, sudden shifts, and unexpected reversals. Kramer explores such timeless themes as parental instability, generational conflict and misunderstanding, and—oh, who are we kidding here? The main themes in this movie involve people being slapped and falling over things, things blowing up and breaking down, large objects and individuals being pushed through windows, unscrupulous ways to steal cars, angry women, impotent men, reckless driving, dead gas stations, and, yes, at the very end, a banana peel to slip on. (Oops—gave away the ending.)

Everyone on earth is in this movie, and, yes, it's annoying, but it's pretty funny all the way through, too. Ready for a shock? The director's cut was five and a half hours long, but audience members kept dying of messy cerebral hemorrhages in previews, so they had to cut it down.

★ 1963, 154 minutes, color, not rated.

★ With: Spencer Tracy, Milton Berle, Ethel Merman. Director: Stanley Kramer.

★ *What star made his (or her) last film appearance in this movie?* (Answer on page 84.)

"It's the Big W, I tell you! The Big W!"

—Suddenly every A-list comedian in Hollywood is staring up at some . . . well, let's not spoil the surprise.

For a great double feature, rent it with *The Great Race.*

Seen it but in the mood for something similar? Try *Those Magnificent Men in Their Flying Machines.*

Answer to page 180 trivia question: *The Yearling.*

Comedy

Jason and the Argonauts

Cheap thrills.

People thought it was a big deal when director Frank Capra got his name above the title on movie posters. Where does that leave Ray Harryhausen, who didn't even direct *Jason and the Argonauts* yet is the main (only?) name anyone associates with this memorable adventure film? Harryhausen's special effects are still spellbinding, even in our high-tech age of cinematic morphing, full-scale explosions, and computer-altered footage. It's not that you don't *see* the technological limitations of his walking skeletons, winged tormentors, and huge sea gods; you do, but everything is executed so crisply, and with such an air of confidence, that you happily consent to being awestruck whenever you're supposed to be.

Who cares if the otherworldly creatures of, say, *Casper,* are more seamless? This film is 20 times more fun; it's a perfect example of a movie that can keep you hooked despite mediocre acting from start to finish. The principals are stiff and sound eerily dubbed, even though the movie is in English, but they're never more than a few minutes away from a confrontation with something spectacular. Personally, I like to think the leaden acting values were a conscious production choice, meant to offer contrast with the lively stop-motion effects.

★ 1963, 104 minutes, color, not rated.

★ With: Todd Armstrong, Gary Raymond, Nancy Kovack. Director: Don Chaffey.

★ *What modern science fiction trilogy was profoundly influenced by Harryhausen's work?* (Answer on page 8.)

Fantasy

Jean de Florette

Spring? What spring?

If a beautiful stretch of French countryside isn't worth swindling someone for, what is? Clearly recognizable good guys and bad guys are, after the exquisite landscape photography, the most prominent feature of this stylish, attractive melodrama. The picture follows the efforts of two scheming farmers (Yves Montand and Daniel Auteil) who launch a plot against a boozing, inexperienced newcomer to the country (Gerard Depardieu). The hunchbacked Depardieu has no idea a precious spring flows across his property; Montand and Auteil aim to keep it that way.

Fine performances throughout, especially Depardieu's; director Claude Berri's pacing and confident use of the magnificent outdoor locations are pretty close to perfect. The visuals alone will leave you breathless. Not, perhaps, the subtlest plot you're going to come across all year, but a lovely ride all the same.

★ 1986, 122 minutes, color, PG.

★ With: Yves Montand, Gerard Depardieu, Daniel Auteil. Director: Claude Berri.

★ *Name the actress who plays Depardieu's daughter in the sequel,* Manon of the Spring. (Answer on page 5.)

"Othentics?"

—The puzzled Daniel Auteil thinks they're a kind of plant; Gerard Depardieu has been discussing "authentic farming."

For a great double feature, rent it with
Manon of the Spring.

Seen it but in the mood for something similar? Try
The Return of Martin Guerre.

Answer to page 151 trivia question:
The Deer Hunter (1978).

Foreign

Jesus of Nazareth

The greatest version ever filmed.

"I'd like to tell you a story."
—Robert Powell's declaration brings silence to the room. The story is that of the Prodigal Son.

For a great double feature—nah, forget it. Just watch this three-cassette masterpiece, then go to bed.

Seen it but in the mood for something similar? Try

Brother Sun, Sister Moon.

Answer to page 187 trivia question:

Leo McKern, who played the bad guy in *Help!*

Franco Zeffirelli, whose previous films include innovative, moving adaptations of the life of St. Francis of Assisi and of Shakespeare's *Romeo and Juliet,* here offers what may very well be the finest film account of the life of Jesus. Zeffirelli knows, first and foremost, how to shoot faces; although the settings in the Holy Land are spectacular, and although the screenwriters have managed, somehow, to add TV-miniseries plot points to the story without doing violence to the Gospel narratives, the main thing you'll remember about this production is the director's masterful rendering of the faces of his all-star cast. With Zeffirelli's help Robert Powell, in the title role, gets more done with his eyes than any actor has a right to. Overcome whatever must be overcome to rent this superb video; even if you don't like religious dramas, even if you don't like television miniseries, even if you don't like long (read: three-cassette) evenings, you will be transfixed by this masterful piece of work.

★ 1977, 371 minutes, color, not rated.

★ With: Robert Powell, Anne Bancroft, James Mason, Rod Steiger, Olivia Hussey, Sir Laurence Olivier. Director: Franco Zeffirelli.

★ *What Mel Gibson action flick did Zeffirelli direct?*
(Answer on page 47.)

Jezebel

*The movie that made David O. Selznick
Scarlett with rage.*

Bette Davis's Oscar-winning performance as a calculating southern belle in *Jezebel* reportedly infuriated the legendary producer David O. Selznick. Although the picture was based not on Margaret Mitchell's novel but on a successful Broadway play, it sure looked and sounded a lot like Selznick's property *Gone with the Wind*, then in its early stages of development. In one scene, for instance, Davis shocks the guests at a ball by wearing a thoroughly scandalous red dress. If *you* were planning the big ballroom scene for *GWTW*, what would *you* have thought?

Davis probably lost the chance to portray Scarlett O'Hara as a result of being cast in *Jezebel*, but she's brilliant enough here to give you a pretty good idea of what she would have done with the coveted role. Featuring a very young Henry Fonda as the beau Davis pushes a little too far, then begs for forgiveness when he falls ill. One of the high points in Warner Brothers studio history.

★ 1938, 103 minutes, B&W, not rated.

★ With: Bette Davis, Henry Fonda, George Brent. Director: William Wyler.

★ *How did Wyler leave audiences with the impression that they were seeing Davis in a bright red dress in this black and white film?* (Answer on page 126.)

"Child, you're out of your mind. You can't wear red to the Olympus ball."
—You'd think people would learn to stop telling Bette Davis what she can and can't do.

For a great double feature, rent it with
Now, Voyager.

Seen it but in the mood for something similar? Try
Hush . . . Hush, Sweet Charlotte.

Answer to page 223 trivia question:
Jeanne Moreau; the picture was *Jules and Jim.*

Drama

179

Johnny Belinda

Jane Wyman's got a problem. Actually, she's got a couple of problems.

"You're the spittin' image of your father."

—None-too-brilliant rapist Stephen McNally's impromptu remark to Jane Wyman's infant son. Her father, Charles Bickford, puts two and two together.

For a great double feature, rent it with

The Piano.

Seen it but in the mood for something similar? Try

The Glass Menagerie (1950).

Answer to page 258 trivia question:

The Great Race.

These days she's followed around by the phrase *former wife of Ronald Reagan,* but before a political career was even a glimmer in the Gipper's eye Jane Wyman staked out her territory as an actress of the very first order with her unforgettable performance in *Johnny Belinda.* She won a richly deserved Oscar for her turn as a hearing- and speech-impaired young woman who, having been raped, gives birth to her child and faces down the tidal wave of societal misunderstanding that greets her everywhere she turns. Pretty powerful stuff for 1948—or now, for that matter.

Wyman is a beacon of quiet strength and independence; she's quite content to handle the situation she finds herself in, and she doesn't need to ask a man for help. Lew Ayres, as the medical man who falls for Wyman, is terrific too.

A sensitive, superbly rendered drama, *Johnny Belinda* is pretty intense in some sections; you might want to reserve it for adults and middle teenagers.

★ 1948, 103 minutes, B&W, not rated.

★ With: Jane Wyman, Lew Ayres, Charles Bickford. Director: Jean Negulesco.

★ *Name the family classic about a young deer in which Wyman appeared.* (Answer on page 175.)

Judgment at Nuremberg

*And you thought the O.J. jury
had it tough.*

OK, the big war's over. Now it's time to tie together a couple of those pesky loose ends. It's the real trial of the century; Spencer Tracy plays the American judge who must decide how much accountability to assign to those who carried out the most horrific dictates of the Nazi regime. This complex, ambitious study of wartime—and postwar—morality has the courage to give the accused Germans a few high fastballs to throw in the direction of the prosecution.

Made at the height of the cold war, *Judgment at Nuremberg* lets its doomed warlords issue a bitter and mostly accurate condemnation of Soviet expansion; when you find yourself agreeing with them, you get the chills. Similarly, the choice to cast Burt Lancaster as a not-altogether-unsympathetic Nazi adds a welcome note of complexity to this excellent courtroom drama.

Stanley Kramer's somber, formal tone is perfect for the material. The all-star cast also features Maximillian Schell and a surprisingly strong Judy Garland, whose career was thought by many to be over at this point. "Star Trek" fans should keep an eye out for a very young William Shatner.

★ 1961, 178 minutes, color, not rated.

★ With: Spencer Tracy, Burt Lancaster, Maximillian Schell, Richard Widmark, Marlene Dietrich, Montgomery Clift, Judy Garland. Director: Stanley Kramer.

★ *What comedy classic did Kramer direct that featured, more or less, every big comedian in the country?*
(Answer on page 282.)

"What was going to be a passing phase became a way of life."
—Burt Lancaster, on the abuses of the Nazi regime.

For a great double feature, rent it with
Music Box.

Seen it but in the mood for something similar? Try
QB VII.

Answer to page 160 trivia question:
Scrooged.

Jules and Jim

A different kind of buddy picture.

"A girl like that . . .
what is she like?"
—Jeanne Moreau is an
enigma . . . I think.

For a great double
feature, rent it with
Breathless (1959).

Seen it but in the mood
for something similar?
Try
Two English Girls.

Answer to page 195
trivia question:
Angus, Herman,
Vernon, Cecil,
Herbert, and John.

You know the Joni Mitchell song about not knowing what you've got until it's all gone? That's the basic message of *Jules and Jim*, François Truffaut's classic, imaginatively cut study of a complex romantic threesome; each occupant of a point on the triangle experiences great longings and great restlessness, but nothing pays off as it's supposed to. No one, in short, ever latches onto the Great Ice Cream Cone in the Sky. Such is love, *oui?*

This stylish, visually adventurous, and generation-defining film helped to secure Francois Truffaut's reputation as one of the world's most accomplished directors; he had already stunned the film establishment with the release, two years earlier, of the masterful *Four Hundred Blows.*

Henri Serre and Oskar Werner play the unexpectedly cooperative French and Austrian men in the equation (in a few years the two countries will be at war); Moreau is radiant as a woman who demands the right to live life on her own terms—even if that means destroying people she loves.

The on-screen depiction of a ménage à trois wasn't exactly common in 1961; the film was banned in the United States by the Catholic Legion of Decency.

★ 1961, 104 minutes, B&W, not rated.

★ With: Oskar Werner, Jeanne Moreau, Henri Serre. Director: François Truffaut.

★ *In what film did Oskar Werner play a fireman?* (Answer on page 315.)

Kafka

If this isn't Kafkaesque, nothing is.

tylish, creepy paranoia. Director Steven Soderbergh, who set the world on its ear with 1989's *sex, lies, and videotape,* played his trump card with the follow-up, this visually intriguing fantasia on the life and works of Franz Kafka.

Jeremy Irons is superb as the brilliant, baffled writer; his unnerving world is populated by a host of menacing and seemingly unescapable authority figures. Joel Grey is cast yet again as a small man with a vicious smile. He's great, though. See what happens when you direct a big hit movie? You get to work with all the cool people.

Irons is in search of a friend who has disappeared mysteriously; the numbingly massive bureacracy at the insurance company where he works may or may not have had something to do with the fellow's sudden departure.

This one's about as different in style and theme from *sex, lies, and videotape* as you can get, although each film does concern itself with lurking artistic types who are fine on their own until a woman comes along to draw them out. *Kafka* offers inspired, dreamy weirdness in abundance; don't be surprised when it rattles the bars of your cage a little too loudly for comfort.

★ 1991, 98 minutes, B&W with color inserts, PG-13.

★ With: Jeremy Irons, Theresa Russell, Joel Grey, Alec Guinness. Director: Steven Soderbergh.

★ *Name the film in which Jeremy Irons left us with "no idea" as to whether or not he killed his wife.* (Answer on page 26.)

"I write about nightmares. You've created one."

—Things are getting a little too bizarre for even Jeremy Irons.

For a great double feature, rent it with *Brazil.*

Seen it but in the mood for something similar? Try the 1984 remake of *1984.*

Answer to page 231 trivia question: *Romance on the High Seas*; the star was Judy Garland.

The Kid

Can Jackie Coogan steal a scene from Chaplin? You bet.

Charlie Chaplin's first feature film, *The Kid*, upped the ante. The Little Tramp's competitors now had to hold the audience's interest as he had—and keep them laughing as he had—for an hour or more. Good luck.

Although there had been feature-length film comedies before *The Kid*, there had never been anything quite like this gentle, touching tale of two outcasts. Heavy on pathos and light on plot, Chaplin's long-form effort easily won over the audiences of the day, and it remains a classic. The story, such as it is, involves Charlie's "adoption" of an adorable orphan (Jackie Coogan). The plot evolved through improvisation over a period of months in the studio—and tense, expensive months, at that.

Coogan became a child star as a result of his fine work in the picture. The little fella holds his own with the Tramp here, and that's saying something. *The Kid* is goopily sentimental in places, but that's really no surprise with Charlie at the helm, is it? It's still a delight to watch.

Most cassettes also include the short *The Idle Class*.

★ 1921, 60 minutes, B&W, not rated.

★ With: Charlie Chaplin, Jackie Coogan, Edna Purviance. Director: Charles Chaplin.

★ *Coogan went on to star in a hit sixties television series. Name it.* (Answer on page 51.)

The Kids Are Alright

Rent this in a hotel room, then throw the television out the window.

Via concert footage, interviews, and clips from old television appearances, we watch the Who change from sneering, petulant adolescents to seasoned artistic professionals.

This exhilarating documentary is equal parts nostalgia trip, career retrospective, and rock show. You come away tapping your toes, but you're also impressed by the band's ability to survive the party. (Sadly, though, drummer Keith Moon, the band's most outrageous barrier pusher, died not long after the group's postfilm *Who Are You* release.)

Among the high points: a spirited skeet-shooting session, with gold records as targets; the group's gleefully chaotic destruction of their instruments on a "The Smothers Brothers Comedy Hour" episode; and Moon's response to Pete Townshend's rhetorical query during a group meeting concerning whether the group should continue to be "a circus act." (Moon promptly stands on his head.) A good group rent; you can gather a bunch of friends, enjoy some great, gut-wrenching rock and roll, and be glad you didn't die before you got old after all.

★ 1979, 108 minutes, color, PG.

★ With: the Who, Ringo Starr, Steve Martin, Tom Smothers. Director: Jeff Stein.

★ *What film based on a landmark album by the Who featured a memorable explosion of baked beans?*
(Answer on page 73.)

"Hope I die before I get old."
—A babyfaced Roger Daltrey delivers the line that would come back to haunt the band.

For a great double feature, rent it with
Gimme Shelter.

Seen it but in the mood for something similar? Try
Quadrophenia.

Answer to page 4 trivia question:
Henry Miller's *Tropic of Cancer.*

Documentary

King Creole

Call it luck, call it an optical illusion, call it what you will; when it's over, you will believe Elvis can act.

"I'm not a hoodlum, I'm a hustler. I've had to be."
—Elvis has learned a little about survival from all those years spent on the wrong side of the tracks.

For a great double feature, rent it with

The Big Easy.

Seen it but in the mood for something similar? Try

Jailhouse Rock.

Answer to page 38 trivia question:

The Adventures of Priscilla, Queen of the Desert.

Director Michael Curtiz (of *Casablanca* fame) does the impossible here—he makes a damn good movie out of what has every right to be a predictable Elvis Presley vehicle.

Elvis is the wrong-side-of-town nightclub singer who's been cheated out of a normal childhood; he gets mixed up with a gang of hoodlums and might just end up on the wrong side of the law for good. But he's got one thing going for him; he can sing—and how.

So it's not exactly a Pulitzer Prize–winning script; the execution is quite startlingly strong. Curtiz knows how to set up a shot, and he also knows how to pry the performance of a lifetime from his leading man. The movie is a testament to inspired black-and-white moviemaking—and to Presley's folly in selling his soul to Tom Parker and submitting to the wagonloads of drek that would mark the rest of his cinematic career. Don't let the awfulness of, say, *A Change of Habit* blind you to the significant pleasures hiding here; *King Creole* is really a first-rate effort.

★ 1958, 116 minutes, B&W, not rated.

★ With: Elvis Presley, Carolyn Jones, Dolores Hart, Walter Matthau. Director: Michael Curtiz.

★ *For what record label did Elvis Presley record "That's All Right Mama"?* (Answer on page 130.)

Musical

King Lear

Olivier's last, and greatest, lead role.

Talk about a must-see. Nearly every one of the *supporting* players in this monumental 1984 production turns in the performance of a lifetime. Leo McKern's headstrong Gloucester carries all the power of a tragic lead character; Diana Rigg's Regan is a terrifying portrait of misdirected sexuality and calculated evil who needs no zippered catsuit to hold your attention; David Threlfall's homeless, howling Edgar explores the limits of love and human endurance; and Colin Blakely, as the ever-loyal Kent, sets his huge, rough will and his sharp tongue against the forces of destruction—making us long for a victory that does not materialize.

Now, then: you were wondering, maybe, about the lead actor? Sir Laurence Olivier serves up his last (and arguably greatest) leading-role screen performance here. Olivier's technique is, as always, iron-sure—but there is also an emotional depth in his portrayal of the mad, embittered king that establishes this production as a standard not likely to be surpassed for generations. Warning: The production pulls no punches; it contains several violent scenes that make it inappropriate for younger viewers, notably the on-screen blinding of Gloucester.

★ 1984, 158 minutes, color, not rated.

★ With: Laurence Olivier, Leo McKern, Colin Blakely, Diana Rigg, Dorothy Tutin. Director: Michael Elliott.

★ *What member of the cast appeared in a movie with the Beatles?* (Answer on page 178.)

"Who is it that can tell me who I am?"
—Olivier has a big-time identity crisis.

For a great double feature, rent it with *Prospero's Books.*

Seen it but in the mood for something similar? Try *The Entertainer.*

Answer to page 72 trivia question: *Monsieur Verdoux.*

Drama

King of Hearts

It's a mad, mad, mad, mad world.

"Long live the King of Hearts."

—The people of the town salute their sovereign.

For a great double feature, rent it with

Mediterraneo.

Seen it but in the mood for something similar? Try

Monty Python and the Holy Grail.

Answer to page 106 trivia question:

Alfie.

I t's World War I; Alan Bates plays a Scottish infantryman whose mission as bomb defuser takes him into a booby-trapped town that's been abandoned by the townspeople—and taken over by the inmates of a local lunatic asylum. Each of the town's new inhabitants has taken on the role best suited to his or her particular delusion; together they're earnest enough to fool Bates and inventive enough to set up a run of inspired gags.

The strange situation gives rise to the film's central question: Is a town run by lunatics really any crazier than a world that insists on destroying itself? Philippe De Broca's engaging, modestly scaled examination of the frailties of the human condition isn't the artistic achievement of the century, but it's sweet enough to make a good impression, which is enough.

★ 1966, 102 minutes, color, not rated.

★ With: Alan Bates, Genevieve Bujold, Pierre Brasseur. Director: Philippe De Broca.

★ *What U.S. film offering a variation on the who's-really-mad-here-after-all theme became the first motion picture since* It Happened One Night *to sweep all the major Academy Awards?* (Answer on page 304.)

King Rat

King of the hill.

ey, whatever happened to George Segal? Films like *Fun with Dick and Jane* and *Where's Poppa?* proved that he could turn in accomplished comic performances; and in *King Rat* he's unforgettable in the title role as the cold, calculating POW who rises to the top of the heap in a hellish Japanese prison camp during World War II.

How, you may ask, does a prisoner of war manage to walk around with perfectly coiffed hair and immaculately pressed uniforms? The answer, my friend, lies in simple economic ruthlessness. Segal's callous disregard for his starving fellow inmates is just this side of unbearable to watch, in no small degree because we know what the prisoners do not: the war is nearing its end, and there's a reckoning on the way. Keep an eye out for the scene in which he fries a precious egg in front of his ravenously hungry cellmates; it encapsulates the whole film into a single scene.

This one's an overlooked classic that boasts taut, intense direction and superb performances from Segal and Tom Courtenay. The latter's complex relationship with the king carries both suppressed eroticism and an uneasy distance.

★ 1965, 133 minutes, B&W, not rated.

★ With: George Segal, Tom Courtenay, James Fox. Director: Bryan Forbes.

★ *Can you spot the future game show host in the cast?* (Answer on page 319.)

"I'm not the people, am I, Max?"
—George Segal has set himself up in another league.

For a great double feature, rent it with
Where's Poppa?

Seen it but in the mood for something similar? Try
Stalag 17.

Answer to page 13 trivia question:
Who's Afraid of Virginia Woolf?

Action

Kings Row

*Not exactly the small-town values the
Gipper would later extol.*

*"Where's the rest of
me?"*

—Ronald Reagan realizes he's
dealing with a new set of
circumstances.

**For a great double
feature, rent it with**

Casablanca (just so
you can try to picture
Reagan in the male
lead, which he nearly
got).

**Seen it but in the mood
for something similar?
Try**

Peyton Place.

**Answer to page 47
trivia question:**

Tippi Hedren, who
starred in a pair of
Hitchcock features,
including *The Birds.*

The good people of Warner Brothers left no stone
unturned in their quest to make this sturdy, watchable melodrama about scandal and hypocrisy in the
heartland pay off for the audiences of the forties.
This precursor to *Peyton Place* explores the familiar
notion that things are not always what they seem in a
sleepy little burg; it's aided immensely by William
Cameron Menzies's sets, Erich Korngold's fine score, and,
yes, the greatest performance of Ronald Reagan's career.

The picture has aged surprisingly well; it's got some
great character studies and acres of creepy cover-ups. It's
also probably the only movie of the forties to feature a
vindictive doctor (Charles Coburn) who performs
unnecessary amputations when the mood strikes him.
(Perhaps this is what inspired 1993's unfortunate *Boxing
Helena*, but I doubt it.) A very worthwhile rental, especially for those who are, as I was, a bit skeptical of our former president's ability to turn in a truly fine piece of
acting work.

★ 1942, 127 minutes, B&W, not rated.

★ With: Ann Sheridan, Robert Cummings, Ronald
Reagan. Director: Sam Wood.

★ *What Ronald Reagan–Shirley Temple film is considered
by connoisseurs of bad cinema to be one of the worst
pictures of all time?* (Answer on page 291.)

Drama

Koyaanisqatsi

*A graat fliqk,
but diffiqlt to spaal.*

Every once in a while you come away from a movie wondering how on earth it ever managed to get made at all. That can either be a bad thing or a good thing; in the case of *Koyaanisqatsi* it's a good thing. This collage of sound and picture, nine years in the making, forgoes traditional narrative, relying instead on images of incredible natural beauty and sickening man-made ugliness to make its points about the way humans abuse the environment.

Because the picture has no dialogue, director Godfrey Reggio must rely on an extraordinary visual sense and a hypnotic score by composer Phillip Glass to pull the picture off. It all works! Give *Koyaanisqatsi* a try; what sounds like a tract for tree huggers is in fact one of the most exhilarating, visually adventurous pictures of the eighties.

An inferior sequel, from the same director, followed in 1988. It's probably a mistake to try to make a movie like this more than once; *Koyaanisqatsi* is best regarded as a genre unto itself. (By the way, the impossible-to-remember title is Hopi for "life out of balance." If the store clerk is bilingual in English and Hopi, you're in luck. Just in case, though, you might want to write it down.)

★ 1983, 87 minutes, color, not rated.

★ With: various natural objects, strange women from Las Vegas. Director: Godfrey Reggio.

★ *Name the sequel.* (Answer on page 135.)

"Dun dun dun dun dun dun dun."
—Phillip Glass's throbbing soundtrack.

For a great double feature, rent it with
2001: A Space Odyssey.

Seen it but in the mood for something similar? Try
Dersu Uzala.

Answer to page 81 trivia question:
The film was presented in 3-D format.

Documentary

The Krays

They can't get no satisfaction.

Peter Medak's chilling portrait of the sociopathic twins who rose to the highest ranks of the British crime scene in the 1960s makes for harrowing, unforgettable viewing. The idea of twin mod-era English mobsters offers considerable dramatic potential; picture the anti-Establishment pose of the Who's *Quadrophenia* transposed to the rough-and-tumble world of the hardcore British murder and protection rackets, and you've got an idea of this picture's peculiar appeal.

Ronald is the twin who takes the lead, as ruthless as he is brilliant; Reginald is the one who follows along and might conceivably have constructed a normal life for himself had he not found himself paired with a monster. The brothers achieved a position of prominence in England that was accompanied not only by fear and loathing on the part of the general public (which you would expect) but also by a surprising amount of hero worship.

In this excellent film account of their underworld career, the twins' pursuit of power is second only to their unswerving devotion to their imperious, overprotective mother. Top-notch acting from all makes this a must-see.

★ 1990, 119 minutes, color, R.

★ With: Billie Whitelaw, Gary Kemp and Martin Kemp (who are real-life brothers but not twins), Susan Fleetwood. Director: Peter Medak.

★ *Casting look-alike actors is one way to portray twins on-screen, but what actor played both lead roles in a film that told the story of twin gynecologists gone mad?* (Answer on page 43.)

Kung Fu (1972)

Half the fun is watching the cowboys grumble about how Chinese Carradine looks.

This nifty pilot for the celebrated cult TV series was the source of an intriguing coupling of ideas in one character: the laconic Gary Cooper–style loner of Hollywood legend and a vaguely Taoist half-Chinese priest with a price on his head who has an unshakable commitment to spiritual values.

As anyone who has seen the much-parodied network series knows, "Kung Fu" made extensive use of flashbacks to recall the training and youth of David Carradine's character in a Shaolin monastery. The less-well-known pilot episode features the obligatory "pluck the pebble from my hand, Grasshopper" scenes, but it also provides the details behind Carradine's decision to flee China for America. (Admit it—you never did get that part straight.) The stateside portion of the plot yields a surprisingly responsible, historically accurate treatment of a group of Chinese railroad workers whose lives are considered expendable by their white boss.

This pilot is easily a notch or two above the average episode of the original series; it should not be confused with the undistinguished 1986 movie featuring Carradine and Brandon Lee.

★ 1972, 75 minutes, color, not rated.

★ With: David Carradine, Keye Luke, Philip Ahn. Director: Jerry Thorpe.

★ *What actor, slated to play Caine in the series, was rejected because network executives feared audiences would not accept an Oriental lead?* (Answer on page 13.)

"In the Shaolin temple, we have never accepted anyone of other than full Chinese birth. There is a first for everything."

—Good thing, too, since David Carradine looks about as Asian as a tin of Spam.

For a great double feature, rent it with *Dragon: The Bruce Lee Story.*

Seen it but in the mood for something similar? Try *Little Buddha.*

Answer to page 16 trivia question:

He was an acrobat— just like Cary Grant.

La Dolce Vita

A huge statue of Christ floats over a beachful of bathing beauties—Fellini, right?

"There are three things I love the most: Love, love, love."
—No prizes for guessing what's on Anita Ekberg's mind.

For a great double feature, rent it with
Roman Holiday.

Seen it but in the mood for something similar? Try
Fellini's Roma.

Answer to page 50 trivia question:
Barton Fink.

Marcello Mastroianni is a glitzy reporter out to win the gold medal in the Shallowness Olympics. He finds himself smitten with the considerable charms of a curvaceous film star (Anita Ekberg) and pursues her even though the one woman capable of truly loving him is in the hospital, recovering from a suicide attempt. Mastroianni seems to want to be there for her, but he's constantly distracted by the lures of "the sweet life"—which it is his job to chronicle and which the vivacious, brainless Ekberg personifies.

Which woman is right for him? Has modern society turned its back on God? Will Ekberg fall out of her dress? For the answer to these and other burning questions, check out Federico Fellini's multilayered early-sixties classic.

★ 1960, 175 minutes, B&W, not rated.

★ With: Marcello Mastroianni, Anouk Aimee, Anita Ekberg. Director: Federico Fellini.

★ *Ekberg's description of what she wears to bed at night ("my favorite perfume") was lifted from what real-life Hollywood star's remark?* (Answer on page 77.)

The Lady Eve

*Shipboard shark swindles
sucker at sea.*

Card shark Barbara Stanwyck, who's pretending to be an innocent young thing to help out in her father's shipboard swindle, has Henry Fonda wrapped around her little finger before she's even met him. Fonda has just come on board after a long trip down the Amazon; he's a babe in the woods when it comes to women. Stanwyck is all but licking her chops in anticipation of bleeding him dry. Of course, after she gets to know her prey, she falls in love with him. Before she has a chance to tell him the truth about who she really is, he finds out himself and drops her like a hot potato—and then the real fun starts.

Preston Sturges wrote and directed this hilarious romantic farce; his taut script fairly crackles with one-liners. There's just enough slapstick, and the costumes are nothing short of spectacular. This film showcases Fonda and Stanwyck at their very best.

★ 1941, 94 minutes, B&W, not rated.

★ With: Barbara Stanwyck, Henry Fonda, Charles Coburn. Director: Preston Sturges.

★ *Name the husbands cited in the honeymoon suite.*
(Answer on page 182.)

"What's your weakness, brother?"
—Barbara Stanwyck's got a pretty good idea already.

For a great double feature, rent it with
Raising Arizona.

Seen it but in the mood for something similar? Try
Ball of Fire.

Answer to page 84 trivia question:
Jean de Florette.

Comedy

The Lady in White

What kind of ghost story is it when the ghosts are the good guys?

"*It was All Hallow's Eve, and I, still locked behind the cloakroom door, suddenly felt a wind sweep through the darkness, chilling me to the bone.*"

—Brrrr. Alex Rocco's got the chills.

For a great double feature, rent it with

The Haunting of Julia.

Seen it but in the mood for something similar? Try

The Shining.

Answer to page 119 trivia question:

Animal House.

It's not the spooks in this story that are scary; the real monster is all too human. While locked in a closet as the result of a schoolboy prank, a youngster sees a vision of a little girl's murder some years earlier. It turns out that there's a serial killer loose in the town, but none of the adults want to talk about it, because that sort of thing simply doesn't happen.

Who's the bad guy? As we learn the answer, we come to see the face of horror as seen through the eyes of a child.

This taut chiller regularly lulls you into a sense of false security, then hits you with a terrific sucker punch; it also mines a good many genuinely humorous moments, in part because the line between the scary and the hilarious is so much fuzzier to children than it is to adults. There are moments of genuine whimsy as well; if it's possible for a film to be both charming and drop-dead scary, *The Lady in White* is that film.

A word of warning: Although this picture accurately depicts a child's sensibility, and although there is not a moment of gore in the film, the plot unfolds some truly horrific events. This is *not* a family film!

★ 1988, 112 minutes, color, PG-13.

★ With: Lukas Haas, Len Cariou, Katherine Helmond, Alex Rocco. Director: Frank LaLoggia.

★ *What television sitcom made Katherine Helmond a star?* (Answer on page 311.)

Ladybird, Ladybird

That's Rock, R-O-C-K; you'll be hearing more from her.

Every once in a while a movie comes and goes without finding its audience, despite having nearly everything working in its favor. *Ladybird, Ladybird* is such a film; it's a powerful, affecting drama that features what has to be one of the finest lead performances of recent years, but it was simply lost in the shuffle when it was released on a limited basis in 1994.

In an extraordinary screen debut Crissy Rock plays a poverty-stricken London mother whose children have been taken away by local social agencies after a devastating fire. She wants 'em back. Rock's character endures the trials of Job and reacts accordingly, but this is no formulaic melodrama with easy-to-pigeonhole good guys and bad guys.

Ladybird, Ladybird poses a number of difficult questions about parenthood and social responsibility, and it doesn't pretend to have all the answers. A gripping piece of work, with a performance you will not soon forget; go out of your way to track it down.

★ 1993, 102 minutes, color, not rated.

★ With: Crissy Rock, Vladimir Vega, Sandie Lavelle. Director: Ken Loach.

★ *What gritty portrait of contemporary British working-class life did Loach direct in 1992?* (Answer on page 55.)

"He's not yours; he's my son."
—Crissy Rock tries to straighten out a social worker.

For a great double feature, rent it with
Not Without My Daughter.

Seen it but in the mood for something similar? Try
An Angel at My Table.

Answer to page 24 trivia question:
City Slickers.

The Last Hurrah

Vote often and early for James Michael . . . er,
Frank Skeffington.

"Politics is the greatest spectator sport in the country."

—And Spencer Tracy thinks he's still got what it takes to pack 'em in.

For a great double feature, rent it with

The Candidate.

Seen it but in the mood for something similar? Try

Ragtime.

Answer to page 58 trivia question:

Rochester on "The Jack Benny Show."

Once upon a time, the roguish ways of Boston's Irish politicians made for great newspaper copy . . . but rarely led to the kind of story that would upset the city's basic power structure. (These days the Boston media won't let you get away with much of anything, and the mayor's not even Irish!)

This is a funny, intelligent screen adaptation of Edwin O'Connor's barely veiled portrait of the final act of legendary Boston pol James Michael Curley's career; it provided Spencer Tracy with one of his great later roles. The picture was also a welcome excuse to round up some of the "mature" character actors of the day and let them have a little fun. *The Last Hurrah* is a thoroughly satisfying portrait of a politician from the old school who tries to apply an outdated campaign formula to a new series of electoral problems.

Sad but true department: a profoundly flattered James Michael Curley, whose misadventures inspired the "fictional" Frank Skeffington, worshipped O'Connor's book, even though it was not, shall we say, uniformly flattering toward him.

★ 1958, 121 minutes, B&W, not rated.

★ With: Spencer Tracy, Pat O'Brien, John Carradine. Director: John Ford.

★ *Why was the material close to home for John Ford?*
(Answer on page 139.)

Laura

Vincent Price as a southern rogue?

Otto Preminger's study of a detective's obsession with a murder victim is a strange kind of film noir; it's got daylight scenes aplenty, but the dark passages are very dark indeed, even though they take place in the best parts of town rather than in seedy alleyways or cheap hotels.

Gene Tierney plays the title role, an advertising executive who rose steadily through the ranks by virtue of her charm and vivaciousness and was, to all appearances, universally admired by those around her. How, then, to explain the appearance of her buckshot-ridden corpse in her apartment?

Dana Andrews, as the police detective with an obsessive—no, make that near-pathological—devotion to the case, has a feeling either Clifton Webb (the radio personality who made Tierney's career possible) or Vincent Price (the southern ne'er-do-well) had a hand in the murder. The facts of the case, however, are a little more complex than Andrews—or the audience—suspects.

Laura is a spellbinding whodunit with an unforgettable twist that explores the limits, and the consequences, of illicit passions.

★ 1944, 85 minutes, B&W, not rated.

★ With: Gene Tierney, Dana Andrews, Clifton Webb, Vincent Price. Director: Otto Preminger.

★ *Which director of what cult-hit TV show was profoundly influenced by* Laura? (Answer on page 246.)

"You belong in an institution; I don't think they've ever had a patient who fell in love with a corpse before."

—Dana Andrews gets his comeuppance for being just a little too deeply involved in his work.

For a great double feature, rent it with the first episode of "Twin Peaks."

Seen it but in the mood for something similar? Try *Gilda.*

Answer to page 92 trivia question: *Ran.*

Suspense

Lenny

Tell joke; go to jail; do not pass Go;
do not collect $200.

"If I repeat what words specifically, your honor?"

—Dustin Hoffman wants some guidance from the Court on exactly how he should tone down his act.

For a great double feature, rent it with
Raging Bull.

Seen it but in the mood for something similar? Try
Bird.

Answer to page 127 trivia question:
Roald Dahl.

Before Eddie Murphy, before Richard Pryor, before George Carlin, there was Lenny Bruce. The scathing, brilliant, envelope-pushing comedian and social critic, who dared to incorporate into his act such topics as religious bigotry, drug use, racial injustice, and, yes, even a few oblique references to sex was vilified as "bad taste personified" during his heyday, the late fifties and early sixties.

Lenny, which boasts Dustin Hoffman's powerhouse performance as Bruce and Bob Fosse's tight-as-a-drum direction, follows the comic's rise from obscurity, his run-ins with the law, and his complex personal life. (Valerie Perrine does a star turn as Bruce's exotic, emotionally unstable wife.) The film is essentially a meditation on the often-insurmountable obstacles a free thinker faces when he puts himself on a collision course with society by deciding to tell the truth about it. Shot in sumptuous black and white, bless Fosse's heart.

★ 1974, 112 minutes, B&W, R.

★ With: Dustin Hoffman, Valerie Perrine, Jan Miner. Director: Bob Fosse.

★ *In what later film did director Bob Fosse include a brief homage to a very* Lenny-*like film, supposedly directed by Roy Scheider?* (Answer on page 299.)

The Letter

The message:
Don't mess with Bette.

Bette Davis walks down the front steps of a large plantation house, unloading a gun into an unidentified man. He's staggering backward; she's marching forward. She's shooting. She wants this guy dead—very dead. And that's just the opening scene. Let's just say that Davis plays a woman of great passion here, and that means she can launch one of the great manic performances of the era.

She plays the wife of a rubber plantation owner in Singapore who was planning on leaving her. (Not anymore, he isn't.) So what happens? Well, she's rich, she's white, and she says she didn't do it, so it stands to reason that she can't be convicted. Or can she? When she looks up from the screen shrouded in her pure white lace veil, she looks like a saint. Will she get away with murder? One glance at those big eyes, and you have to wonder.

This top-notch melodrama boasts a great story by Somerset Maugham, a strong supporting cast, and the steady directorial hand of William Wyler.

★ 1940, 95 minutes, B&W, not rated.

★ With: Bette Davis, Herbert Marshall, James Stephenson. Director: William Wyler.

★ *Name two other films in which Wyler directed Davis.*
(Answer on page 323.)

"Yes, I killed him! And I'm glad, I tell you. Glad, glad, glad!"
—So what are you saying, Bette?

For a great double feature, rent it with
A Letter to Three Wives.

Seen it but in the mood for something similar? Try
Beyond the Forest.

Answer to page 33 trivia question:
The Thomas Crown Affair.

Libeled Lady

No, there's no murder to solve.

"She may be his wife, but she's engaged to me."

—Spencer Tracy knows that some principles are worth standing up for.

For a great double feature, rent it with

The Thin Man.

Seen it but in the mood for something similar? Try

Without Love.

Answer to page 67 trivia question:

Musicals: he directed, for instance, *Singin' in the Rain.*

Surprise, surprise! The best film William Powell and Myrna Loy ever made together *wasn't* an entry in the immortal *Thin Man* series. It was this delightful screwball comedy about a socialite (Loy) who decides to sue a publisher (Spencer Tracy) for libel. Tracy uses William Powell and—fourth star alert—Jean Harlow, in an elaborate plot to frame Loy. It's so good, you won't miss the little dog.

Director Jack Conway, who would go on to direct features like *Saratoga,* with Clark Gable and Harlow, keeps things humming in this fast-paced comic gem. Things get a little frivolous now and then, but there's nothing wrong with that when the leads are effectively setting the laugh lines up and effectively knocking 'em down. All four of them are doing just that here, and they appear to be having the time of their lives. This one's a great deal of fun; don't miss it.

★ 1936, 98 minutes, B&W, not rated.

★ With: William Powell, Myrna Loy, Spencer Tracy, Jean Harlow. Director: Jack Conway.

★ *What is the name of the dog in the Nick and Nora Charles movies?* (Answer on page 81.)

Little Big Man

What was a short Jewish guy doing at Custer's Last Stand?

One of the most improbably satisfying roles of Dustin Hoffman's career came early. In 1970 he starred in this film as Jack Crabb, the sole white survivor of the storied Battle of Little Big Horn.

In this one-of-a-kind western Hoffman, via flashback, recalls his youth (he was raised by Indians and is the adopted grandson of Chief Dan George's superbly played Old Lodge Skins); he reminisces about his friendship with Wild Bill Hickok; and he recounts his experiences at Custer's Last Stand. Not exactly what one would have expected from Hoffman after the triumphs of *The Graduate* and *Midnight Cowboy*, but a rousing, magnificent addition to a genre still prone, in 1970, to racist stereotypes.

A major-league gamble that pays off, *Little Big Man* carries some powerful emotions and unexpected twists. Let's hear it for actors who know how to take a risk once in a while. (In the same vein, see also the listing for Hoffman's fine effort in *Straight Time*.) Based on Thomas Berger's novel of the same name.

★ 1970, 150 minutes, color, PG.

★ With: Dustin Hoffman, Faye Dunaway, Chief Dan George. Director: Arthur Penn.

★ *How old is Jack Crabb at the end of the film?* (Answer on page 22.)

"There is an endless supply of white men, but there has always been a limited number of human beings."
—Chief Dan George identifies a pressing problem.

For a great double feature, rent it with
A Man Called Horse.

Seen it but in the mood for something similar? Try
Dances with Wolves.

Answer to page 101 trivia question:
Flower Drum Song.

Little House on the Prairie, the Premiere Movie

I know what you're thinking, but trust me for a minute.

"We're home."
—Michael Landon knows it when he sees it.

For a great double feature, rent it with
Anne of Green Gables.

Seen it but in the mood for something similar? Try
The Yearling.

Answer to page 137 trivia question:
Crimes of the Heart.

You're probably wondering what on earth this video is doing in a book that's supposedly about movies you *haven't* seen before. I'm betting, though, that you and your family are more familiar with the weekly episodes from the endearing but goopy network smash than you are with this superb hour-and-a-half-long pilot. This is the initial small-screen foray into the work of Laura Ingalls Wilder; it has the good sense to follow the author's lead in recounting the trials of mid-nineteenth-century life on the frontier.

The extended pilot episode is blissfully free of pretense or self-parody—something that could not, alas, always be said of the series it inspired. Michael Landon, a headliner but not yet a tabloid icon, directs and stars in what may be the single strongest undertaking of his long career. Fans of the subsequent TV series will probably be flabbergasted by the strength this fine family drama shows when the familiar characters actually encounter the challenges intended for them by Wilder.

★ 1974, 100 minutes, color, not rated.

★ With: Michael Landon, Melissa Gilbert, Melissa Sue Anderson, Karen Grassle. Director: Michael Landon.

★ *What horror flick launched Michael Landon's film career?* (Answer on page 145.)

Little Miss Broadway

Depression?
Not with Shirley around!

urprise! Shirley Temple finds herself about to be adopted yet again, this time by the owner of the Hotel Variety, a home for vaudevillians. Among the many eccentric residents of the home is Jimmy Durante; next door lives George Murphy. Like all of their predecessors given the thankless role of being Temple's screen partner, Durante and Murphy struggle mightily to keep up with the kid.

The unusual setting lends the movie a bizarre, near-freak-show quality at times, but don't worry; Shirley's not out to score points for surrealism here. *Little Miss Broadway* is really a supremely charming diversion that benefits from all its studied quirkiness.

Now this is probably going to come as a shock, but the hotel gets into financial trouble, and it's up to Temple and Murphy to prove to the owner of the building that these vaudevillians are professionals and that, given the right opportunity, they could all become big stars. Think they'll pull it off? What if Shirley gets all her friends to put on a show right in the courtroom where the judge is to decide her adoption and the fate of her friends?

★ 1938, 70 minutes, B&W, not rated.

★ With: Shirley Temple, George Murphy, Jimmy Durante. Director: Irving Cummings.

★ *What high-profile job did George Murphy hold down after his showbiz career?* (Answer on page 295.)

"You old pumpkin head!"
—Smile when you say that, Shirley.

For a great double feature, rent it with
42nd Street.

Seen it but in the mood for something similar? Try
Rebecca of Sunny-brook Farm.

Answer to page 29 trivia question:
Benjamin Braddock in *The Graduate.*

Family

A Little Romance

Perhaps the perfect first-date movie.

"If you kiss under the Bridge of Sighs, you will be in love forever."

—So promises Laurence Olivier.

For a great double feature, rent it with

The Boy Who Could Fly.

Seen it but in the mood for something similar? Try

Small Change (L'Argent du Poche).

Answer to page 63 trivia question:

My Brilliant Career.

A bright American lass's new-blooming affections for an equally sharp Parisian boy are not well received by the adults in her world. This enchanting picture tells a familiar story, but it sustains a dreamy, deliciously youthful feel that's guaranteed to spark new flames or rekindle old ones, as the situation requires. (If you use it to do *both*, but with different people, shame on you.)

A Little Romance is a constantly charming little comedy that never fails to entertain; Laurence Olivier provides a delightful supporting turn as a world-weary French pickpocket who knows just how much first love can mean. In a personal triumph Lord Olivier, a trouper all the way, rides a bicycle during the film without summoning a stunt double, despite his frail physical condition at the time of the shooting.

This movie is great fun from beginning to end, and it boasts the perfect scene for you to plant a kiss on your companion. You'll know when it comes; trust me.

★ 1979, 108 minutes, color, PG.

★ With: Thelonious Bernard, Diane Lane, Laurence Olivier. Director: George Roy Hill.

★ *Name Laurence Olivier's first, second, and third wives.*
(Answer on page 242.)

Local Hero

An offer they can refuse.

Formulas, formulas, formulas. You've seen it all before, right? Anal-retentive American oil company representative travels to surrealistically eccentric Scottish fishing town with the aim of buying it out and turning it into an industrial wasteland but finds that he's unexpectedly started becoming a human being in the process.

You say you *haven't* heard that one before? Come to think of it, neither have I. Actually director Bill Forsyth's one-of-a-kind comedy is a blow against conventional movie plotting, and God bless him for it. Virtually nothing that happens in this gloriously offbeat film can be seen coming ahead of time by Peter Riegert, the (initially) ugly American—or by the audience, for that matter. It all pays off quite nicely, though.

The picture features a delightful turn from Burt Lancaster as Riegert's stargazing boss back in Texas. This is an appealing, low-key movie that makes up its own obscure rules and follows them scrupulously the whole way through.

★ 1983, 111 minutes, color, PG.

★ With: Peter Riegert, Burt Lancaster, Fulton MacKay. Director: Bill Forsyth.

★ *In what film did Lancaster play a football and Olympic great?* (Answer on page 149.)

"Breakfast isn't till eight, seven in the fishing season. It's not the fishing season."
—Innkeeper Denis Lawson, explaining why Peter Riegert will have to wait for a meal.

For a great double feature, rent it with
Crossing Delancey.

Seen it but in the mood for something similar? Try
Gregory's Girl.

Answer to page 97 trivia question:
Macaroni.

Lolita

Count the double entendres.

"You really must come and see my garden."
—Whaddya suppose Shelley Winters has in mind?

For a great double feature, rent it with
Tess.

Seen it but in the mood for something similar? Try
Rambling Rose.

Answer to page 132 trivia question:

Nothing. He was fitted with a glovelike prosthesis. When Lloyd climbs the sky-scraper/clock tower in *Safety Last,* he's using only one hand to support his weight.

It was 1962; the only way the studio was able to release the picture at all was to bowdlerize the plotline of Vladimir Nabokov's classic novel. Fortunately Nabokov himself won the job of doing the bowdlerizing. The result is a delicious, witty, nod-and-a-wink kind of picture in which James Mason's Humbert Humbert falls for a decidedly chesty, rather than prepubescent, Lolita (Sue Lyon).

The weird thing is that between Nabokov's wickedly sharp script and Stanley Kubrick's inspired direction, even the picture's concessions to the moral dictates of the time are more than a little incendiary. Half the fun—maybe more than half the fun—is watching Nabokov and Kubrick play with double meanings. Even with the knee-bendings it had to perform to get past the censors, *Lolita* is a rebellious piece of work worthy of the great novel that inspired it; scandalous at the time of its release, it shows more class than 95 percent of the gratuitous "sex comedies" taking up space on video shelves these days.

Everyone will get a kick out of it, but those who've read the book are in for a special treat. Featuring memorable performances from Shelley Winters (as Lyon's pathetic mom) and Peter Sellers (as Mason's rival).

★ 1962, 152 minutes, B&W, not rated.

★ With: James Mason, Sue Lyon, Shelley Winters, Peter Sellers. Director: Stanley Kubrick.

★ *What song by the Police makes reference to Nabokov's masterpiece?* (Answer on page 85.)

Comedy

Long Day's Journey into Night

Table for four, please, and a side order of morphine for the lady.

No punches are pulled in this faithful film adaptation of Eugene O'Neill's shattering, claustrophobic family drama, based on the playwright's own dysfunctional home life. Pretty decent cast if you like that screen-legends-at-the-top-of-their-form thing: Katharine Hepburn plays the morphine-addicted mom, Ralph Richardson the miserly stage legend father, Jason Robards the alcoholic older son, and Dean Stockwell the younger son, who is dying of tuberculosis.

Hey, no one said it was a *comedy*. This is the superlative screen version of O'Neill's most acclaimed play; it was made for a paltry $400,000 because the principals agreed to accept minimum scale. Apparently they didn't want the chance to work together on this O'Neill masterpiece to pass them by because of financial issues. A little depressing, maybe, but spellbinding from start to finish.

★ 1962, 136 minutes, B&W, not rated.

★ With: Katharine Hepburn, Ralph Richardson, Jason Robards, Dean Stockwell. Director: Sidney Lumet.

★ *What film star married playwright O'Neill's daughter Oona?* (Answer on page 39.)

"Watch out for me, kid."
—Jason Robards warns his brother Dean Stockwell about following a bad example.

For a great double feature, rent it with
Desire Under the Elms.

Seen it but in the mood for something similar? Try
Suddenly, Last Summer.

Answer to page 5 trivia question:
Ten Little Indians.

Drama

The Long Good Friday

Happy Easter.

"*Colm never hurt a fly . . . unless it was necessary.*"
—Bob Hoskins can't understand why one of his hit men has been blown to smithereens.

For a great double feature, rent it with
Scarface (1932).

Seen it but in the mood for something similar? Try
Scarface (1983).

Answer to page 10 trivia question:
"Happy Anatomy."

Bob Hoskins may be best known on this side of the Atlantic for his work in such big-studio smasheroos as *Hook* and *Who Framed Roger Rabbit*, but before he started cutting package deals and rubbing elbows with Julia Roberts he turned in the performance of a lifetime in this extraordinary mobster movie. Hoskins plays Harold Shand, a driven cockney crime boss who prides himself on his accomplishments as a peacemaker—but thinks nothing of hanging his rivals from meat hooks when he finds himself challenged by an unknown competitor.

The hypnotic, elliptical script doles out its plot points cautiously but effectively; the ambiguity produces not confusion but a welcome emphasis on the often-contradictory passions of the central character. It would all fall apart in a heartbeat if there weren't some major-league acting moves from the tough little guy in the middle of it all.

Not to worry; nothing falls apart. This exuberant, extremely violent film may not always be easy to watch, but it is in a league with such films as *The Godfather* and *GoodFellas* in its portrait of power pursued, attained, and lost. An extraordinary achievement.

★ 1981, 114 minutes, color, R.

★ With: Bob Hoskins, Helen Mirren, Pierce Brosnan. Director: John Mackenzie.

★ *What British television series starring Bob Hoskins was the basis of a Steve Martin film?* (Answer on page 365.)

Drama

Lost in America

Headin' down the HIGH-way . . .
in a Winn-uh-BAY-go . . .

Dennis Hopper and Peter Fonda stumbled across the dark heart of America with only countercultural vision and a big drug deal to guide them in 1969's *Easy Rider,* but Albert Brooks and Julie Hagerty took on the task with a little more cash in store. Brooks, an out-of-work ad agency executive who shows less-than-perfect grace when passed over for a promotion, persuades his wife (Julie Hagerty) to buy out of the American Dream—and cruise the country in a Winnebago fitted out with all the comforts of home.

After a disastrous visit to Las Vegas, the Mecca of the materialistic society they claim to be rebelling against, the pair bounce uneasily against a landscape populated almost exclusively by oddballs. Without stuff, the two have, alas, no purpose in life.

Brooks is at his best in this film, perhaps his only fully realized comedy. (Check him out as he drools over the old guy's Mercedes.) Hagerty is even more deliriously loopy than she was in *Airplane!*

★ 1985, 92 minutes, color, R.

★ With: Albert Brooks, Julie Hagerty. Director: Albert Brooks.

★ *Who plays the casino manager?* (Answer on page 9.)

"Don't use 'nest.' Don't use 'egg.' If you're in the forest, you can point: 'The bird lives in a round stick.' And you can have two things over easy with toast."

—Julie Hagerty has gambled away their life savings, but Albert Brooks isn't the kind of guy to hold a grudge about it.

For a great double feature, rent it with
Easy Rider.

Seen it but in the mood for something similar? Try
Melvin and Howard.

Answer to page 39 trivia question:
Richard Pryor.

Comedy

Love Finds Andy Hardy

Let's see: Judy Garland or Lana Turner?
Some guys have all the luck.

"She doesn't want to swim, she doesn't want to play tennis, go for walks. All she wants to do is kiss. I'm a nervous wreck!"

—Every guy in the country sympathizes with Mickey Rooney's predicament.

For a great double feature, rent it with

Girl Crazy.

Seen it but in the mood for something similar? Try

Babes in Arms.

Answer to page 73 trivia question:

"Mister Rogers' Neighborhood."

The Andy Hardy movies may be a little hokey around the edges, but they're never less than charming.

As Andy, Mickey Rooney's the kind of boy who just wants to do the right thing when it comes to love—or anything else, for that matter. Judy Garland, for her part, is the kind of girl who'll wait patiently for her guy to realize how great she really is. If the way she belts out a tune doesn't get his attention, though, you have to wonder whether anything ever will. Lana Turner is Judy's competition; she's got something besides good vocals to turn Rooney's head with, and, gee, you can't blame a guy for getting distracted. What to do?

Luckily for Rooney, he has the world's wisest dad and a mom who's always got fresh-baked pie waiting on the window sill. So Mickey's gonna be OK.

Take a break; sit back and spend some time in the simple, nearly perfect world of the Hardys, the Brady Bunch of the prewar years. This is easily the best entry, thanks to the strong work the supporting cast turns in, in a series of funny, sweet movies I hope we never become too sophisticated to enjoy.

★ 1938, 90 minutes, B&W, not rated.

★ With: Mickey Rooney, Judy Garland, Lana Turner. Director: George B. Seitz.

★ *The studio bosses at MGM wanted to make the most of Judy Garland's little-girl image; how did they minimize her womanly appearance during adolescence?* (Answer on page 6.)

Comedy

Love with the Proper Stranger

Sexual revolution, anyone?

T his tender, modestly scaled love story blew away such high-ticket competitors as *Cleopatra* and *How the West Was Won* in 1963. The epics were elbowed aside by an envelope-pushing, naturalistic story of two people who find themselves falling in love in an unorthodox way: pregnancy first, courtship second. Natalie Wood hunts down Steve McQueen, an out-of-work musician, at the local union hall. She slept with McQueen the summer before (it was her first time); now she's going to have a baby, and she comes to him not because he's the father, which he's not, but because she has nowhere else to turn. She wants McQueen to help her make the problem go away, but, truth be told, he doesn't quite remember her. A distraught Wood leaves abruptly. McQueen, however, has been bitten by the bug. (Hey, it's Natalie Wood.)

The story, quite racy for the era, begins with a harsh edge, but as the principals become more emotionally involved, a welcome softness and humor come to the fore. This is probably Natalie Wood's best work; the movie made Steve McQueen a star.

Warning: This gem is not to be confused with the execrable *Love with a Perfect Stranger* (1988).

★ 1963, 100 minutes, B&W, not rated.

★ With: Steve McQueen, Natalie Wood, Edie Adams. Director: Robert Mulligan.

★ *In what movie did Steve McQueen have his first starring role?* (Answer on page 48.)

"I'm pregnant."
—Natalie Wood tells Steve McQueen how things stand; he's trying to figure out who he's talking to.

For a great double feature, rent it with
The Snapper.

Seen it but in the mood for something similar? Try
Marty.

Answer to page 107 trivia question:
Brief Encounter.

Drama

213

Lust for Life

As Van Gogh always said, "Huh?"

"I work in haste from day to day, as a miner does who knows he's facing disaster."

—Kirk Douglas has apparently been reading a little too much Sylvia Plath.

For a great double feature, rent it with

The Agony and the Ecstasy.

Seen it but in the mood for something similar? Try

Moulin Rouge.

Answer to page 12 trivia question:

Anne Shirley played Anne Shirley; she liked the part so much she kept it as her stage name.

Based on the popular book by Irving Stone, this account of the life of the great Dutch painter Vincent Van Gogh frames its story with excerpts of actual letters from the artist to his brother Theo, lending an autobiographical feel to the proceedings.

Director Vincente Minnelli, best known for his work in big-budget musicals, here shows an unerring sense for both drama and color. (In fact the tones he uses throughout the course of the film support and reinforce the images created on Van Gogh's canvases.)

It is often the artist's lot to be fluent in his chosen medium but to fail miserably in his efforts to communicate with other human beings; it was, of course, this way with Van Gogh, and Minnelli's picture captures with admirable skill the many painful ironies of Vincent's passions, visions, and yearnings. Featuring an exuberant performance by Kirk Douglas in the lead and some fine supporting work from Anthony Quinn as Paul Gauguin.

★ 1956, 122 minutes, color, not rated.

★ With: Kirk Douglas, Anthony Quinn, James Donald. Director: Vincente Minnelli.

★ *In what unfortunate film did Anthony Quinn costar with Kevin Costner?* (Answer on page 127.)

Biography

The Magnificent Ambersons

Wouldn't you know it? The one time you want a special release of the director's final cut, it doesn't exist.

Orson Welles's "other" directorial masterpiece, a stunning, self-assured adaptation of the Booth Tarkington novel, was so good that even the tampering with, and telescoping of, the final print by studio hacks couldn't obscure its status as a classic. One wonders, though, what might have been had RKO opted to let the director oversee the editing work himself. You suppose he was tough to work with or something?

The picture charts the decline of a prominent midwestern family that isn't quite ready for the age of the motorcar and follows its youngest representative, Tim Holt, through his haughty days, yea, even unto his just desert.

A breathtaking achievement of balance and rhythm in black and white; Welles and cameraman Stanley Cortez actually manage to expand on the endlessly inventive visual sense that supplied such a kick in *Citizen Kane*. Holt and Mercury regulars Agnes Moorehead and Joseph Cotten turn in fine performances, but the real star is Welles, whose presence looms unseen thanks to his spoken narration.

★ 1942, 88 minutes, B&W, not rated.

★ With: Joseph Cotten, Agnes Moorehead, Tim Holt. Director: Orson Welles.

★ *Who called Cotten one of the "three scariest men in film"?* (Answer on page 174.)

"Automobiles are a useless nuisance. They'll never amount to anything but a nuisance. They had no business to be invented."

—Joseph Cotten, clearly in touch with the trends of the times, has his opinions.

For a great double feature, rent it with
Citizen Kane.

Seen it but in the mood for something similar? Try
The Third Man.

Answer to page 46 trivia question:
Gang of Four.

Drama

Major Barbara

Not to be confused with Private Benjamin.
For one thing, no one here was ever on "Laugh-In."

"I am a millionaire. That is my religion."
—Wendy Hiller learns that her father is a man of principle after all.

For a great double feature, rent it with
Pygmalion.

Seen it but in the mood for something similar? Try
The Importance of Being Earnest.

Answer to page 80 trivia question:
The royal birthmark on the royal heir's royal backside.

D o-gooders can be such a pain in the neck sometimes, can't they? That's Wendy Hiller (later *Dame* Wendy Hiller) in the title role of this classic George Bernard Shaw comedy; she's an idealistic rich girl who joins the Salvation Army even though it ticks off her dad.

This is a thoughtful, elegantly structured examination of the power of cold, hard cash and the crippling effects of poverty. It's funny and quite powerful in places; the film still hits a couple of raw nerves connected to social issues that remain unresolved today.

Even with all its period costuming and academy-level diction, *Major Barbara* comes across as a piece that's willing to stare real-world dilemmas (like ethically suspect defense-contracting windfalls) right in the face. Just goes to show you what a great piece of writing can do when you throw some great actors at it and get out of its way. Deborah Kerr's movie debut; she is only one of about a half dozen superlative actors to make memorable contributions to this worthy, entertaining film.

★ 1941, 135 minutes, B&W, not rated.

★ With: Wendy Hiller, Rex Harrison, Robert Morley, Emlyn Williams, Deborah Kerr. Director: Gabriel Pascal.

★ *In what film did Deborah Kerr make quite a stir by having an affair with a younger man?* (Answer on page 283.)

The Mambo Kings

*The neckties alone are worth
the rental fee.*

The *Mambo Kings Play Songs of Love*, the acclaimed novel by Oscar Hijuelos, here receives a vibrant, energetic film treatment that showcases a very different side of the fifties from the staid conformism we're used to watching Hollywood parody.

This stylish tale of Cuban musicians on the way up in the United States features powerhouse performances from Armand Assante and, in his first English-speaking film role, Antonio Banderas. The sacrifices and transformations the two brothers make toward the cherished goal of prominence in their new homeland carry a resonant power that will remind you, just a little, of the struggles the Corleone family faced in the first two *Godfather* pictures.

If you're after sharp, character-first drama, this movie has it; if you're after great music and dancing, this movie has it (witness the presence of Tito Puente); if you're after exhilarating visual style, this movie's got it; and, yes, if you're after Desi Arnaz, Jr., playing the part of his father and stepping into an old episode of "I Love Lucy," it's got that, too.

★ 1992, 104 minutes, color, R.

★ With: Armand Assante, Antonio Banderas, Cathy Moriarty, Desi Arnaz, Jr., Tito Puente. Director: Arne Glimcher.

★ *In what picture did Cathy Moriarty make her acting debut?* (Answer on page 316.)

"You write the music, let me worry about the business, and together we're going to be rich and famous."
—Armand Assante's got it all figured out.

For a great double feature, rent it with
The Fabulous Baker Boys.

Seen it but in the mood for something similar? Try
The Idolmaker.

Answer to page 115 trivia question:
Jamie Lee Curtis.

Drama

The Man Who Would Be King

Or: The many virtues of quitting while you're ahead.

"We're not little men, so we're going away to be kings."
—Words to live by for Sean Connery and Michael Caine

For a great double feature, rent it with
The Treasure of the Sierra Madre.

Seen it but in the mood for something similar? Try
The Wind and the Lion.

Answer to page 28 trivia question:
Mariette Hartley.

I defy you to watch any five-minute section of this film and not get hooked. Having tasted the thrill of battle at the far reaches of Victoria's empire, a pair of cockneys (Sean Connery and Michael Caine) decide they aren't about to head back to the mother country and get real jobs. On their own, they head into the heart of Kafiristan, a locale to which no white man since Alexander the Great has journeyed and returned to tell the tale. They survive an encounter with the natives—but only because the natives think they're gods.

This rousing sand-and-battle picture is great fun to watch, in no small degree because Connery and Caine obviously had a great deal of fun making it. The picture boasts fine, outrageously scaled performances from each of the principals; what it lacks in verisimilitude it more than makes up for in panache.

A satisfying parody of the imperialistic urge, *The Man Who Would Be King* showcases two hustlers who boast of being Englishmen and opine that that's the next best thing to being gods. But what happens when the people they encounter can't tell the difference?

★ 1975, 129 minutes, color, PG.

★ With: Sean Connery, Michael Caine, Christopher Plummer. Director: John Huston.

★ *The actress who plays Roxanne did so only on the agreement that she would not have to speak. Who is she, and why was she on location?* (Answer on page 27.)

The Man with the Golden Arm

Old Blue Eyes rides the big white horse.
And no, it's not a western.

In the barroom scene that starts a few minutes after this movie begins you'll see all the important characters in musician (and recovering morphine addict) Frank Sinatra's life. There, in that dark, smoky room, is everyone who will either hasten his fall back into addiction or help move him toward a life free of drugs. He's close, agonizingly close, to making a new life for himself, but the road the recovering Sinatra faces is full of traps, most of them connected to the influence of "friends" he'd be better off never having met.

This gritty 1955 drama is the first realistic film portrayal of an addict's life. It looks unflinchingly at Sinatra's shoot-up sessions and his agonizing withdrawal sequences. (Earlier films employed discreet fade-outs when the going got tough.) Through it all, a young, vacuous Kim Novak does her best to stand by her man.

Don't be put off by the stagy look of the film's early sequences; *The Man with the Golden Arm* quickly moves into harrowing realism—at a time in Hollywood history when such a style was far from commonplace. The picture represented a considerable gamble for Sinatra; it required extraordinary commitment and acting ability and was certainly not standard fare for fifties subject matter. The gamble paid off.

★ 1955, 119 minutes, B&W, not rated.

★ With: Frank Sinatra, Eleanor Parker, Kim Novak. Director: Otto Preminger.

★ *What punk-crushing detective was Frank Sinatra slated to portray until he injured his wrist?* (Answer on page 52.)

"You know what you're letting yourself in for? It ain't pretty, and it could be dangerous."
—Frank Sinatra isn't sure Kim Novak knows exactly what she's getting into.

For a great double feature, rent it with
Pal Joey.

Seen it but in the mood for something similar? Try
From Here to Eternity.

Answer to page 62 trivia question:
The Princess and the Pirate, with Bob Hope.

Drama

The Manchurian Candidate

*Don't you hate it when your brain comes back
from the cleaners with too much starch?*

*"Raymond, why don't
you pass the time by
playing a little
solitaire?"*
—A mysterious caller tells
Laurence Harvey the game's
about to begin.

**For a great double
feature, rent it with**
*The Man with the
Golden Arm.*

**Seen it but in the mood
for something similar?
Try**
Jacob's Ladder.

**Answer to page 96
trivia question:**
Saratoga.

Laurence Harvey is a jerk, and everyone in his army squadron knows it. Why, then, after they all return from Korea, do the men start praising him to the heavens? Why do they all use the exact same description of the improbable hero—"the finest man I've ever known"? The answer has something to do with the Communist Menace—and a deck of cards.

This classic cold war thriller features some of the best screen acting ever turned in by Frank Sinatra, who was far more deserving of attention from the Academy Awards committee for this film than for his work in *From Here to Eternity.*

The quirky script features a good number of pleasantly disconcerting plot points that seem not to add up to much of anything: Sinatra reads books compulsively and with no apparent concern for their content; Janet Leigh engages Ol' Blue Eyes in some surrealistic dialogue in a creepily erotic scene in a train. Then there's the unforgettable garden party scene, as out-of-left-field (so to speak) as anything Fellini might have served up.

By turns amusing and horrifying, the film tosses out paradoxes even stranger than, say, the fact that Angela Lansbury is several years younger than Laurence Harvey, who plays her son.

★ 1962, 126 minutes, B&W, not rated.

★ With: Frank Sinatra, Angela Lansbury, Laurence Harvey, Janet Leigh. Director: John Frankenheimer.

★ *In what other film does Angela Lansbury portray a mind-game-playing heavy?* (Answer on page 74.)

Suspense

The Manhattan Project

What if Oedipus had had the bomb?

John Lithgow plays the new man in town; he has eyes for Chistopher Collet's mother, Jill Eikenberry. At first she turns down his offer for a dinner date, but when her son enters the room with a copy of *Popular Science* under his arm, Lithgow spies an in. You see, he's a big-time scientist. As a matter of fact, he's working secretly for the government on a new weapon. When Collet, who's something of a boy genius, gets a look at Lithgow's lab, he recognizes the bottles of glowing fluid as plutonium.

Christopher, aside from being smart, is going through some very confusing emotions right now. He resents Lithgow, in a refreshingly Freudian way, so he steals the plutonium from Lithgow's office and makes his own atomic bomb for the science fair. Gee, what ever happened to putting your old tooth into a glass of cola overnight?

So: how is Lithgow going to win the trust of the boy, get the bomb, save the town, and still get a date with Mom?

★ 1986, 117 minutes, color, PG.

★ With: John Lithgow, Christopher Collet, Cynthia Nixon, Jill Eikenberry. Director: Marshall Brickman.

★ *John Lithgow tried his hand at a role that William Shatner originated on TV. Can you name the part?*
(Answer on page 230.)

"I never thought I would say this to anybody, but I've got to get the atomic bomb out of my car."
—John Lithgow is hoping not to have to duck and cover.

For a great double feature, rent it with
War Games.

Seen it but in the mood for something similar? Try
Real Genius.

Answer to page 44 trivia question:
The Exorcist.

Suspense

Manon of the Spring

Payback time.

"Don't be enticed by a pretty face."

—Yves Montand issues his warning, but he's too deeply in debt to the karma bank for it to make much difference.

For a great double feature, rent it with

Jean de Florette.

Seen it but in the mood for something similar? Try

The Return of Martin Guerre.

Answer to page 131 trivia question:

"Northern Exposure."

Ready for a fascinating, leisurely, female-Hamlet routine set in the French countryside? Sure you are—Yves Montand's got it coming to him from the last picture, remember? This satisfying conclusion to *Jean de Florette* (see page 177) pits the beautiful shepherdess daughter (Emmanuelle Beart) of a dead farmer against the unscrupulous neighbors responsible for his undoing. It takes its time in spinning out its straightforward revenge plot, but you don't mind because you're in the presence of both accomplished acting and the most magnificent country scenery imaginable.

Actually, I shouldn't belittle the bare-bones plot; it's got a nifty twist toward the end. Beart is wonderful, and the bad guys from the last go-around are even more fun when they realize the *merde* is about to hit the fan.

Basic message: it's not nice to fool around with Mother Nature. Captivating, steadily paced, and just as beautiful as the first film; I strongly recommend that you see *Jean de Florette* first, though.

★ 1986, 113 minutes, color, PG.

★ With: Yves Montand, Emmanuelle Beart, Daniel Auteil. Director: Claude Berri.

★ *How much time elapsed between the release of* Jean de Florette *and* Manon of the Spring *in the United States?* (Answer on page 131.)

Map of the Human Heart

Rent this for anyone who tells you there's no way to put a new twist on a World War II film.

It's unlikely that anyone else is going to deliver another Eskimo-youth-confronting-Freudian-sexual-dilemmas-during-World-War-II epic in the near future, but director Vincent Ward did, and thank goodness.

As a half-white, half-Eskimo RAF pilot, Jason Scott Lee turns in an exquisite performance that straddles races, social structures, and the better part of four decades. During the war he falls in love with his childhood sweetheart, the lovely French aerial photo analyst Anne Parillaud . . . but after the bombing stops, some seemingly insurpassable roadblocks to their romance arise.

This massively scaled, visually striking film offers invaluable lessons on the notable advantages of cultures white people are often tempted to dismiss as "primitive," and it uses some wildly disparate effects to get its points across: it features eye-popping battle scenes, extended meditations on the nature of the body, and enough crossed sexual wires to keep an analyst busy for life. Through it all, *Map of the Human Heart* traces out one of the most unlikely extended love stories you'll ever see.

★ 1993, 126 minutes, color, R.

★ With: Anne Parillaud, Patrick Bergin, Jason Scott Lee, John Cusack. Director: Vincent Ward.

★ *What actor who shows up in a cameo here appeared in a groundbreaking 1961 picture that also concerned a romantic triangle?* (Answer on page 179.)

"If you don't behave like a half-breed, then anything is possible."
—Patrick Bergin will find out that all sorts of things are possible for his young charge, including some fun on top of a dirigible.

For a great double feature, rent it with
Dragon: The Bruce Lee Story.

Seen it but in the mood for something similar? Try
The Blue Kite.

Answer to page 32 trivia question:
Movie Movie.

Drama

223

Marat / Sade

*You can say a lot of things about the Marquis de Sade,
but you have to admit the guy was never boring.*

"We want our revolution . . . now."
—The inmates/actors/disgruntled revolutionaries are getting restless.

For a great double feature, rent it with
Lenny.

Seen it but in the mood for something similar? Try
Sweeney Todd.

Answer to page 66 trivia question:
Nastassja Kinski and Malcolm McDowell.

Peter Weiss's very nearly indescribable stage hit of the sixties set Broadway on its ear; the film adaptation, directed by Peter Brook, retains the creepy, theater-of-cruelty edge of the original and comes at you like a freight train.

The complex story concerns a performance of a play written by that notable traverser of boundaries, the Marquis de Sade. The actors are the inmates of the insane asylum at Charenton; the topic of de Sade's script is the murder of the French revolutionary Jean-Paul Marat. *Marat/Sade* is an intricate, intellectually demanding tour of a house of mirrors where madmen always seem to stare back. Its themes—betrayed idealism, the inherent disregard of political systems for the citizenry, and the impossibility of a truly successful revolution—are all the more relevant after the collapse of the international Communist movement.

This film is best saved for the adults in the group; the script's quite deliberate excesses make this piece inappropriate for younger viewers (who probably wouldn't get much from the provocative political and social commentary anyway). The top-notch ensemble cast features Glenda Jackson in her first film appearance.

★ 1966, 115 minutes, color, not rated.

★ With: Patrick Magee, Glenda Jackson, Clifford Rose. Director: Peter Brook.

★ *What is the movie's full title?* (Answer on page 243.)

Master Harold and the Boys

Think of this as a lesson in respect.

By the time Hollywood got around to making movies like *A Dry White Season,* the world had pretty much figured out that apartheid stank to high heaven. Part of the reason people knew this lay in the inspired writing of Athol Fugard, which explored the perils of racism on both the small and large scale. This script is ample evidence of the gifted writer's talents. Matthew Broderick shines as the youngster on the verge of manhood who must decide the new social footing on which he and his longtime friend and father figure, Zakes Mokae, will operate.

The piece is rooted in the political and racial turmoil of South Africa before the release of Nelson Mandela, but its examination of the limits of friendship, the tragedy of reducing others to objects, and the catastrophic effects of failing to reach true maturity still ring true. The picture is a reminder that human beings, not institutions, build the walls that divide them.

★ 1984, 90 minutes, color, not rated.

★ With: Matthew Broderick, Zakes Mokae, John Kani. Director: Michael Lindsay-Hogg.

★ *In what John Hughes film did Matthew Broderick play hooky for a day because life is short?* (Answer on page 320.)

"None of us know the steps, and there is no music."
—Matthew Broderick gets a difficult lesson on the dances of life.

For a great double feature, rent it with
Careful, He Might Hear You.

Seen it but in the mood for something similar? Try
The Power of One.

Answer to page 100 trivia question:
Plan Nine from Outer Space.

Drama

Mediterraneo

"Dedicated to all of those who are running away."

Early in World War II a band of Italian sailors on a reconnaissance mission in Greece land on what appears to be a deserted island. Not long afterwards the Americans destroy their ship, and it looks like the men are going to be spending some time in Nowheresville until someone rescues them.

Someone does—but it's not who they expect. The island turns out to be inhabited . . . primarily by old men and very, very beautiful young women. Tough assignment, eh? All the young men of the town have gone off to war. After a period of adjustment, and, yes, some fun, the men of the unit find the strangest outcome to their mission: a period of profound self-assessment. One of them starts out repainting the frescoes of the old village just to pass the time . . . and ends up doing the Michelangelo bit.

A very satisfying meditation on war, passion, and the soothing nature of the passage of lots and lots of time. If you can get over the initial feeling of being driven slowly insane.

★ 1991, 92 minutes, color, not rated (but features profanity and nudity).

★ With: Diego Abatantuono, Claudio Bigagli, Giuseppe Cederna. Director: Gabriele Salvatores.

★ *Which brother impregnated the shepherd girl?*
(Answer on page 292.)

The Member of the Wedding

Get out of here, kid, you bother me.

Remember those can't-help-growin'-up blues? They're the subject of Julie Harris's film debut—she's great as an awkward 12-year-old who is forced to make adjustments to the adult world after a friend dies and her brother decides to get married.

Things get a little strained when Harris sets her heart on accompanying the bride and groom on the honeymoon. For some reason the idea doesn't catch on. Brothers can be so selfish, can't they?

A sensitive examination of the adolescent need to belong; the picture is a little stagy (it's adapted from Carson McCullers's Broadway success), but it's involving enough to get away with it. Fine supporting work from Ethel Waters, as Harris's nanny, and Brandon de Wilde, as her devoted cousin. If you follow the movie on its own leisurely terms, you'll probably find it quite moving.

★ 1953, 91 minutes, B&W, not rated.

★ With: Julie Harris, Ethel Waters, Brandon de Wilde. Director: Fred Zinnemann.

★ *How old was Harris when she played a 12-year-old girl in this film?* (Answer on page 136.)

"All people belong to the 'we' except me."

—Julie Harris is feeling a little left out of things.

For a great double feature, rent it with

A Tree Grows in Brooklyn.

Seen it but in the mood for something similar? Try

To Kill a Mockingbird.

Answer to page 315 trivia question:

Peter Shaffer, author of *Amadeus.*

The Men

Marlon Brando's film debut.

"I'm not the same person I was. I'm not the same man I was."

—So maybe if they'd given Brando an Oscar for this one, he'd have been able to accept it?

For a great double feature, rent it with

Coming Home.

Seen it but in the mood for something similar? Try

The Purple Hearts.

Answer to page 336 trivia question:

Gig Young.

An uncompromising film that examines the lives of the men who came home from World War II with devastating injuries. Unlike, say, *The Best Years of Our Lives,* it never indulges in mawkish sentimentality.

In his screen debut Brando plays a virile young lieutenant who's still desperately in love with the beautiful woman he planned to marry after the war. He is, however, a paraplegic, which means, in this case, that everything's changed. Brando's depiction of a man trying to make his way through an emotional train wreck was so realistic, and so new, that I think he scared some of the critics of the day. They weren't really sure this guy was *just* acting. (The whole Method thing wasn't well understood yet.)

This is a brave film with some extraordinary performances and a terrific script. Long before Jon Voight came home, Brando did. And Brando didn't have Jane Fonda waiting for him.

★ 1950, 85 minutes, B&W, not rated.

★ With: Marlon Brando, Jack Webb, Teresa Wright. Director: Fred Zinnemann.

★ *In what film did Brando get to show off his singing and dancing talents?* (Answer on page 44.)

Mephisto

Psst. Hey, buddy.
Wanna sell your soul?

Mephisto, or Mephistopheles, is the incarnation of the devil who is said to have struck a deal with Dr. Faustus: you give me your soul, I hand over youth, knowledge, and magical power for you to enjoy as you see fit . . . for a while. Such a deal! Well, maybe not.

In *Mephisto*, Klaus Maria Brandauer plays an ambitious German actor in the 1930s whose signature role is the tempter of medieval lore. Heck of a coincidence, too, since he's basically selling out to the Nazis to keep his career on the fast track. You'd think he'd realize how this story ends, wouldn't you?

Brandauer is perhaps best known to American audiences for his supporting work as Not Robert Redford in *Out of Africa*. (You remember: he was the one who had the bad taste to give Meryl Streep a social disease.) He turns in a magnificent, get-the-hell-out-of-my-way lead performance in this Hungarian production. It may be possible for an actor to take total command of a picture more authoritatively, but I'm betting you'll be hard put to recall anything quite like the gloriously theatrical turn Brandauer displays in *Mephisto*. There's a lesson here: When the devil offers, just say no. The picture won an Oscar for Best Foreign Film.

★ 1981, 135 minutes, color, not rated.

★ With: Klaus Maria Brandauer, Krystyna Janda, Karin Boyd. Director: Istvan Szabo.

★ *In what adaptation of a Jack London classic did Brandauer appear?* (Answer on page 14.)

"You love yourself, Heinz, and then not even enough."

—Klaus Maria Brandauer is going to work on that self-absorption thing.

For a great double feature, rent it with *Colonel Redl.*

Seen it but in the mood for something similar? Try *The Pawnbroker.*

Answer to page 309 trivia question:
40 Acres and a Mule Filmworks.

Foreign

229

Metropolis

*I have seen the future,
and it is big.*

"What will you do if
they turn against you
someday?"

—Brigitte Helm's titanium
bra shall lead them.

**For a great double
feature, rent it with**

Brazil.

**Seen it but in the mood
for something similar?
Try**

Modern Times.

**Answer to page 221
trivia question:**

The nervous flyer in
*The Twilight Zone—
The Movie.*

Legend has it that Fritz Lang modeled the extraordinary sets in his futuristic silent epic after the skyline of New York City, which he had recently visited for the first time. This towering story of class conflict is set in the first third of the 21st century; an elite, leisured society lives a life of pleasure above ground, while a class of miserable drones works endlessly beneath them, in massive, man-made underground canyons. If you ask me, it sounds less like Manhattan than Disney World, but I digress.

This is one of the most influential science fiction films of all time; its startling images and relentless visual ingenuity were breathtaking in 1926, and they're breathtaking today.

Much of the original film has been lost (the original running time is said to have been over 200 minutes), but what remains is masterful. Eugen Schufftan supervised the groundbreaking special effects work.

★ 1926, 120 minutes, B&W, not rated.

★ With: Brigitte Helm, Alfred Abel, Gustav Froelich.
Director: Fritz Lang.

★ *What famous rock group used images from the film in a video?* (Answer on page 78.)

Midnight Lace

Doris Day loses it.

One of Doris Day's few dramatic roles, and it's a doozy. Someone's out to kill her, and her hysteria actually begins to grow on you. (It's a little grating at first, but stick with her.) Hey, it's not easy walking through the London fog while a menacing unseen voice tells you that your time on this earth is running out. Or to figure out what to say when you pick up the phone and hear an evil, high-pitched voice telling you that you're about to die. The problem is, no one else has heard this guy's voice or seen his shadow in the alley, like Day has. Is she really in danger, or is she just going loony?

The movie has lots of surprises and a delicious cast of would-be killers, each of whom is apparently just as likely to be the stalker as the next guy. Her husband, played by Rex Harrison at the height of his charm, certainly hasn't been much help, but he does seem very concerned for her sanity. Too concerned, perhaps? Then there's that handsome young architect working on the building next door. Who's behind the weirdness? And where the hell is Rock Hudson? A top-notch whodunit and a nice stretch for Day.

★ 1960, 108 minutes, color, not rated.

★ With: Doris Day, Rex Harrison, Myrna Loy. Director: David Miller.

★ *Can you name Doris Day's first feature film and the star who was originally slated to play her part?*
(Answer on page 183.)

"I've come to keep our appointment."
—The caller is there for Doris Day.

For a great double feature, rent it with
Romance on the High Seas.

Seen it but in the mood for something similar? Try
The Man Who Knew Too Much (1955).

Answer to page 364 trivia question:
The Philadelphia Story.

Midnight Run

Are you asking me if this is a good movie?
Are you asking me?

Robert De Niro plays the bounty hunter, and Charles Grodin plays the bad guy he has to track down. Yes, that's right, this supremely watchable comedy-action entry has the guts to let De Niro, the prototypical Urban Tough Guy, carry his fair share of the comic load. Guess what? He's hilarious, and he manages to hold his own with Grodin in the laconic, deadpan, I-can-under-play-you-any-day-of-the-week competition.

Grodin isn't exactly *dangerous*—he's an accountant who *works* for the Mr. Big the authorities are after—but he sure knows how to get on De Niro's nerves. It's as though Oscar were to find himself locked in a train compartment with Felix and would lose a big bet if he threw Felix out the window.

The script crackles along nicely, distributing snappy lines, unexpected twists, and enough zippy action scenes to make for a nice, even mix. Director Martin Brest never lets the pace slacken; he's not out to make an ambitious motion picture, and he knows it. Those who are familiar primarily with De Niro's more intense screen roles should definitely give this film a look.

★ 1988, 128 minutes, color, R.

★ With: Robert De Niro, Charles Grodin, Yaphet Kotto, John Ashton. Director: Martin Brest.

★ *For what role did Robert De Niro win his first Academy Award?* (Answer on page 312.)

A Midsummer Night's Dream (1935)

Bard enchant pic boffo for WB.

Just about every star on the Warner Brothers lot at the time showed up for this adaptation of the classic Shakespeare comedy. The picture is a lot of fun and user-friendly enough to serve as a good introduction to the Bard's work for younger members of the family or those who were forced to endure boring lectures about Shakespeare from bad high school English teachers.

The plot, as you may remember, has to do with the struggle between the king and queen of a kingdom of fairies and the misadventures of a couple of pairs of human lovers who stumble into the enchanted domain. Although Mickey Rooney does an energetic enough turn as Puck, you may feel as though you've seen enough of his routine about halfway through; the real reasons I kept watching were the unexpectedly strong performance of James Cagney as Bottom, the marvelous Mendelssohn music, and the enchanting cinematography of Hal Mohr. A pleasant, funny romp that will prove to the skittish that Shakespeare doesn't bite after all.

★ 1935, 117 minutes, B&W, not rated.

★ With: Pretty much everyone under contract at the time, including Olivia de Havilland, James Cagney, and Mickey Rooney (but where the hell is Bogey?). Directors: Max Reinhardt, William Dieterle.

★ *What was special about the Academy Award the film received for best cinematography?* (Answer on page 56.)

"If I do it, let the audience look to their eyes; I will move storms."

—James Cagney's confident he's about to leave 'em crying in the aisles.

For a great double feature, rent it with
Much Ado About Nothing.

Seen it but in the mood for something similar? Try
A Midsummer Night's Dream (1968).

Answer to page 143 trivia question:
That man was trying to interfere with my personal life.

Comedy

Miss Firecracker

It's a blast!

"Don't make me treat you like dogs."
—Tim Robbins gets rid of some unwanted female attention.

For a great double feature, rent it with *Crimes of the Heart.*

Seen it but in the mood for something similar? Try *The Positively True Adventures of the Alleged Texas Cheerleader-Murdering Mom.*

Answer to page 359 trivia question: *The Turning Point.*

Holly Hunter works in a factory extracting the guts from fish; she's dyed her hair bright red for the upcoming Miss Firecracker Pageant, held every year in Yazoo City, Mississippi. Her cousin Elaine won a few years ago and this year will be giving a speech entitled "My Life as a Beauty." Hunter has a lot at stake; if she can win, she knows she will be afforded the respect that her cousin has, which will help her turn around her reputation as the town's resident "hot tamale." Then she'll be able to leave her tiny town with her bright-red head held high.

Her dress is being prepared by Alfre Woodard, as Popeye, whose name arose from a childhood accident she had after putting ear drops in her eyes. Sometimes she can hear out of them. Then there's Tim Robbins, Hunter's other cousin, who, after spending some time in a very comfortable mental institution, has been cleaning up roadkill out on the interstate. He, too, is ready for a change in his life.

All of these nutballs will convince you that Tennessee Williams characters look pretty normal by comparison. At least this batch of southern weirdos is *likable.* This is a truly original movie that introduces you to a bunch of people you may not want to live next door to but certainly would enjoy spending an evening with.

★ 1989, 102 minutes, color, PG.

★ With: Holly Hunter, Alfre Woodard, Tim Robbins, Mary Steenburgen. Director: Thomas Schlamme.

★ *In what film did Alfre Woodard's character fall in love with Danny Glover's character?* (Answer on page 140.)

Modern Times

Watch that conveyor belt.

It's the Little Tramp against the machine age, and the results are comic magic. This send-up of "better living through technology" is probably even more relevant to our time than it was to Charlie Chaplin's. Back in the thirties the idea that the boss could spy on you electronically was the most far-fetched science fiction. These days it's cold, hard fact.

The impetus behind the picture, of course, was Chaplin's own discomfort with certain rapidly advancing film technologies. It was 1936; everyone was wondering whether Charlie would bow to the realities of the age by incorporating sound and dialogue in one of his pictures.

In *Modern Times*, he came up with a nifty conceit that allowed him to duck the issue for another few years: the only understandable spoken words in this satire of an automation-crazy world are those issued by machines or the people speaking through them. When Charlie does use his own voice, he spouts only gibberish in a delightful nonsense musical number. These are inspired touches, one of many in this satire that dares you to take a stand with people, rather than things, lest you become one of the latter. It's one of the master's very best. What do you think's up with that joy powder in the saltshaker?

★ 1936, 89 minutes, B&W, not rated.

★ With: Charlie Chaplin, Paulette Goddard, Chester Conklin. Director: Charles Chaplin.

★ *In what all-female picture did Goddard appear?*
(Answer on page 247.)

"Humanity crusading in the pursuit of happiness."
—Legend that appears on-screen immediately before Chaplin cuts to a shot of sheep rushing through an entryway.

For a great double feature, rent it with
Metropolis.

Seen it but in the mood for something similar? Try
The Great Dictator.

Answer to page 299 trivia question:
Friz Freleng.

Mon Oncle d'Amerique

That's "My American Uncle" to you, bub.

"A living creature is a memory that acts."

—Dr. Henri Laborit argues that all human—and animal—behavior is the result of both conditioning and mental codes that have been deeply imprinted on us from the moment of conception. Translation: If we screw up, it may be because we can't help it.

For a great double feature, rent it with

The Last Metro.

Seen it but in the mood for something similar? Try

A Clockwork Orange.

Answer to page 334 trivia question:

Olivia Hussey.

Hard to describe, even harder to stop watching, this unusual French entry showcases a very young Gerard Depardieu as a textile plant manager who has an affair with a striking actress (Nicole Garcia). Depardieu's actions are being observed by a behavior scientist (Henri Laborit), whose incisive commentaries on the proclivities of various mammals—including, most notably, humans—provides the picture with its distinct, detached tone.

Deliciously odd in structure, and punctuated at intervals by a blend of fascinating scientific commentary and weird imagery, *Mon Oncle d'Amerique* offers some surprising insights into why we do what we do. Alain Resnais directs this fragile, carefully assembled series of meditations on human relationships with insight and precision; Depardieu gives notice that he intends to hold our attention for some time to come.

★ 1980, 123 minutes, color, PG.

★ With: Gerard Depardieu, Nicole Garcia, Henri Laborit. Director: Alain Resnais.

★ *In what adaptation of an Edmond Rostand classic did Depardieu star in 1990?* (Answer on page 300.)

Monster in a Box

No peeking.

The follow-up to Spalding Gray's fascinating tour-de-force *Swimming to Cambodia,* this film chronicles the monologuist's real-life attempt to write his auto-biography and raises some illuminating questions about life, death, and human frailty. It sounds like pretty heady stuff, but Gray is such an accomplished raconteur that he's more than up to the task of holding our interest with his vivid, one-of-a-kind confessional rants, which take you from California (during an earthquake) to China.

You may feel skeptical about one-person-shows as a genre, but Gray is the perfect performer to convince you of the viability of his undertaking. He is brutally, hysterically honest, capable of finding connections among the most unlikely bits of material, and in possession of a razor-sharp comic sense that often doubles back on him. This is the kind of picture that makes you wonder why movie studios don't make more one-performer films; the budget has to be easy to manage, and the material, when developed and delivered by a master like Gray, is spellbinding.

★ 1992, 96 minutes, color, PG-13.

★ With: Spalding Gray. Director: Nick Broomfield.

★ *What classic of the American stage does Gray report as having been marred by an unfortunate vomiting incident during a production in which he was a cast member?* (Answer on page 324.)

"It's a book I've been working on for the past two years, entitled Impossible Vacation, *due to be published by Knopf, in hardcover, two years ago."*
—Spalding Gray's got deadline problems.

For a great double feature, rent it with
My Dinner with Andre.

Seen it but in the mood for something similar? Try
Swimming to Cambodia.

Answer to page 355 trivia question:
Key of Keys.

Comedy

The Morning After

Talk about waking up on the wrong side of the bed.

For a great double feature, rent it with

Gaslight (1944).

Seen it but in the mood for something similar? Try

Jagged Edge.

Answer to page 290 trivia question:

Watch the actor who has the right build; that might not be him in all of the shots.

Jane Fonda has been drinking way too much lately. She's been having these unfortunate blackouts. When she comes to one morning, she finds herself lying in bed next to the body of a very dead guy with a very big knife in his chest. One too many Harvey Wallbangers, huh?

After a mild panic attack, Fonda does what any smart woman would do; she cleans the apartment from top to bottom, erasing any evidence of her having been there. She's hoping to leave in the clear, but it appears that she was never alone in that apartment after all. While she was cleaning, someone was watching, and that someone is after her.

This is a great edge-of-your-seat thriller that relies on smart characters and a taut, smart script. Every character in the film is flawed (including the mysterious Jeff Bridges, who may or may not be in a position to help Fonda), but the acting is not. The two principals, each from a storied Hollywood family, do their respective daddies proud.

★ 1986, 103 minutes, color, R.

★ With: Jane Fonda, Jeff Bridges, Raul Julia. Director: Sidney Lumet.

★ *Which film with Jane Fonda made the shag haircut a fashion sensation?* (Answer on page 82.)

Moulin Rouge

Little guy gets ahead.

What do you suppose Jose Ferrer's knees felt like when they finished shooting this one? John Huston directed this lush account of the life of the legendary French artist Henri de Toulouse-Lautrec; Ferrer got to wobble around on his knees in the long shots and wait, no doubt with ever-decreasing patience, for the close-ups, in which the illusion of the artist's deformity was not necessary.

The picture features some breathtaking recreations of 19th-century Parisian nightlife, any number of familiar images and faces from that art history class you probably weren't paying enough attention to, and more spirited cancan dancing than you'll know what to do with (*Scandaleuse!*). Ferrer is magnificent as the eccentric artist with a distorted world view that screws up his personal life but serves him quite well when it comes to developing a unique artistic vision.

The film received well-deserved Oscars for Best Set Decoration, Best Costumes, and Best Art Direction. The last award was particularly appropriate; Huston, who used only hues from Lautrec paintings, was quoted as saying he wanted the picture to look as though Lautrec directed it. It does.

★ 1952, 123 minutes, color, not rated.

★ With: Jose Ferrer, Zsa Zsa Gabor, Peter Cushing. Director: John Huston.

★ *What famous big-band singer was Jose Ferrer's wife?* (Answer on page 23.)

"Marriage is like a dull meal, with the dessert at the beginning."
—Jose Ferrer figures he probably isn't missing much.

For a great double feature, rent it with *Lust for Life.*

Seen it but in the mood for something similar? Try *Immortal Beloved.*

Answer to page 325 trivia question: *Kramer vs. Kramer* (1979).

Drama

The Mouse That Roared

Get me Washington. First, tell them who we are.
Then tell them we give up.

"As long as no one gets hurt."
—The Queen's wary condition for approving a declaration of war on the United States.

For a great double feature, rent it with

Being There.

Seen it but in the mood for something similar? Try

Dr. Strangelove or: How I Learned to Stop Worrying and Love the Bomb.

Answer to page 346 trivia question:

To Kill a Mockingbird (1962).

This devastatingly on-target satire of international superpower relations provides Peter Sellers with the opportunity to deliver yet another sterling comic performance. No, make that *performances.* Here he plays three roles in what amounts to a warm-up for his unforgettable tour-de-force performance in *Dr. Strangelove or: How I Learned to Stop Worrying and Love the Bomb* five years later.

The cute conceit runs like this: financially strapped leaders of a tiny country (the Duchy of Grand Fenwick—great name, eh?) decide that if getting beaten by the United States can bring prosperity to Japan or Germany, it might do them some good, too. Accordingly, they declare war on America. Kind of like the whole Grenada thing, except that in the case of *The Mouse That Roared* it almost makes sense, and the little guy starts it. Followed by a cute little sequel, *The Mouse on the Moon,* but as usual, the first offering is the best.

★ 1959, 83 minutes, B&W, not rated.

★ With: Peter Sellers, Peter Sellers, Peter Sellers, Jean Seberg. Director: Jack Arnold.

★ *How many Academy Awards did Peter Sellers win as Best Actor?* (Answer on page 146.)

Movie, Movie

Watch it twice!

Critics weren't quite sure what to make of this inspired twin parody of thirties double features. Structurally adventurous, it offers *both* an over-the-top, self-lampooning Busby Berkeley–style musical *and* a melodramatic spoof of Clifford Odets's *Golden Boy.* Folks, I'm here to tell you, this swell idea works like gangbusters—and if two movies for the price of one isn't just what Mr. and Mrs. John Q. Public are after in times like these, then, gosh, I guess I have some funny ideas about what makes America great. (Sorry. Got caught up in the spirit of things for a moment.)

Great cast, with George C. Scott allowed the rare opportunity to display his impeccable comic timing; a young Harry Hamlin shines in the boxing segment. Larry Gelbart and Sheldon Keller fashioned the screenplay for this clever, affectionate tribute to all that was great, and not so great, about formulaic moviemaking; director Stanley Donen achieved the perfect look and pace. Don't miss it.

★ 1978, 107 minutes, color (with B&W inserts), PG.

★ With: George C. Scott, Trish Van deVere, Eli Wallach, Harry Hamlin. Director: Stanley Donen.

★ *Name the pictures in the picture.* (Answer on page 296.)

"How hard it is to say what there are no words for! But when a man speaks what's true and what's right, then his mouth is 10 feet tall."
—Whatever Harry Hamlin's point is, he couldn't have put it better.

For a great double feature, rent it with
42nd Street.

Seen it but in the mood for something similar? Try
Young Frankenstein.

Answer to page 172 trivia question:
Sam Peckinpah.

Comedy

Mr. Blanding Builds His Dream House

Cary Grant and Myrna Loy bring down the house.
Literally.

C ary Grant, the master of the slow burn, the wry look, and the air of bemused befuddlement, meets his comedic match here in Myrna Loy, and they both meet their match when they try to build what turns out to be the house from hell.

Director H. C. Potter makes the most of the material's considerable comic potential; this film is one of Hollywood's classic screwball comedies, and it's a damn shame that more people have probably seen *The Money Pit*. This is a video to buy as a housewarming gift for anyone buying or (God forbid) building a home. The Blandings learn, as all who do not know their place must learn, that wailing and gnashing of teeth await those who offend the deities of real estate and construction. No matter that the project at first seems complex but nothing two halfway intelligent people can't pull off; there will inevitably follow a fiasco of such expense and duration as to instill permanent mental imbalance.

Everyone will enjoy this film; those who have built their own home and can identify with the special pain associated with blindly writing checks for horrific sums because some guy says you have to will find redemption. They will know, at long last, that they are not alone.

★ 1948, 94 minutes, B&W, not rated.

★ With: Cary Grant, Myrna Loy, Melvyn Douglas. Director: H. C. Potter.

★ *Why is Cary Grant linked forever with Mae West in film history?* (Answer on page 305.)

Mr. Hulot's Holiday

Out of order.

I t was the 1950s; who on earth gave this man permission to make a silent movie? Actually, *Mr. Hulot's Holiday* isn't exactly dialogue-free, but it might as well be. Jacques Tati, both director and star here, offers the first screen appearance of the well-intentioned but mechanically challenged Mr. Hulot, who takes a vacation trip to a French resort town and encounters any number of uncooperative inanimate objects.

Comedy is a subjective thing, of course: some people worship Beavis and Butt-head; others consider them a sign of the imminent collapse of civilization. It's hard, though, to imagine anyone not giving the thumbs-up to this consistently inventive display of sustained physical comedy.

Describing the specifics of the Hulot comedies is a little like giving a minute-by-minute account of a ballet or a tap dance; words aren't really the point. Suffice it to say that Tati, with his Hulot character, took the distrust of technology evident in Chaplin's *Modern Times* and gave it a refreshing, distinctly Gallic twist. Hulot's misadventures continued in the equally hilarious *Mon Oncle*.

★ 1953, 86 minutes, color, not rated.

★ With: Jacques Tati, Nathalie Pascaud, Michelle Rolla. Director: Jacques Tati.

★ *Who went Tati one further and made an honest-to-goodness silent picture that was a hit in the 1970s?*
(Answer on page 150.)

"   "

—There aren't a lot of subtitles to worry about in this foreign film.

For a great double feature, rent it with
Modern Times.

Seen it but in the mood for something similar? Try
Mon Oncle.

Answer to page 224 trivia question:
The Persecution and Assassination of Jean-Paul Marat as Performed by the Inmates of the Asylum of Charenton, Under the Direction of the Marquis de Sade.

Foreign

Murder by Death

Easily the finest film of Truman Capote's acting career.

Neil Simon's inspired spoof of 1940s detective dramas probably features more A-list actors making gloriously bad jokes than any picture this side of *It's a Mad, Mad, Mad, Mad World.* While that sprawling all-star yuk fest scored its points with, shall we say, occasional comic excesses, *Murder by Death* is a restrained, civilized little send-up of the mystery genre in a single location.

It features an assemblage of the world's greatest detectives, each of whom bears a passing resemblance to a screen icon of yesteryear. Nick and Nora Charles, Sam Spade, Charlie Chan, Miss Marple, Hercule Poirot—they're all in attendance to solve a crime "that has not yet been committed." Well, their comic equivalents are all here, with names slightly altered; it's Sam Diamond and Inspector Perrier who show up at the house of a mysterious mystery fan.

This is a great rent: you get to watch Peter Falk, David Niven, Maggie Smith, and company poke exquisite fun at—sorry, *pay tribute* to—the actors of an earlier generation, and they do it with a script in which Neil Simon skewers—sorry, *pays tribute* to—Agatha Christie, Dashiell Hammett, and Raymond Chandler.

★ 1976, 94 minutes, color, PG.

★ With: Truman Capote, James Coco, Peter Falk, Alec Guinness, David Niven, Peter Sellers, Maggie Smith. Director: Robert Moore.

★ *Name the Oscar winners in the cast.* (Answer on page 86.)

My Beautiful Laundrette

Punks on the spin cycle.

This satisfyingly realistic portrait of life on the fringes in modern-day London features a very early performance from Daniel Day-Lewis (he's the one with the skunk do). Day-Lewis falls in love with a handsome Pakistani teenager (Gordon Warnecke). The two want to open a laundromat together, but they have a hard time convincing others that they deserve a chance to pull it off: for one thing, they're low-level punks, and for another, they're gay.

The picture is a pleasantly wise examination of how different groups react to the same stifling social conditions. For the white street toughs the urban decay that surrounds them is proof of their relegation to the bottom end of the hierarchy; for the Pakistanis a European urban wasteland is the necessary backdrop to an often slow, often illicit, but always steady, ascent to a better situation.

My Beautiful Laundrette is, like many other entries in this book, proof that you can make a damn good movie on an almost nonexistent budget.

★ 1985, 98 minutes, color, R.

★ With: Saeed Jaffrey, Roshan Seth, Daniel Day-Lewis, Gordon Warnecke. Director: Stephen Frears.

★ *What provocative Frears film created a stir when Prince Charles and Lady Di attended the premiere?* (Answer on page 40.)

"I'm a professional businessman, not a professional Pakistani."
—Saeed Jaffrey finds himself firmly stuck within the British class system.

For a great double feature, rent it with
Sammy and Rosie Get Laid.

Seen it but in the mood for something similar? Try
My Own Private Idaho.

Answer to page 165 trivia question:
Shane.

Drama

My Dinner with Andre

If they'd only been able to work in a car chase . . .

Director Louis Malle plunks a camera down in the middle of a restaurant and films a scripted, but seemingly off-the-cuff, extended conversation about life, the internal universe versus the external universe, and anything else that comes to mind.

As the film opens, frumpy playwright Wallace Shawn (playing himself) isn't really looking forward to his dinner with brilliant theater director Andre Gregory (playing himself)—his intimidation in the face of high-octane intellectualism is one that any number of viewers will share. This film, which consists almost entirely of two men sitting at a table, is never boring; on the contrary, its collection of mental and emotional fireworks set seamlessly into the fabric of the real world offers an evening of real human contact of the kind that one enjoys only once or twice in a lifetime. The picture scales extravagant intellectual heights and a moment later addresses the pesky details of making a living and getting through the day; whenever *Andre* gets too smart for its own good, it has the sense to gleefully puncture its own bubble.

★ 1981, 110 minutes, color, PG.

★ With: Wallace Shawn, Andre Gregory. Director: Louis Malle.

★ *In what fantasy film directed by Rob Reiner did Shawn play a heavy?* (Answer on page 10.)

Drama

Mystic Pizza

A movie with the works.

This film is that rarity, a top-notch coming-of-age movie that focuses on young *women*. In a New England resort town three friends—Julia Roberts, Annabeth Gish, and Lili Taylor—learn of the pains, pleasures, and perils of love. Lower-middle-class Roberts meets a boy from the right side of the tracks and dreams of doing something more interesting with her life than working behind a pizza counter; Taylor ponders whether to get married to the local fisherman who is smitten with her and dreams of doing something more interesting with her life than working behind a pizza counter; Gish moonlights as a baby-sitter, nearly has an affair with the married man who's hired her, and dreams of doing something more interesting with her life than working behind a pizza counter. All the hard lessons get learned, all the important friendships survive, and you feel a heck of a lot better about life than you do at the end of, say, *Taps*.

★ 1988, 94 minutes, color, R.

★ With: Julia Roberts, Annabeth Gish, Lili Taylor. Director: Donald Petrie.

★ *What is the meaning of the film's title?* (Answer on page 7.)

"I'm going to be slinging pizza here for the rest of my life."
—Julia Roberts has bigger dreams.

For a great double feature, rent it with
Foxes.

Seen it but in the mood for something similar? Try
Gas Food Lodging.

Answer to page 235 trivia question:
The Women.

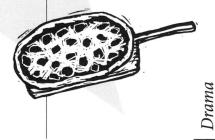

Drama

Naked Lunch

That's one excited typewriter.

"It's a very literary high. A Kafka high. It makes you feel like a bug."

—Nobody has to twist Peter Weller's arm after a description like that.

For a great double feature, rent it with

Kafka.

Seen it but in the mood for something similar? Try

Brazil.

Answer to page 273 trivia question:

What the Butler Saw.

Somebody, somewhere, must have collected big-time on a private bet upon the release of this ambitious adaptation of the crazed William S. Burroughs classic. The novel is easily among the most unfilmable literary efforts ever set down on paper, and it faced long odds against ever being made into a movie. Believe it or not, though, this picture works.

Peter Weller's creepy, lean-boned performance as the Burroughs-like William Lee adds a welcome point of view to the often unnerving proceedings; we follow him through a series of hallucinatory encounters with various menacing, alluring, and/or enigmatic oddballs. Weller is hooked on cockroach pesticide dust, y'see, and we're never quite sure which of his paranoid conquests is rooted in what *we* would call reality.

Naked Lunch is a series of disturbing, on-target burlesques in which inanimate objects take on a life of their own, huge insects hold extended conversations with the main character, and everyone really *is* out to get you after all. Comic fun for the whole family, with a special musical appearance by the Muppets. (See—now *you're* starting to hallucinate.)

★ 1991, 115 minutes, color, R.

★ With: Peter Weller, Judy Davis, Ian Holm. Director: David Cronenberg.

★ *In what picture does Burroughs himself play a defrocked priest?* (Answer on page 49.)

Drama

248

Formerly rich SWM wishes to meet extremely rich SWF.

Walter Matthau plays a boorish, asexual snob who has no skills or interests other than spending his money. After he's spent almost all of it, he has no recourse but to marry a rich girl. He borrows enough money from his rich uncle to keep up appearances for six weeks, with the understanding that if he cannot find a bride in the allotted time all of Matthau's remaining collateral will revert back to his uncle, leaving him even poorer than before.

Matthau sets to work as he's never worked before; the bride (Elaine May) proves surprisingly easy to find. She's a bookish, clumsy botanist who proves herself to be as socially inept as Matthau is emotionally inept. Together they make a better match than either of them has a right to expect.

This truly funny script was written by May, who also directs; Matthau quickly proves himself equal to the quirky leading part. *A New Leaf* is a rare treat, a picture that is smart, romantic, and very funny from beginning to end. A great find.

★ 1971, 102 minutes, color, G.

★ With: Walter Matthau, Elaine May, Jack Weston, James Coco. Director: Elaine May.

★ *Elaine May holds the distinction of directing what massively unsuccessful tribute to the Hope and Crosby road pictures?* (Answer on page 128.)

"I can engage in any romantic activity with an urbanity born of disinterest."

—Walter Matthau, one of the most Jewish actors on the face of the planet, does his turn as a Brahmin. Good thing Elaine May's on the same wavelength.

For a great double feature, rent it with
The Odd Couple.

Seen it but in the mood for something similar? Try
The Heartbreak Kid.

Answer to page 6 trivia question:
Charles Grodin.

Comedy

Night on Earth

Hey, call me a cab.

"*I'm a cab driver. And that's what I do.*"
—Winona Ryder, who doesn't know she's supposed to want more from life, is happy in her little corner of the world.

For a great double feature, rent it with

Taxi Driver.

Seen it but in the mood for something similar? Try

Stranger than Paradise.

Answer to page 40 trivia question:

Radio City Music Hall.

Independent-minded director Jim Jarmusch, who gave vacuity a good name in *Stranger than Paradise,* took on an unusual premise in this offbeat international comedy. He tossed out most of the conventional Hollywood requirements for audience buy-in—plot continuity, three-act structure, even the semblance of a single protagonist—all to follow five cabbies and their passengers through a series of bizarre journeys in five different cities.

The string of one-act plays hangs together nicely, thanks to Jarmusch's intelligent handling of the single, loose-fitting idea that unites them. A series of comic high-wire acts through Los Angeles, New York, Paris, Rome, and Helsinki, *Night on Earth* reaffirms Jarmusch's unique style and spotlights his masterful ability to build tension from the most unlikely material. You may never step into a cab—or look at a sheep—in quite the same way again.

★ 1991, 125 minutes, color, R.

★ With: Winona Ryder, Gena Rowlands, Giancarlo Esposito. Director: Jim Jarmusch.

★ *What happens to the priest in the back of the cab?* (Answer on page 176.)

Comedy

Nineteen Eighty-Four (1984)

Doubleplusgood film.

Richard Burton turned in his final screen performance in this faithful, finely crafted adaptation of the classic George Orwell novel; he's magnificent. Burton and John Hurt represent the two most perfect pieces of casting imaginable for the male leads.

The look of the film is similarly unwavering in its devotion to Orwell's (often all-too-prophetic) anti-utopian masterpiece. Director Michael Radford does a masterful job of evoking the era in which the novel was written *and* convincing us that our own future may well hold the horrors chronicled in the film. If a film can be both nostalgic and futuristic at the same time, this is the one. It's as if the technology of 1948 has not advanced but simply expanded in every conceivable direction.

Bringing a modern classic to life and making viewers care about the outcome of a story many of them probably know almost word for word are tough assignments. The movie pulls it off, however, in part because it's a little like an Edward Hopper painting: a bleak vision of unexpected, stark beauty that you can't manage to pry your eyes from, even though you may wish you could. An interesting side note: The shooting took place during the exact time and place specified in Orwell's novel.

★ 1984, 115 minutes, color, R.

★ With: John Hurt, Richard Burton, Suzanna Hamilton. Director: Michael Radford.

★ *What John Hurt starring role never revealed his face?*
(Answer on page 284.)

"Who controls the past, controls the future. Who controls the present, controls the past."

—Memory is a tricky commodity in Oceania, and Richard Burton knows it.

For a great (if lengthy and somewhat depressing) double feature, rent it with *Brazil.*

Seen it but in the mood for something similar? Try *THX-1138.*

Answer to page 74 trivia question: Tom Selleck.

Drama

No Time for Sergeants

Pre-Mayberry gold and essential viewing.

For a great double feature, rent it with

Stripes.

Seen it but in the mood for something similar? Try

Buck Privates.

Answer to page 108 trivia question:

He wears a black suit and carries a guitar case.

A hayseed (a very young Andy Griffith) is inducted into the military, where he runs into problems with a troublesome commanding officer. Not the most original premise, perhaps, but the picture is well worth checking out because of the hilarious work turned in by Andy Griffith. The film established him as a gifted comic actor, a label that stuck and that resulted in a storied television career . . . and an unfortunate bout of typecasting. (For proof that the Genial One is in fact capable of serious dramatic work, see *Hearts of the West* and *A Face in the Crowd*.)

This one's a classic, though, and worth watching anytime you need a lift. I dare you to get through the lavatory scene without laughing. Tenn-*hutt!*

★ 1958, 111 minutes, B&W, not rated.

★ With: Andy Griffith, Myron McCormick, Nick Adams. Director: Mervyn LeRoy.

★ *Who wrote the play on which the film is based?*
(Answer on page 317.)

Comedy

Now, Voyager

Bette Davis, a shrinking violet?

ette's mother is a jerk. She's browbeaten her daughter for years, until all that is left of what was once a pretty girl on the verge of womanhood is an overweight bun-headed spinster. After all, if you let children blossom, they might leave you, and then who will take care of you in your old age? That's Mom's thinking, anyway. Luckily for Bette, a kind relative notices that she's on the brink of a breakdown and helps her sneak off to a sanitarium to find herself.

Boy, does she ever. The now-glamorous Bette, with a new do and a smashing new wardrobe, is off on a steamer to Europe to see what else she can find. Enter Paul Henreid, the handsome misunderstood married man; I'll leave the rest to your imagination. (Even if it is very uncool to smoke, Henreid will have you thinking how really suave it can be to light one up.) A supremely romantic early-forties envelope pusher.

★ 1942, 117 minutes, B&W, not rated.

★ With: Bette Davis, Paul Henreid, Claude Rains. Director: Irving Rapper.

★ *What are they cooking in the fireplace at the end of the film?* (Answer on page 28.)

"Let's not reach for the moon when we have the stars."

—Bette Davis offers a poetic justification for an unconventional domestic arrangement.

For a great double feature, rent it with *Dark Victory.*

Seen it but in the mood for something similar? Try *Casablanca.*

Answer to page 11 trivia question: Michael Crichton.

Romance

The Nun's Story

Hey, it's not all glamour.

"You must bend or you will break."
—Audrey Hepburn receives a warning from the Mother Superior.

For a great double feature, rent it with

Two Mules for Sister Sarah.

Seen it but in the mood for something similar? Try

Black Narcissus.

Answer to page 78 trivia question:

American Graffiti.

This one offers a glimpse into the world of a novice nun and does a good job of dramatizing the significant trials of a life spent in that vocation. When Audrey Hepburn says good-bye to her family, we get the first glimmer of what she will have to leave behind; in her new world, friendships outside the order are out of bounds—they're considered a distraction and a selfish indulgence. To scrub the floor well and then take pride in the job would be a sin. To become a nurse so as to help people is to lose sight of your job as a servant to God. In the order, He comes before everything, including what might seem the most laudable Christian ideal.

Tough job, especially if you consider you never get a single day off. It's particularly tough for Hepburn, not merely because she has a very limited wardrobe but because she's perfectly suited for a job as nurse in a hospital in the Congo. She's from a medical family and is easily the best in her class, but if she can't learn to do things God's way, she won't be allowed to do them at all.

This is a totally engrossing tale of one young woman's dream—and the sometimes paradoxical choices that accompany that dream.

★ 1959, 149 minutes, color, not rated.

★ With: Audrey Hepburn, Peter Finch, Edith Evans. Director: Fred Zinnemann.

★ *What television icon played a nun in an Elvis Presley vehicle?* (Answer on page 158.)

The Nutty Professor

OK, maybe just maybe, the French have a point.

In this, the funniest solo Jerry Lewis movie, the star finds a plot that lets him alternate between nerdy anti-hunk and supermacho ladies' man. It works, in no small degree because the tough-guy Buddy Love persona effectively lampoons that of Lewis's estranged partner, Dean Martin.

The gags may be a trifle over the top in places, and the film's view of women may incline toward the prefeminist, nay, even unto the Cro-Magnon viewpoint, but let's face it: when the guy's on, he's on.

Check out the superamplified sound effects when Lewis is suffering from a hangover and the subsequent inspired mugging he serves up in reaction to the cacophony only he can hear. Similarly on-target ideas bounce past every scene or so.

Even when something doesn't quite work, Lewis's confidence and, one senses, his joy at finally having found a vehicle worthy of comparison with his earlier films with Martin carry the day.

★ 1963, 107 minutes, color, not rated.

★ With: Jerry Lewis, Stella Stevens, Del Moore. Director: Jerry Lewis.

★ *In what film did Jerry Lewis play a Johnny Carson–like talk show host?* (Answer on page 53.)

"Every move a picture."
—Jerry Lewis, in his incarnation as Buddy Love, likes what he sees of himself.

For a great double feature, rent it with
The Absent Minded Professor.

Seen it but in the mood for something similar? Try
Hollywood or Bust.

Answer to page 45 trivia question:
Patty Hearst, with Natasha Richardson in the title role.

Comedy

Of Mice and Men (1992)

Will work for puppies.

"We're gonna have a cow and a pig, and some chickens . . . a field of alfalfa. . . ."
—Gary Sinise and John Malkovich share an impossible dream.

For a great double feature, rent it with
Cannery Row (1982).

Seen it but in the mood for something similar? Try
Charly.

Answer to page 79 trivia question:
He claimed to be allergic to the Hollywood air; supposedly, it played havoc with his asthma.

This poignant adaptation of the John Steinbeck classic features a glove-fitting screenplay by Horton Foote, an impressive two-for-the-price-of-one trick by Gary Sinise (he plays George *and* directs the picture), and, last but not least, a true star turn by John Malkovich as the powerful, simpleminded Lenny.

Malkovich's performance is all the more remarkable when you take into account that he delivers all the immense strength and physical bulk required by the role—yet is not a large man and doesn't really pretend to be. Malkovich's is an eerily on-target performance; his scenes with the sultry Sherilyn Fenn radiate equal measures of naivete and physical energy, and it's hard to tell which gives you the creeps more.

Steinbeck's unforgettable story of life on the edge during the Depression years in California receives a top-notch treatment here, complete with the hard-hitting ending sequence the makers of the 1939 film version, starring Burgess Meredith, could only hint at.

★ 1992, 110 minutes, color, PG-13.

★ With: Gary Sinise, John Malkovich, Sherilyn Fenn. Director: Gary Sinise.

★ *Name the Chicago theater group where Sinise and Malkovich first came to prominence.* (Answer on page 75.)

Oklahoma Kid

He's a rootin', tootin', singin', shootin' cowboy!

This classic western has it all. Not only does James Cagney play the rough-and-tumble cowboy with the heart of gold, but he also starts a barroom brawl, jumps on the back of a horse from the second story of a building, kills several bad guys (all in self-defense), and wins the heart of the girl in the gingham dress. Did I mention he also sings a lullaby in Spanish?

Cagney's performance is a real gem. We believe him in the role—and, more important, we like him. This role was a hard-won victory for Cagney, who had, before this film, been typecast in his financially successful—but, from his perspective, artistically limiting—gangster parts. Cagney clearly enjoys the stretch, and so will you.

The baffling (yet oddly enjoyable) miscasting of Humphrey Bogart as a black-hatted cowboy is the only misstep in what is otherwise probably one of the greatest Hollywood films of the genre. Some people belong only in the 20th century, and Bogey's one of them.

★ 1939, 85 minutes, B&W, not rated.

★ With: James Cagney, Humphrey Bogart, Rosemary Lane. Director: Lloyd Bacon.

★ *In what film did James Cagney make his last on-screen appearance?* (Answer on page 132.)

"You all know the Oklahoma Kid. Don't ya?"
—Humphrey Bogart introduces James Cagney to the gang.

For a great double feature, rent it with
The Bride Came C.O.D.

Seen it but in the mood for something similar? Try
Destry Rides Again.

Answer to page 113 trivia question:
Prizzi's Honor (1985).

Western

Operation Petticoat

The brassieres on the periscope alone are worth the price of admission.

"Never have so few stolen so much for so many."
—Cary Grant looks the other way while Tony Curtis gets shipshape.

For a great double feature, rent it with
Destination Tokyo.

Seen it but in the mood for something similar? Try
The Great Race.

Answer to page 17 trivia question:
To raise money for a mental-health organization.

Is there some kind of karmic boat principle swirling around Gavin McLeod, or what? You take this movie (where he plays a guy with a lewd tattoo), combine it with McLeod's stint on "McHale's Navy," then throw in "The Love Boat," and you get an idea why he always seemed so happy on "The Mary Tyler Moore Show": he was on dry land for a change.

Anyway, Tony Curtis was supposedly very nervous indeed when it came time to shoot his scenes with Cary Grant in this film; Curtis had lampooned him mercilessly in *Some Like It Hot,* but Grant, legend has it, was a great sport.

In this gleefully sexist comedy Grant plays a stately commanding officer who has to deal with an unexpected personnel addition: a group of women (most of them quite buxom) must be accommodated on his submarine during wartime, and the passageways are all suddenly narrower than they seemed before. Grant's timing is, as usual, impeccable; he underplays while Curtis goes for the obvious gags, and between the two of them they pick up just about every possible laugh.

★ 1959, 124 minutes, color, not rated.

★ With: Cary Grant, Tony Curtis, Dina Merrill.
Director: Blake Edwards.

★ *What other film did Tony Curtis make with Blake Edwards?* (Answer on page 180.)

Comedy

Outland

How can you tell when it's high noon in space?

I f there's been a more seamlessly satisfying union of not two but *three* disparate movie genres than *Outland*, it's sure hard to think of. This supremely gratifying Sean Connery adventure effectively unites the best features of the science fiction yarn, the classic film noir, and, perhaps most noticeably, the one-good-man-up-against-a-world-of-trouble western. (Keep an eye out for the script's subtle Gary Cooper references.)

Connery's the only straight shooter on a remote space station. Sinister forces are feeding the workers amphetamines to boost their output, but the drugs have an unfortunate side effect: after a while they turn folks into murderous psychopaths. That's not exactly pleasant in a confined environment several million miles away from civilization, and neither is the way material witnesses have of exploding at inopportune times.

Connery turns in yet another standout performance, solidifying his credentials as both the thinking person's action hero and, just perhaps, the single coolest individual on the face of the earth (or elsewhere, for that matter). The consistently underrated Frances Sternhagen offers some top-notch supporting work as the surly, space-weary doctor.

★ 1981, 109 minutes, color, R.

★ With: Sean Connery, Frances Sternhagen, James B. Sikking. Director: Peter Hyams.

★ *What James Bond reference appears on a computer screen during the course of the film?* (Answer on page 306.)

"If you're looking for sterling characters, you've come to the wrong place."

—Frances Sternhagen has been in space long enough to know who she's sharing it with.

For a great double feature, rent it with
High Noon.

Seen it but in the mood for something similar? Try
Blade Runner.

Answer to page 51 trivia question:
Murphy's Romance.

The Ox-Bow Incident

*Henry Fonda gets drunk, picks a fight, and throws up—
all in the first five minutes.*

In a nondescript stretch of the West in 1885, word gets out that a rancher has been killed by cattle rustlers. Who did it? Well, a group of bored townspeople think they have a pretty good idea. Lacking anything better to do, they organize a lynching party and apprehend three suspects.

William A. Wellman's striking, carefully observed film is a searing examination of issues of responsibility, conscience, and group hysteria—a kind of *Twelve Angry Men* on the frontier. Nominated for Best Picture in 1943, *The Ox-Bow Incident* was a breakthrough western, the first picture in the genre in which character and motivation outweighed action. Rather than lionizing the strong-willed, authoritarian figures it portrayed, as other films might have done, it examined the consequences of following such people heedlessly.

★ 1943, 75 minutes, B&W, not rated.

★ With: Henry Fonda, Harry Morgan, Francis Ford, Anthony Quinn. Director: William A. Wellman.

★ *In what other famous film did Francis Ford (John Ford's father) play a cowboy?* (Answer on page 321.)

Western

260

The Paper Chase

Law students as heroes—and it works, too!

One of Hollywood's most reliable formulas is the boot-camp drama, in which our hero or heroes encounter an uncompromising drill instructor and emerge from camp better for the experience. The adaptable idea has led to a number of audience-pleasing pictures (*Buck Privates, The D.I., At War with the Army, An Officer and a Gentleman, Stripes, Private Benjamin,* etc., etc.), but it has probably never been refitted to a *non-military* setting to better effect than in *The Paper Chase*.

In place of boot camp, insert Harvard Law School during the students' first grueling year; in place of Jack Webb, Louis Gossett, Jr., or whoever else would have been yelling at the recruits, insert the supremely cantankerous John Houseman, who won the Oscar for his portrayal of the pupil-shredding professor.

This literate, funny movie offers an insider's view of the challenges of first-year law studies at an Ivy League institution as seen through the eyes of an idealistic young student (Timothy Bottoms). He must try to answer a different, but just as demanding, kind of bugle call. Based on John Jay Osborne's novel.

★ 1973, 111 minutes, color, PG.

★ With: Timothy Bottoms, Lindsay Wagner, John Houseman. Director: James Bridges.

★ *In what film did Houseman play the big cheese in an all-seeing, multinational corporation that had replaced all those pesky governments?* (Answer on page 63.)

"Call your mother and tell her you will never be a lawyer."

—John Houseman is engaged in his usual terrorize-the-students routine.

For a great double feature, rent it with
Reversal of Fortune.

Seen it but in the mood for something similar? Try
Gross Anatomy.

Answer to page 112 trivia question:
Duke Kahanamoku in 1910.

Comedy

Paper Lion

It seemed like a good idea at the time, doctor.

"Last-string quarter-back."

—At least George Plimpton's job description with the Detroit Lions leaves little doubt about what's expected of him.

For a great double feature, rent it with

The Longest Yard.

Seen it but in the mood for something similar? Try

It Happens Every Spring.

Answer to page 120 trivia question:

Andy Griffith, Lee Remick, and Anthony Franciosa.

Alan Alda stars in this film adaptation of George Plimpton's most famous story: his ground-level foray into the world of the National Football League. Now, any number of writers can write about the NFL from a distance; the lanky, erudite Plimpton decided to take a new approach by writing from a player's perspective . . . even though he knew he was unlikely to be confused for a legitimate NFL prospect by anyone who might be scouting him, including Ray Charles.

Plimpton showed up at the doorstep of the Detroit Lions organization, secured a uniform number, worked out during training camp, took some ribbing, and actually appeared in a scrimmage. Most important of all, he lived. It's a pretty cool story, and it's also a pleasant, diverting little comedy with some nice work from Alda and plenty of celebrity sports cameos. The intriguing fish-out-of-water angle makes this a sports picture even non-football fans will get a kick out of.

★ 1968, 107 minutes, color, G.

★ With: Alan Alda, Lauren Hutton, Alex Karras. Director: Alex March.

★ *Name the film in which a hard-slugging Karras knocks out a horse.* (Answer on page 293.)

Paris, Texas

An American in Paris.

It's a little weird, but stick with it. This is a film to rent when you feel like complaining about the shallowness of standard, formulaic Hollywood moviemaking.

We're never quite sure where Sam Shepard's eccentric screenplay is going, but Wim Wenders's perceptive direction makes this a compulsively watchable study of loss, memory, and unfulfilled longing.

Paris, Texas summons up the nearly deserted expanse of an America on the fringes, a vast, empty canvas where only the most fitful attempts at human contact are possible.

People with ragged edges have always been Shepard's stock in trade; here he provides two oddballs of memorable dimensions: Harry Dean Stanton is a mysterious wanderer, and Nastassja Kinski is the young, beautiful wife he left behind . . . and now pursues through the desert.

Rent it for the confident direction; rent it for the magnificent Shepard monologues (arias, really); rent it for the first-rate performances of actors who know they're not working with the clearest story in the world but are nevertheless the beneficiaries of some great writing.

★ 1984, 150 minutes, color, R.

★ With: Harry Dean Stanton, Nastassja Kinski, Dean Stockwell, Hunter Carson. Director: Wim Wenders.

★ *What was Dean Stockwell's first film musical?*
(Answer on page 137.)

"Do you know what side of the border you're on?"
—Harry Dean Stanton realizes the question is a little more complicated than it may seem on first hearing.

For a great double feature, rent it with
Wings of Desire.

Seen it but in the mood for something similar? Try
The Curse of the Starving Class.

Answer to page 23 trivia question:
Apocalypse Now.

Drama

The Pawnbroker

No man is an island—not even on the island of Manhattan.

*"I didn't die. Every-
thing I loved was
taken away from me,
and I did not die."*

—Steiger's got some survival
guilt.

**For a great double
feature, rent it with**

Mephisto.

**Seen it but in the mood
for something similar?
Try**

Sophie's Choice.

**Answer to page 20
trivia question:**

My Favorite Wife.

You think *you've* got troubles. Rod Steiger stars—and
I do mean stars—as a Jewish pawnbroker in Harlem
whose wartime experiences in the Nazi death camps
still haunt him. Astounding flashback sequences
make it immediately clear that this is not your average
alienated-protagonist picture. *The Pawnbroker* is a staggering, unforgettable portrait of a survivor who is forced
to emerge from his self-imposed exile.

One of Steiger's very best roles, although he lost out
to Lee Marvin in *Cat Ballou* at that year's Academy
Awards presentation. As good as Marvin was . . . oh,
never mind.

Director Sidney Lumet got the most out of his on-
location New York shoots; he also ignored a long-unchal-
lenged boundary by incorporating some brief but
unapologetic shots of bare female breasts—something no
major U.S. director in memory had dared to do. The flus-
tered officials of the Production Code office ordered
Lumet to remove the scenes, but he refused and eventually won release of the picture as he had assembled it. The
Catholic Church, outraged by the few seconds in question, banned the movie. Seems like a tempest in a teapot
nowadays, given the overall strength of the picture, but it
was 1965.

★ 1965, 116 minutes, B&W, not rated.

★ With: Rod Steiger, Geraldine Fitzgerald, Brock Peters.
Director: Sidney Lumet.

★ *What picture earned Steiger an Oscar as Best Actor?*
(Answer on page 104.)

Drama

264

The Pee-wee Herman Show

I know what you're thinking.
"If you love it so much, why don't you marry it?"

Not—repeat, not—a family rental! That's the whole point, folks. Before Paul Reubens had to clean up his act for network television, HBO let him try out his act in an hour-long, distinctly adult-oriented special. Not that this inventive collection of sophomoric gags is any more sophisticated than the stuff you're used to from Reubens; the double entendres are just a little more pointed. So is Captain Carl when he catches sight of a very buxom Miss Yvonne, for that matter, but let's not get into that here.

If you enjoyed the Pee-wee movies or the marvelous kids' show, and you're ready for a few surprises, you'll get a kick out of this. Truth in advertising disclaimer: some of the routines revel gloriously in their lameness.

★ 1982, 60 minutes, color, not rated.

★ With: Pee-wee Herman (Paul Reubens), Phil Hartman, John Paragon. Director: Marty Caliner.

★ *In what film did Reubens play a vampire?*
(Answer on page 156.)

"I'm not wearing underpants."
—No peeking, Pee-wee!

For a great double feature, rent it with
An Evening with Robin Williams.

Seen it but in the mood for something similar? Try
Pee-wee's Big Adventure.

Answer to page 54 trivia question:
A plane.

Comedy

Pennies from Heaven

Steve Martin challenged his audience, and the silence was so deafening he'll probably never try it again.

"Every time it rains. . . ."

—Sing-alongs anyone? No matter what sheet music salesman Steve Martin may have to offer, the Depression is still pretty depressing.

For a great double feature, rent it with

42nd Street.

Seen it but in the mood for something similar? Try

Cabaret.

Answer to page 57 trivia question:

Cactus Flower, for which she was named Best Supporting Actress.

Warning: *It's not a comedy!* This uncompromising musical portrait of the grim doings of a Depression-era sheet music salesman was a hard-hitting British television series before it was a feature film. Steve Martin saw it, loved it, and decided he'd star in it.

Writer Dennis Potter's use of ironic, surrealistic lip-synchings of the popular songs of the day provides a running commentary on the downbeat plot. The courageous decision to retain the story's dark undercurrents results in some brilliant filmmaking; unfortunately for Martin, the picture came as a surprise to those who were expecting something along the lines of *The Jerk II.*

Pennies from Heaven is an ambitious, intermittently brilliant musical with exquisite sets, choreography, and costumes. The picture, which deals with the mechanics of denial, is no laugh riot, but that's disappointing only if you think the only thing Steve Martin should do is make us laugh. If you haven't seen *Pennies from Heaven,* you've missed some of Martin's very best work. Keep an eye out for the elaborate re-creations of Edward Hopper tableaux and for the delicious slow-motion dance sequence in which coins fall from the heavens.

★ 1981, 107 minutes, color, R.

★ With: Steve Martin, Bernadette Peters, Christopher Walken. Director: Herbert Ross.

★ *Who played the lead role in the* BBC *series on which the film was based?* (Answer on page 45.)

The Petrified Forest

Poet/philosopher versus gun-toting maniac.
Place your bets.

From the good old days, when bad guys were just bad guys and you didn't have to worry about any of that knee-jerk, sociological liberalism. An early, break-through performance for Humphrey Bogart is only one of the attractions of this extraordinary crime picture about a bunch of gangsters on the run from the law. They hole up in a modest little Arizona cafe and keep things really, really creepy for a while.

Leslie Howard and Bette Davis are the biggest reasons to watch this superb effort; they are extraordinary. Bogart's superb supporting work is unalloyed Hollywood magic; his electrifying performance made audiences sit up and take notice of him for the first time. The part served to launch a tough-guy image that would endure to this day. In the following year he was given the lead in *Dead End*, a role that was powerful enough to catapult him to the front rank of Hollywood's leading men. It wouldn't have been possible without his unforgettable performance as a sociopathic hood in *The Petrified Forest*.

★ 1936, 83 minutes, B&W, not rated.

★ With: Leslie Howard, Bette Davis, Humphrey Bogart. Director: Archie Mayo.

★ *What member of the cast insisted on Bogart's appearing on-screen in the supporting role that had been a triumph for him on stage?* (Answer on page 15.)

"Living, I'm worth nothing to her. But dead, I can buy her the tallest cathedrals, golden vineyards, and dancing in the street."
—Leslie Howard realizes he can give Bette Davis the ultimate gift—he just won't get much fun out of it.

For a great double feature, rent it with
Public Enemy.

Seen it but in the mood for something similar? Try
Dead End.

Answer to page 91 trivia question:
Boyz N the Hood.

Action

Picnic at Hanging Rock

Virgins lie down on a big rock . . . hmmm. . . .

"What we see and what we seem are but a dream . . . a dream within a dream."

—That's all very well for the narrator to say, but the fact of the matter is that someone's misplaced the virgins.

For a great double feature, rent it with

Don't Look Now.

Seen it but in the mood for something similar? Try

Where the Green Ants Dream.

Answer to page 126 trivia question:

Gower Champion.

You'll never forget Peter Weir's unsettling, surrealistic examination of the consequences of a seemingly innocent Valentine's Day outing by students at a 1901 Australian school for girls. At a distance the young ladies in their white gowns and parasols look like figures in a Degas painting; up close Weir puts them to sleep next to strange bugs and snakes and summons up visions closer to those of Salvador Dali.

What strange force possesses these innocent-looking girls and has the potential to turn them into screaming animals? Well, my bet is that it has something to do with the libido, but I'm just guessing. The constant sexual imagery, side by side with all the very prim demeanors and high collars, creates a sensuality and tension that Weir maintains with something very like a master's touch. Don't make the mistake of turning the VCR off once the credits start rolling; this is one picture it pays to watch *all the way to the bitter end.* Trust me.

★ 1975, 110 minutes, color, PG.

★ With: Rachel Roberts, Dominic Guard, Helen Morse. Director: Peter Weir.

★ *What Oscar-nominated film starring Robin Williams did Weir direct?* (Answer on page 79.)

Pillow Talk

Doris Day and Rock Hudson give phone sex a good name.

A frothy, fast-paced vehicle for Rock Hudson and Doris Day that stands out as their strongest collaboration. The two share a party line and (guess what?) can't stand each other.

Day is a modern, hardworking single woman with no intention whatsoever of getting married; Hudson is a hard-living playboy songwriter who seems to be singing the same love song to a new woman every time Day picks up the line. Day happens to be decorating the apartment of the big backer of Hudson's new Broadway show (Tony Randall, who is hilarious). Both Randall and Hudson fall for Doris.

Knowing that Day would never fall for the next-door neighbor she despises, Hudson tries an elaborate subterfuge based on assuming a swaggering Texas persona, but that backfires when Randall finds out what he's up to. Things get pretty complicated, and Day, who also gets wise to Hudson's evil ploys, decides to have her revenge by doing up his bachelor pad in Early Hideous Purple Bordello. I don't want to ruin anything for you, but let's just say that true love finds a way to conquer all.

★ 1959, 105 minutes, color, not rated.

★ With: Doris Day, Rock Hudson, Tony Randall, Thelma Ritter. Director: Michael Gordon.

★ *Why was the film a personal landmark for Doris Day?*
(Answer on page 184.)

"I don't have any bedroom problems. There's nothing in my bedroom that bothers me."
—Perhaps Doris Day doth protest too much.

For a great double feature, rent it with
The Goodbye Girl.

Seen it but in the mood for something similar? Try
Send Me No Flowers.

Answer to page 27 trivia question:
"Oxis on the conoxis." Indisposed as he was, Fields did not appear that evening.

Comedy

The Pirate

Gene Kelly in shorts.
'Nuff said.

"Why, if he saw a
woman he wanted,
he'd just come and
take her and carry her
off on his ship—but
he'd treat her like a
queen!"

—Judy Garland gets swept up
in the reverie.

**For a great double
feature, rent it with**

Captain Blood.

**Seen it but in the mood
for something similar?
Try**

Summer Stock.

**Answer to page 61
trivia question:**

17.

Yes, that's really Gene Kelly walking the tightrope above the town square. Kelly prided himself on doing his own stunts—and he horrified studio executives by insisting on at least one bona fide acrobatic move in every one of his pictures.

This film flopped, but *not* because it's bad. It made some theatrical in-jokes that may have gone over the heads of its intended audience.

Did you really *want* a plot summary of a classic MGM musical? OK, it's set in the Caribbean, there's this guy named Don Pedro who thinks he's going to marry Judy Garland even though Kelly's the lead (dream on), and there's a wild production number with flames and ropes and sails and really tight shorts. And Judy sings "Mack the Black" and (with Kelly) "Be a Clown." Have fun.

★ 1948, 101 minutes, color, not rated.

★ With: Gene Kelly, Judy Garland, Walter Slezak. Director: Vincente Minnelli.

★ *Who wrote the score?* (Answer on page 313.)

Musical

Play It Again, Sam

Bogey is virile; Woody—well, let's just say he makes an effort.

You expect tons of movie references from a Woody Allen script, and sure enough, in this one, adapted from the Bespectacled One's Broadway hit, the allusions come at you thick and fast: subtle (and not-so-subtle) references to *The Seven Year Itch, A Star Is Born,* and *Across the Pacific* fly past. But the heart of the movie is, of course, Allen's ongoing dialogue on the war between the sexes with *Casablanca*'s Rick Blaine (played by Jerry Lacy, a ringer for Humphrey Bogart).

Allen plays a lonely nebbish who falls in love with the woman trying to set him up with dates: Diane Keaton, wife of the proto-yuppie Tony Roberts. (Oh, the hell people went through before cellular phones.) After each of Allen's disastrous blind dates Keaton is there to cheer him up. Soon they find themselves comparing prescriptions and theorizing about what True Love might look like if they ever were to come across it. The neat ending deftly parallels Bogey's unforgettable airstrip farewell to Bergman.

The film, based on his own play but directed by Herbert Ross, is a good example of Allen's early slapstick style. Allen's fixation on relationships in general and on Keaton in particular foreshadows greater things to come, in *Annie Hall.*

★ 1972, 87 minutes, color, PG.

★ With: Woody Allen, Diane Keaton, Tony Roberts. Director: Herbert Ross.

★ *This is one of the rare Allen films not shot in New York City. Why?* (Answer on page 57.)

"Dames are simple; I never met one that didn't understand a slap in the mouth or a slug from a .45."
—Bogey takes the direct approach in explaining women to Woody Allen.

For a great double feature, rent it with
Casablanca (what else?).

Seen it but in the mood for something similar? Try
The Purple Rose of Cairo.

Answer to page 95 trivia question:
His cowboy hat; he wore the same one in each western he appeared in.

Comedy

The Playboys

Sounds like the name of a bad rock group,
doesn't it? Read on.

"It's a lucky woman
that catches a
dreamer."
—Aidan Quinn thinks he's
quite a catch.

For a great double feature, rent it with

The Snapper.

Seen it but in the mood for something similar? Try

Love with the Proper Stranger.

Answer to page 130 trivia question:

The Muppet Christmas Carol; everyone else was a Muppet.

No, it's not a *Commitments* rip-off. Robin Wright, better known these days for her work in *Forrest Gump,* shines in this melancholy portrait of a woman who refuses to submit to the narrow-minded social constraints of a rural Irish village in the 1950s. The stigma of single motherhood, explored to deeply satisfying comic effect in *The Snapper,* here takes on tragic overtones in an Ireland of a few decades earlier.

The film features some magnificent sequences of traveling actors who make their living by barnstorming through the provinces; one of them, Aidan Quinn, is Wright's key to sanity in an impossible situation.

The picture features standout performances from Wright, Quinn, and Albert Finney as the menacing police sergeant. Parts of the story are based on actual events from the childhood of coscreenwriter Shane Connaughton; the dreamy, dark feel of the movie strangely complements its appealing romantic elements.

The Playboys is both a love story and an intriguing examination of the danger faced by people whose only crime is not quite fitting into the boxes designed for them by others.

★ 1992, 113 minutes, color, PG-13.

★ With: Albert Finney, Aidan Quinn, Robin Wright. Director: Gillies Mackennon.

★ *In what picture did Robin Wright win her first starring role?* (Answer on page 141.)

Prick Up Your Ears

Do you suppose there could be a double entendre at work in that title?

If British playwright Joe Orton *wasn't* an attitude-laden reincarnation of Oscar Wilde, then he was damn close. This engrossing, surefooted biopic is an in-your-face account of a man who lived an in-your-face life and wrote several decidedly in-your-face plays that are now recognized as comic masterpieces.

Gary Oldman is wonderful as the brilliant, sharp-tongued writer, but Alfred Molina's scary turn as his obsessive, less-gifted lover is what will keep you hooked. This is an unsentimental portrait of a gifted, anarchistic writer who stomped mightily, helping to bring about the first tremors of the social upheavals of the sixties; he tried to knock down nearly every social barrier he encountered and at the same time led a risky, cruel, and, ultimately destructive personal life. Sometimes, a joke *does* go too far.

★ 1987, 108 minutes, color, R.

★ With: Gary Oldman, Alfred Molina, Vanessa Redgrave. Director: Stephen Frears.

★ *What Orton play concludes with the presentation of a small object believed to be Winston Churchill's private parts?* (Answer on page 248.)

"I'm from the gutter, and don't you ever forget it, because I won't."
—Gary Oldman makes a point of remembering his roots.

For a great double feature, rent it with *Sid and Nancy.*

Seen it but in the mood for something similar? Try *The Picture of Dorian Gray.*

Answer to page 31 trivia question: A 12-ish Donald O'Connor.

Biography

Enjoy it.
A prime lasts only so long.

"My girls are the crème de la crème."

—Maggie Smith's girls may not be as lucky as she makes them out to be.

For a great double feature, rent it with

The Missionary.

Seen it but in the mood for something similar? Try

Dead Poets Society.

Answer to page 65 trivia question:

Nat King Cole.

Maggie Smith is a teacher who's less interested in formal academics than in inspiring her charges. She teaches in 1930s Edinburgh, at a private school for well-to-do girls. She's a bit of a crackpot, with a headful of sketchy political passions and a passionate love of the great, misunderstood artists of history. She's having an affair—for now, until it bores her, as she knows it will—with the art teacher (Robert Stephens). Then her plan is to marry Gordon Jackson, another teacher at the school. Jackson is her ace in the hole, so to speak.

This is a very funny film with an edge; Smith has a great deal of power over the girls in her charge, and she is quite insistent that, although society's rules need not always be followed, her example always should be. She's very modern, very forthright, and in some way correct. But all too often she is blinded by romantic notions, and she has a nasty habit of pigeonholing her girls into roles they're not prepared for. Sometimes it works. Sometimes it doesn't.

★ 1969, 116 minutes, color, PG.

★ With: Maggie Smith, Robert Stephens, Celia Johnson, Gordon Jackson. Director: Ronald Neame.

★ *What Neil Simon picture featured a role that won Smith an Oscar—as an actress who doesn't win an Oscar?* (Answer on page 301.)

The Princess and the Pirate

Who needs Bing?

D o I really have to tell you the plot of this one? Isn't it enough to say that this is one of Bob Hope's best pictures, that he's genuinely funny throughout, and that if you show this to the kids you'll probably both laugh more than you would if you watched *Aladdin* for the 40th time?

Filmed in lush Technicolor (still a cutting-edge innovation in 1944), with fabulous costumes and a great supporting cast, *The Princess and the Pirate* lets Virginia Mayo perform the honors as Hope's straight man, a role usually reserved for Bing Crosby. Victor McLaglen offers plenty of over-the-top-fun, and I dare you, no, I *double-*dare you, to find another pirate movie with Walter Brennan in it.

For those who must have a whiff of plot: Hope plays Sylvester the Great, a prevaudevillian impressionist; Mayo is the princess of the title, traveling incognito. The odd couple find themselves in search of buried treasure and get chased by scruffy pirates; a good time is had by all, including those who make surprise cameos. Don't ask how the treasure map gets tattooed to Hope's chest.

★ 1944, 94 minutes, color, not rated.

★ With: Bob Hope, Virginia Mayo, Walter Brennan, Victor McLaglen. Director: David Butler.

★ *How did the crew overcome the difficulty of making the food look real under the hot Technicolor lights?*
(Answer on page 325.)

"A skull and cross-bones! You know what that means?" "Yeah, iodine—and I have a feeling we're gonna need plenty."
—Bob Hope swoons as pirates loom.

For a great double feature, rent it with *Road to Bali.*

Seen it but in the mood for something similar? Try *Captain Blood.*

Answer to page 99 trivia question: Dabney Coleman.

Family

Prospero's Books

Shakespeare on acid.

"We are such stuff as dreams are made on."
—Gielgud delivers the famous line as though he were conducting his very own Magical Mystery Tour.

For a great double feature, rent it with

A Midsummer Night's Dream (1935).

Seen it but in the mood for something similar? Try

Forbidden Planet (another liberal adaptation of *The Tempest*).

Answer to page 135 trivia question:

He showed up in Jean-Luc Godard's 1987 version of *King Lear*.

H ere's a movie that's both difficult to keep up with and impossible to turn away from, a little like the journey into the "brave new world" described in *The Tempest,* its source text.

Although *Prospero's Books* features a magnificent, complex assault on the role of Prospero by Sir John Gielgud and is well worth renting on that account alone, don't imagine it's going to be a straight-ahead, by-the-numbers adaptation. This is a hypnotic display of visual inventiveness that demands to be watched on its own uncompromising terms.

Gielgud occupies the central position in this unceasing, hallucinatory pageant of detail; Sir John is spellbinding as he assumes the roles of storyteller, stage manager, author, and magician—all of which is fully in keeping with Shakespeare's story. But this daunting, lush production uses that story as a starting point; it takes the text of *The Tempest* apart and puts it back together again, and in the process it gives you the eerie sensation that you've gotten a little bit closer to both Gielgud at the twilight of his career and to Shakespeare at the twilight of his. If you're looking for a challenging, visually stunning experience, *Prospero's Books* is a great choice.

★ 1991, 129 minutes, color, R.

★ With: John Gielgud, Michael Clark, Isabelle Pasco, Michel Blanc. Director: Peter Greenaway.

★ *In what film did John Gielgud promise to "alert the media" regarding an impending bath?* (Answer on page 83.)

Pumping Iron

*Early Arnold.
Check out his neck.*

How many movie legends can you think of who turned a role in a *documentary* into the first step toward stardom? Arnold Schwarzenegger's electrifying appearance in this well-toned look at the world of top-tier bodybuilding hints at bigger things to come, but the picture offers much more of interest than retrospective pec peeks.

Pumping Iron shines a spotlight on a disciplined, lonely world populated by men who have made a major life commitment to the grueling routines of physical development. Oil, muscles, and mirrors are everywhere. Are these just big, lumpy guys with hearts of gold who like to show off? Or is there a deeper sense of mission here?

The contestants, a group that also includes future "Incredible Hulk" Lou Ferrigno, typically started out as average-bodied (or less-than-average-bodied) youngsters; personal commitment and extraordinary goal orientation seem to have played a critical role in their success. This, then, is a movie that looks at titanic physical *and* mental efforts; it's a fascinating ride, whether or not you consider yourself an Arnold devotee. The movie is based on the book of the same title; it gave rise to a sequel, *Pumping Iron II: The Women.*

★ 1977, 85 minutes, color, PG.

★ With: Arnold Schwarzenegger, Lou Ferrigno, Mike Katz. Director: George Butler.

★ *Name the two films Arnold Schwarzenegger made with Danny DeVito.* (Answer on page 24.)

"When he first saw Arnold, he wanted to be Mr. Olympia."
—Lou Ferrigno's father explains his son's early interest in the sport.

For a great double feature, rent it with
The Terminator.

Seen it but in the mood for something similar? Try
Pumping Iron II: The Women.

Answer to page 7 trivia question:
L.A. Story.

Documentary

Rachel, Rachel

A strange, intimate chemistry between star and director. How come?

"Is it that obvious that it's the first time for me?"

—Joanne Woodward isn't fooling anybody.

For a great double feature, rent it with

Mr. & Mrs Bridge.

Seen it but in the mood for something similar? Try

Shirley Valentine.

Answer to page 41 trivia question:

Never Say Never Again.

Never mind what John Mellencamp has to say about the matter; if you don't quite fit in, life in a small town can drive you off the deep end. Joanne Woodward turns in yet another exquisite performance in this picture, the first directed by Paul Newman.

Woodward plays an unmarried schoolteacher who must decide whether she will ever demand more from her life, which so far has been marked by loneliness, work, more loneliness, more work, and, oh yes, the looming presence of her mother. The picture explores an unattached woman's attempts to come to terms with her sexual and emotional yearnings; that's not a groundbreaking theme these days, but it sure was in 1968.

Rachel, Rachel, however, is not a period piece. It's a striking example of a great actress at the top of her game. The supporting cast, which features James Olson as Woodward's brief love interest and Estelle Parsons as her colleague, is marvelous. Rent it if you've got a thing for performances that should have won Oscars but didn't; that's the category Woodward's work here falls into.

★ 1968, 101 minutes, color, R.

★ With: Joanne Woodward, James Olson, Estelle Parsons. Director: Paul Newman.

★ *For what picture did Woodward win an Academy Award as Best Actress?* (Answer on page 147.)

Ragtime

It was the best of times, it was the worst of times.

E. L. Doctorow's smash-hit novel had 15 zillion plotlines; Milos Forman made the wise choice of spending most of his screen time on one of them, that of Howard Rollins's quixotic effort to win justice after being treated spitefully by a passel of redneck firefighters. (The firemen have a problem with the idea that a black man might be able to afford a nice car.) Forman does a wonderful job of exploring the grim perils of racially arranged hierarchies and of tracing the unpredictable effects people can have on one another's lives without meaning to.

The picture features inspired acting work from Rollins and Elizabeth McGovern and a bevy of unexpectedly charming walk-ons by such notables as Norman Mailer (no, really, Norman Mailer) and James Cagney. But don't rent it just because it's Cagney's last film; he shows up for a few scenes, looks tired (which he was), and plays himself. That's all you'd expect, and Cagney's scenes are unobjectionable enough, but the legendary actor's occasionally strained work is by no means the most interesting thing in this superb adaptation of Doctorow's page-turner.

★ 1981, 155 minutes, color, PG.

★ With: James Cagney, Elizabeth McGovern, Howard E. Rollins, Jr. Director: Milos Forman.

★ *What Milos Forman film was the first since* It Happened One Night *to sweep all the major Academy Awards?* (Answer on page 297.)

"That library over there is worth millions, and people keep telling me you're a piece of . . . "
—Howard Rollins may or may not be able to be talked out of an explosive situation.

For a great double feature, rent it with
The Last Hurrah.

Seen it but in the mood for something similar? Try
Hester Street.

Answer to page 75 trivia question:
Ringo.

Drama

The Rainmaker

Hepburn's been looking for a beau, but the well's run dry.

"You're so full of what's right, you can't see what's good."

—Lloyd Bridges's dad tries to set his son's priorities straight.

For a great double feature, rent it with

The African Queen.

Seen it but in the mood for something similar? Try

His Majesty O'Keefe.

Answer to page 109 trivia question:

She's pretty hard to miss, isn't she?

There's a drought here, and it doesn't take a genius to figure out the metaphor. When handsome, smooth-talking Burt Lancaster saunters into town with promises of rain, we know that, one way or another, there's gonna be some kind of cloudburst.

Hepburn plays her part as more tomboy than spinster, which is wise. I don't think anyone would buy someone with as much charm as Katharine Hepburn as anything but a great catch. Lancaster plays his part with bravado and a near-acrobatic flair—as if he's in a musical and everyone else is just in a western. You can see the others in the town looking at him as if he's a true oddball, but before long they're hypnotized by his magnetic charm. So's Katharine . . . but will she end up with him?

I know how I would have played it if I'd been in her place. But then I've always been a sucker for poets.

★ 1956, 121 minutes, color, not rated.

★ With: Katharine Hepburn, Burt Lancaster, Lloyd Bridges. Director: Joseph Anthony.

★ *Lloyd Bridges has two actor sons. Can you name them—and the only film they starred in together?* (Answer on page 244.)

A Raisin in the Sun

You want to live where?

Relax; it's not a civics lesson. This gripping movie adaptation of Lorraine Hansberry's landmark play focuses on an African-American family's struggle to escape from life in a tiny apartment and enter an all-white neighborhood. Its story of intergenerational struggle and the crippling effects of racism is "important" in the sense that it should certainly be seen and remembered by anyone trying to make sense of racial issues, but it's not preachy. Hansberry's extraordinary play succeeded on Broadway because it was an undeniably *human* drama first and foremost. The family is falling apart, and Claudia McNeil simply isn't going to put up with that. The film version, for which Hansberry supplied the screenplay, is just as effective as the stage play, and it boasts monumental performances from McNeil and Sidney Poitier. Danny Glover starred in an equally praiseworthy 1988 remake.

★ 1961, 128 minutes, B&W, not rated.

★ With: Sidney Poitier, Claudia McNeil, Louis Gossett. Director: Daniel Petrie.

★ *What poet wrote the line that is quoted in the film's title?* (Answer on page 151.)

"In my mother's house, there is still a God."
—Claudia McNeil wants it understood that there are certain standards that are not to be compromised.

For a great double feature, rent it with *Lilies of the Field.*

Seen it but in the mood for something similar? Try *A Raisin in the Sun* (1988).

Answer to page 145 trivia question: John Gilbert.

Ran

Domo arigato, Will-san.

"The moment has come to stable the steeds of war and give free rein to peace."

—Tatsuya Nakadai gathers the boys together for a little talk.

For a great double feature, rent it with

The Field.

Seen it but in the mood for something similar? Try

King Lear (1984).

Answer to page 181 trivia question:

It's a Mad, Mad, Mad, Mad World.

This Kurosawa masterpiece, adapted from Shakespeare's *King Lear,* follows the decline of a medieval Japanese warlord. It contains some of the most magnificent battle scenes ever filmed, but this epic, like the play it follows, is essentially a family tragedy.

Kurosawa's account benefits from the stately pace and unforgettable emblems of Noh theater. He makes you forget the tale was ever anything other than Japanese, yet the picture remains accessible throughout for Western audiences.

Tatsuya Nakadai, who plays the old misguided lord, wanders through desolate, ruined fields of war, but he winds up there because the closeted rooms of his palace were the backdrops of betrayal and personal intrigue. Both worlds are dangerously mismanaged; both are rendered with exquisite skill by Kurosawa.

The master filmmaker (75 at the time this film was made) planned *Ran* for 10 years and on a vast enough scale to make him doubt that the picture would ever be produced. Fortunately he was mistaken; he was able to bring this staggering vision of family and social collapse to the screen without cutting any corners. A crowning achievement from one of the world's greatest filmmakers.

★ 1985, 161 minutes, color, R.

★ With: Tatsuya Nakadai, Akira Terao, Mieko Harada. Director: Akira Kurosawa.

★ *What Kurosawa epic is set in Siberia?* (Answer on page 87.)

Random Harvest

Do I know you?

This is the film that won worldwide attention for Greer Garson. But I'm going to level with you. It wasn't just her acting that did the job. That very, very short kilt she wears in her role as the vaudeville performer with the heart of gold helped, too.

After entertaining the troops during World War I, Garson spots a lost soul (Ronald Colman) and falls head over heels for him. He's sweet, handsome, sort of helpless, and very vague about his past. They get married, of course, and for a short time they enjoy a perfect life together. Everything's just ducky—that is, until Colman heads out to buy Garson a gift and gets hit on the head (for the second time, apparently), remembers who he really is, and forgets all about his new life with Garson, darn it.

In his new life . . . I mean his old life . . . it turns out that Colman is a nobleman held in high esteem—and quite rich. Soon he has a new fiancée and is starting a career in politics. But he keeps getting that feeling that he's forgotten something. No, not his keys. Not his wallet. Yes, he turned off the iron. What could it be? Maybe that new redheaded secretary who looks so strangely familiar will help him remember.

★ 1942, 126 minutes, B&W, not rated.

★ With: Ronald Colman, Greer Garson, Susan Peters. Director: Mervyn LeRoy.

★ *What film introduced Greer Garson to American audiences?* (Answer on page 41.)

"Smithy, do I always have to take the initiative? You're supposed to kiss me."
—Ronald Colman has a forgetful side.

For a great double feature, rent it with
The Enchanted Cottage.

Seen it but in the mood for something similar? Try
A Tale of Two Cities (1935).

Answer to page 216 trivia question:
Tea and Sympathy.

Comedy

Real Men

What if everything you read in the Weekly World News *were (gulp) true?*

"It's a thrill, isn't it? You never forget the first time you save the world."

—James Belushi looks at the up side of being a secret agent.

For a great double feature, rent it with

The Blues Brothers.

Seen it but in the mood for something similar? Try

To Catch a Spy.

Answer to page 251 trivia question:

The title role in *The Elephant Man.*

Successfully spoofing the spy thriller genre is a tricky undertaking. Many of the most popular films in the category rely on a tongue-in-cheek, we-don't-really-expect-you-to-buy-this delivery to hold the audience between explosions. (Some of the pictures in the James Bond series come to mind.) If your aim is to get big-time laughs from start to finish in the espionage genre, one good way to do it would be to go *all* the way—and I do mean *all* the way—over the top. In that respect *Real Men* is a resounding success.

The earth is being invaded by aliens; Jim Belushi has to recruit John Ritter, a meek civilian who's a dead ringer for an agent who died at the hands of a rival spy faction. Belushi's got to turn Ritter into a topflight agent whether he likes it or not because (all together now) the fate of the world hangs in the balance.

A profoundly weird little comedy that never takes itself seriously, *Real Men* succeeds where something along the lines of *Spies Like Us* fails. It dares to be ridiculous. You probably won't be surprised to learn that Belushi holds his own here, but those who think of John Ritter as a sitcom actor will be pleasantly surprised at the comic range he displays in this film.

★ 1987, 86 minutes, color, PG-13.

★ With: James Belushi, John Ritter, Bill Morey, Barbara Barrie. Director: Dennis Feldman.

★ *What critically acclaimed television comedy starred John Ritter? Hint: It was bimbo-free.* (Answer on page 11.)

Comedy

Requiem for a Heavyweight

The mighty Quinn.

long, long, time ago, the movies that originated from television shows were based not on instantly recognizable "franchise" characters but on single-episode *stories* from the days of live broadcasting, stories that were strong enough to stand on their own as feature films. The Oscar-winning *Marty* is probably the most famous example of this teleplay-to-screenplay transition, but I've always been of the opinion that *Requiem for a Heavyweight,* which has a similar pedigree, is the better movie.

Originally a live "Playhouse 90" production starring Jack Palance, the script, adapted for the screen, provided Anthony Quinn with the opportunity for an unforgettable performance. Quinn plays a fighter whose ring days are over; he tries in vain to find a dignified place in a decidedly unfriendly postboxing world. He's given everything to a system that still doesn't quite make sense to him, and now he has nothing to show for it.

Although the corrupt world *Requiem for a Heavyweight* spotlights isn't a very attractive one, its telling observations about systems that eat men alive still pack quite a punch. Quinn is magnificent; there's some great supporting work, too.

★ 1962, 100 minutes, B&W, not rated.

★ With: Anthony Quinn, Jackie Gleason, Mickey Rooney. Director: Ralph Nelson.

★ *Who wrote the original "Playhouse 90" teleplay?*
(Answer on page 1.)

"You owe me."
—Anthony Quinn could, in fact, have been a contender.

For a great double feature, rent it with *Raging Bull.*

Seen it but in the mood for something similar? Try *Rocky* (but not one of the sequels!).

Answer to page 314 trivia question: *The Sting.*

Drama

285

The Return of the Secaucus Seven

Low-budget group hug delivers big-time.

John Sayles's extraordinary study of the reunion of a bunch of Vietnam War protesters scores some serious points with its reveries for a lost counterculture. Its arias on the necessity of finding purpose in life without losing sight of the whole idealistic sixties thing are on a par with, if not superior to, those in *The Big Chill,* released three years later.

Granted, Sayles's picture looks a little rough in places—its total shooting budget wouldn't have covered what *Chill* spent on song royalties for the soundtrack—but it's a classic example of how talent, drive, inventiveness, and commitment can deliver moviemaking that stops you dead in your tracks, even if you don't have, you know, a budget.

It would be nice to say that the unknowns who turn in such fine acting work in this picture went on to mainstream stardom, but such is not the case. Sayles, however, went on to direct such fine films as *Matewan* and *Eight Men Out.*

★ 1980, 106 minutes, color, R.

★ With: Mark Arnott, Gordon Clapp, Maggie Cousineau, Adam Lefevre, Bruce MacDonald, Jean Passanante. Director: John Sayles.

★ *Name the film in which John Sayles cast Daryl Hannah as the ugliest lady around.* (Answer on page 29.)

Drama

Reuben, Reuben

Hello, rewrite? Can you help me out with, um, my life?

Tom Conti is bewildered, frequently inebriated, witty in a consistently nasty way, and seemingly incapable of dealing with people in anything resembling a mature fashion. Could he be . . . a *writer?* Bingo, and welcome to the bonus round.

Movies about artists and writers often focus on these creative folks' inability to communicate effectively in any nonartistic medium; Conti's even a step beyond this sorry state, because his best days as a poet are apparently behind him. He's doing his worn-out literary two-step in front of an ever-changing group of undergraduates. Fortunately, lovely young Kelly McGillis (in her film debut) is in one of the audiences he condescends to, and he falls in love with her.

This is a quirky, literate little comedy that suggests that even seemingly washed-up, pretentious writers can win a second chance at happiness. If that's not an optimistic premise, I don't know what is.

★ 1983, 101 minutes, color, R.

★ With: Tom Conti, Kelly McGillis. Director: Robert Ellis Miller.

★ *The picture was inspired by the works of what gifted humorist?* (Answer on page 69.)

"There are no trashy writers, only trashy readers."
—Tom Conti knows where the blame really lies.

For a great double feature, rent it with
Rachel, Rachel. (Sorry, couldn't resist.)

Seen it but in the mood for something similar? Try
American Dreamer.

Answer to page 302 trivia question:
As Mrs. Livingston in "The Courtship of Eddie's Father."

Comedy

287

Richard Pryor—Live in Concert

The one and only.

Forget the accidents, the personal crises, the headlines, and the unfortunate self-indulgent biopic; forget the many, many comedians who followed in Richard Pryor's footsteps and didn't give him anything like the credit he deserved. When Pryor was at the top of his game, he was simply untouchable.

Any who doubt his status as a comedian of the very first order are advised to spend an evening with this hilarious concert movie. This is his first, and best, live-performance film. It's remarkable not so much for the shock value of its routines—later, less talented comics would shatter more boundaries and get less accomplished—but for its unrelenting originality.

All alone on stage, Pryor mounts superb multicharacter sketches involving amorous monkeys, sadistic relatives, muggers, and stuttering Asians. His skills have never served him better than they do here. (The movie will serve as a reminder that Pryor, at his peak, was a superb physical comedian.)

★ 1979, 78 minutes, color, R.

★ With: Richard Pryor. Director: Jeff Margolis.

★ *What did* NBC *censors change about "Saturday Night Live" when Pryor first appeared on the show?* (Answer on page 100.)

Road to Bali

A sarong in their hearts.

My personal favorite of all the Hope-Crosby road pictures, primarily because it's the heaviest on the celebrity cameos. Bob and Bing, out-of-work vaudeville performers, follow a job lead all the way to the South Seas, where they both become enamored of the lovely Dorothy Lamour.

Sound familiar? Sure it does. Go with the flow. In a series of dreamily exotic tropical locales that look suspiciously like stock footage and back lot sets, the two tell jokes that make you laugh or groan, do a few dance numbers in which enthusiasm shines more brightly than pinpoint choreography, and generally refuse to take anything seriously. You never want them to stop.

Of the seven road pictures Hope and Crosby teamed up for, there are a couple of less-than-inspired efforts and even the odd turkey. (Witness the regrettable 1962 trip to Hong Kong.) With this series you quickly get the feeling that you're going to have fun only when the stars do. In *Road to Bali*, everyone, including the audience, has a great time. By the way, any guesses as to who winds up with the girl?

★ 1952, 90 minutes, color, not rated.

★ With: Bob Hope, Bing Crosby, Dorothy Lamour. Director: Hal Walker.

★ *In how many films did Bing Crosby receive top billing?*
  (Answer on page 307.)

"They're not going to torture me—it hurts!"
—Nothing much gets past Bob Hope.

For a great double feature, rent it with
Hollywood or Bust.

Seen it but in the mood for something similar? Try
Road to Zanzibar.

Answer to page 358 trivia question:
Public Enemy.

Family

Rope

Knot to be missed.

"*Murder is, or should
be, an art. And as
such, the privilege of
committing it should
be reserved for those
few who are really
superior individuals.*"

—James Stewart comes to an
ominous conclusion.

**For a great double
feature, rent it with**
Rear Window.

**Seen it but in the mood
for something similar?
Try**
Lifeboat.

**Answer to page 155
trivia question:**
Ishtar.

This film was an experiment for Alfred Hitchcock. He wanted to film a movie using only one set and no jumps in time—which meant, given the technology of the day, a series of uninterrupted 10-minute takes. In other words, Hitch kept the feel—and the intensity—of the original play, which was based loosely on the Leopold and Loeb murder case.

We follow the relentless, tautly delineated story as though we were somehow in on the murder . . . and of course, we are, because we know where the body is hidden. We even catch ourselves, just for a moment, hoping that no one will open the chest in which the body has been concealed. And we wince when John Dall hands the victim's father some books that have been tied with the very rope that served as the murder weapon.

Listen closely to the dialogue in the dark that follows the killing. Could any of these lines have been intended as double entendres?

★ 1948, 80 minutes, color, not rated.

★ With: Farley Granger, John Dall, James Stewart.
  Director: Alfred Hitchcock.

★ *Where's Hitch?* (Answer on page 238.)

Rosencrantz and Guildenstern Are Dead

Two for the road.

Another unlikely success, a play that producers had no doubt been betting for years would never become a film. This screen adaptation of Tom Stoppard's intellectually stimulating comic parody of Shakespeare's *Hamlet* manages to take a dense thicket of ideas and make them cinematically interesting, thanks to a series of inspired visual gags involving famous physics experiments. (Trust me. It works.)

The piece is basically a high-octane updating of Samuel Beckett's *Waiting for Godot,* with lots of cool Shakespeare gags thrown in. The two title characters are minor functionaries in *Hamlet,* frequently confused with one another for centuries by readers and theatergoers, who die more or less pointlessly about two-thirds of the way through Shakespeare's play. Their complete inability to take control of their situation makes up much of the evening's entertainment.

Wickedly funny, but with an edge; *R&G* shows off two lost souls who face a fate many in the modern world will find disconcertingly familiar: being stuck somewhere that makes no sense and not being able to do a thing about it.

★ 1990, 118 minutes, color, PG.

★ With: Gary Oldman, Tim Roth, Richard Dreyfuss. Director: Tom Stoppard.

★ *What futuristic Terry Gilliam comedy did Tom Stoppard help write?* (Answer on page 170.)

"We're actors. We're the opposite of people."
—Richard Dreyfuss seems to call his own existence into question. Tough day at work?

For a great double feature, rent it with
Hamlet (1990).

Seen it but in the mood for something similar? Try
Bagdad Cafe.

Answer to page 190 trivia question:
That Hagen Girl.

Comedy

Ruggles of Red Gap

*Betcha can't watch it
just once.*

"Ah—indubitably."
*"Oh, you speak French
so beautifully!"*
—Mary Boland may want to
consider taking a Berlitz
course.

**For a great double
feature, rent it with**

Rustlers' Rhapsody.

**Seen it but in the mood
for something similar?
Try**

The Canterville Ghost.

**Answer to page 226
trivia question:**

We'll never know; they
both had affairs with
her at, um, roughly the
same time.

As Marmaduke Ruggles, Charles Laughton is the kind of devoted manservant who maintains his composure even when informed by his employer that he, Ruggles, has been lost in a poker game to a frontier-loving American couple. With hardly a murmur Ruggles is off to Washington state to serve his new employers, who aren't exactly models of English propriety but who do know a thing or two about American-style audacity.

Even after a series of unexpected misadventures that test both his poise and his drinking ability, the butler's freewheeling employers teach him that his new country offers something important that England did not: a chance to escape the rigid bonds of a suffocating class system. Much to his surprise, the new country offers the opportunity to open one's own business (the Anglo-American Grill), fall in love with someone other than a servant, and be appreciated for one's own merits.

For his part, Ruggles brings some much-needed gentility to the rough-and-tumble town of Red Gap. A very trim Laughton is hilarious throughout in this fast-paced comedy classic—if you like the Marx Brothers tempo, you'll have a good time here.

★ 1935, 92 minutes, B&W, not rated.

★ With: Charles Laughton, Mary Boland, Charlie Ruggles. Director: Leo McCarey.

★ *For what film did Laughton win an Academy Award as Best Actor?* (Answer on page 66.)

Running Scared (1986)

Eddie who?

etter than *Beverly Hills Cop* (its obvious model), this sparkling little action picture features nonstop wisecracking from Billy Crystal and a nifty performance from Gregory Hines that proves he's quite capable of holding down his side of the screen without donning a pair of tap shoes.

Like Danny Glover in the *Lethal Weapon* movies, Crystal and Hines have decided they're getting too old for this . . . stuff. They want to retire, move to Florida, and open a bar together; when duty calls for one more assignment, they find themselves a little more concerned for their own personal safety than they were a few years back. The two exhibit the perfect personal chemistry crucial to any undertaking like this; if they weren't so good at filling in each other's blind spots, you'd start thinking too much about the plot, which is serviceable but nothing spectacular.

Running Scared features a pre–"L.A. Law" Jimmy Smits as one of the bad guys, loads of chase scenes, and a cool locale: gritty, dirty, snow-blown Chicago. Not to be confused with the Kennedy-era espionage picture of the same name starring Judge Reinhold.

★ 1986, 107 minutes, color, R.

★ With: Billy Crystal, Gregory Hines, Steven Bauer. Director: Peter Hyams.

★ *What is the correct answer to the "Jeopardy" question, supplied on the phone by Billy Crystal?* (Answer on page 18.)

"Hi, we're from Noisebusters. Do you know where the Menudo concert is being held?"

—Billy Crystal is eager to get to where the action is.

For a great double feature, rent it with
White Nights.

Seen it but in the mood for something similar? Try
Red Heat.

Answer to page 262 trivia question:
Blazing Saddles.

Action

The Russians Are Coming! The Russians Are Coming!

Guess who's coming to dinner?

"You help us get boat quickly; otherwise there is World War Three and everybody is blaming you!"
—Alan Arkin takes the subtle approach in enlisting help from the locals.

For a great double feature, rent it with

The Trouble with Harry.

Seen it but in the mood for something similar? Try

It's a Mad, Mad, Mad, Mad World.

Answer to page 171 trivia question:

Hearts of the West.

One of the most engaging fish-out-of-water comedies of the sixties features Alan Arkin as a Russian submariner whose vessel has gone off course and run aground at Gloucester Island, Massachusetts. In search of a boat that will get him off the island and prevent an international incident, Arkin stares, fumes, and slinks his way around the island. He and his men scare the dickens out of the locals, but the only assault Arkin launches is against the English language, and it's great fun to watch. So is the populace's frenzied preparation for the first battle of the impending war.

A well-paced, consistently goofy examination of cold war paranoia, this film probably would have been impossible to make only a few years earlier; I guess Stanley Kubrick loosened things up a bit with *Dr. Strangelove.* Arkin's intense Soviet sailor is hilarious; so is Jonathan Winters, who here offers a memorably overwrought deputy struggling to get organized for the big invasion. It's Barney Fife's worst nightmare come to life.

★ 1966, 126 minutes, color, not rated.

★ With: Alan Arkin, Carl Reiner, Jonathan Winters, Eva Marie Saint, Brian Keith. Director: Norman Jewison.

★ *What actor did Carl Reiner cast as the lead in the pilot for the show that became "The Dick Van Dyke Show"?*
(Answer on page 35.)

Comedy

Rustlers' Rhapsody

What if there was a western that knew it was a western?

Warning: If the great American cowboy movie isn't your cup of tea, this film probably won't be either; if, on the other hand, you know and love the various traditions of the genre, *Rustlers' Rhapsody* is essential viewing.

Tom Berenger shines in this crafty send-up of the B movies of the thirties and forties. The deliciously self-conscious script juxtaposes stereotypes from the naive early days of the genre with those of westerns of later eras.

Imagine Mel Brooks taking on the same material he did in *Blazing Saddles* but deciding to take the high road on every single gag; you don't get the jokes about the gastronomic effects of baked beans, but you do get to watch the white-clad hero patiently explain to an admiring, well-proportioned young lady that he never gets intimate with women because gentlemen simply don't behave that way. Toss in Andy Griffith as the bad guy, and you're in for a lot of good-natured myth puncturing.

★ 1985, 88 minutes, color, PG.

★ With: Tom Berenger, G. W. Bailey, Marilu Henner, Andy Griffith. Director: Hugh Wilson.

★ *In what 1956 film did ultimate cowboy John Wayne and Susan Hayward find themselves exposed to real-life radiation during the shoot?* (Answer on page 108.)

"In the sixties, they started making these spaghetti westerns; I was always jealous of these guys, because they had better background music than we did."

—An unseen narrator complains that the grass is always greener on the other side of the barbed wire.

For a great double feature, rent it with
This Is Spinal Tap.

Seen it but in the mood for something similar? Try
Young Frankenstein.

Answer to page 205 trivia question:
U.S. senator.

Comedy

The Rutles (also known as All You Need Is Cash)

*Watch it backward; they're all saying
Eric Idle is dead.*

"We were stunned."
"Yeah. Stunned."
—Stunned, the lads react to
their manager's sudden
departure from the scene.

**For a great double
feature, rent it with**
The Compleat Beatles.

**Seen it but in the mood
for something similar?
Try**
This Is Spinal Tap.

**Answer to page 241
trivia question:**
Dynamite Hands and
*Baxter's Beauties of
1933.*

I f you liked *This Is Spinal Tap,* you'll get a kick out of
this hilarious, carefully conceived parody of the career
of the Beatles. Monty Python veteran Eric Idle is the
McCartney stand-in (watch him execute the vintage
1964 head bob perfectly), and the rest of the lads from
Rutland follow his confident lead in recounting the
unlikely success of this "legend that will last a lunchtime"
known as the "Prefab Four."

Funny, and surprisingly listenable, parodies of
famous Beatles songs show up every few minutes, and
meticulously assembled re-creations of famous photos
and film clips materialize even more frequently than that.
The piece also boasts plenty of appearances from real-life
superstar rockers willing to go along with the gag. Anyone
who loved the music (and let's face it, that's everyone)
will find plenty to laugh at; serious Beatlemaniacs will
demand repeat viewings to catch all the inside references.

Originally a television special, it got mystifyingly poor
ratings but eventually began to attract a cult following on
video. A heavily disguised George Harrison shows up for
a brief cameo. See if you can spot him.

★ 1978, 70 minutes, color, not rated.

★ With: Eric Idle, Neil Innes, Rikki Fataar.
Directors: Eric Idle, Gary Weis.

★ *What is the name of the McCartney-like Rutle played
by Eric Idle?* (Answer on page 167.)

Saboteur

When in trouble,
ask the bearded lady for help.

This neglected Hitchcock picture was made on a strict budget (thanks to the war), and Hitch had to cut back in a few areas so that he could include the truly remarkable special effects that he knew had to remain in the picture. Now consider, in that light, the casting of Robert Cummings. He's not Robert Donat (the star of *The 39 Steps,* which this film resembles), but he does, in my opinion, help transform the picture into a distinctly American treatment of a classic Hitchcock theme: the wrong man being victimized by circumstances beyond his control. You can't get much more all-American than Cummings, unless perhaps Ronald Reagan isn't doing anything at the time.

Priscilla Lane is fine as the easily manipulated heroine. And about those special effects Hitch was saving up for—they're doozies! There may be nothing more satisfying than seeing a fascist spy fall to his death from the arms of the Statue of Liberty.

A funny, offbeat Hitchcock entry that carries all the irony and thrills you've come to count on. Not to be confused with Hitchcock's *Sabotage* (1936).

★ 1942, 108 minutes, B&W, not rated.

★ With: Robert Cummings, Priscilla Lane, Norman Lloyd. Director: Alfred Hitchcock.

★ *What hospital TV series did Norman Lloyd appear in?*
(Answer on page 341.)

"Isn't there anyone we can trust?" "Yeah, all of them. Only which one?"
—Robert Cummings is a little paranoid, but can you blame him?

For a great double feature, rent it with
The 39 Steps.

Seen it but in the mood for something similar? Try
North by Northwest.

Answer to page 279 trivia question:
One Flew Over the Cuckoo's Nest.

Suspense

Sabrina (1954)

Somebody's first love, somebody else's last chance.

"Sabrina, darling,
where have you been
all my life?" "Right
over the garage."

—Audrey Hepburn may not
have been under William
Holden's nose, but she was
certainly in the neighborhood.

**For a great double
feature, rent it with**

Roman Holiday.

**Seen it but in the mood
for something similar?
Try**

Breakfast at Tiffany's.

**Answer to page 166
trivia question:**

A street light burned
out just before filming,
allowing Muni to
disappear into total
darkness.

At first glance Humphrey Bogart may seem terrifi-
cally miscast as the romantic lead in this comedy
about a chauffeur's daughter (Audrey Hepburn)
who gets just what she always wished for . . . and
suddenly realizes it's all wrong. But as usual, Bogart pulls
the part off.

As the picture opens, Hepburn's idealized dream man
is none other than Bogart's younger brother, played by
William Holden with his customary charm and suave-
ness. Holden seems to offer everything a young woman
could want in a man . . . at least that's what his three former wives thought. In fact, he's a cad. Bogey, the responsible one, initially sees Hepburn as little more than an
obstacle to his high-stakes business plans, but the chauffeur's daughter, who has come back from a Parisian cooking school as quite a dish herself, proves to him that
there's more to life than dollars and cents.

Sentimental and sweet, the film gets plenty of early
mileage out of our willingness to drool over the sophisticated, romantic personas of Hepburn and Holden; the
surprise comes toward the end, when Bogey convinces
you that he's capable of turning in a sensitive, sympa-
thetic portrayal of a man who may have just come across
his last chance for love.

★ 1954, 113 minutes, B&W, not rated.

★ With: Audrey Hepburn, Humphrey Bogart, William
Holden. Director: Billy Wilder.

★ *Name the only film in which William Holden wore a
sarong.* (Answer on page 360.)

Comedy

A Salute to Chuck Jones

It wasn't Einstein who reinvented Newtonian physics.
It was Chuck Jones.

This is the big one, friends. Some of the finest animation Hollywood ever produced is on display here, including the classic Daffy Duck entry, "Duck Dodgers in the 24½ Century" and the sublime "One Froggy Evening." Hilarious stuff; all the shorts are magnificent artistic achievements in their own right.

I'm not going to pretend all of this is going to be brand-new to you, but I will wager you'll relish the opportunity to see all this masterful work in crystal-clear, commercial-free format. Jones's timing is, of course, legendary; his routines are so good that it has been appropriated by professional comedians as home study material. Mel Blanc (vocals) and Carl Stallings (music) lend invaluable support to these masterpieces.

★ 1960, 56 minutes, color, not rated.

★ With: Daffy, Bugs, and the gang. Director: Chuck Jones.

★ *What director colleague of Chuck Jones in the Warner Brothers animation studio often found his own first name woven into many of the backdrops of Jones's cartoons?* (Answer on page 235.)

"You're making me very angry."
—Daffy may have met his match in the strange visitor from another planet.

For a great double feature, rent it with
A Salute to Friz Freleng.

Seen it but in the mood for something similar? Try
The Adventures of Rocky and Bullwinkle–Mona Moose.

Answer to page 200 trivia question:
All That Jazz.

It don't come easy.

"*We make a mistake, and some guy don't walk away. Forevermore, he don't walk away.*"

—John Wayne has a good reason for the high standards he expects his men to meet.

For a great double feature, rent it with

Bataan.

Seen it but in the mood for something similar? Try

They Were Expendable.

Answer to page 236 trivia question:

Cyrano de Bergerac.

This superb World War II picture won John Wayne an Oscar nomination. (He would have to wait 20 more years before he actually won an Academy Award, though. Maybe if he had put on an eye patch for *this* picture . . .) Wayne plays a tough Marine Corps sergeant whose young troops can't stand him—until they figure out that he's being hard-nosed only so he can bring as many people back alive as possible.

Wayne's chief problem, besides the Japanese, is John Agar, whose dad was Wayne's commanding officer. Agar, who detests military life, smells a little too much of his own old man in the Duke. Sparks fly—and, of course, shells do, too.

Although the picture is no antiwar tract (big surprise), it does have the honesty to admit that being a soldier can be a very frightening thing indeed. ("I'm always scared," Wayne admits in one striking moment.) The battle scenes are staged spectacularly and are combined with actual battle footage for an authentic feel. The screenplay won an Oscar.

★ 1949, 110 minutes, B&W, not rated.

★ With: John Wayne, John Agar, Forrest Tucker. Director: Allan Dwan.

★ *Who was John Agar's 17-year-old, real-life bride?* (Answer on page 105.)

Say Anything

The thinking person's teen movie.

Let's hear it for director Cameron Crowe, who here delivers a movie about teenagers that *isn't* a predictable coming-of-age story embellished with gratuitous scenes of getting laid and throwing up. *Say Anything* is—are you ready for this one?—about the *interior lives of the characters* and their struggles to make the right life choices for themselves and the ones they love. This movie gently reminds us that teenagers are people, too, that they make mistakes every once in a while, but that adults do, too.

John Cusack speaks with the simple, inscrutable voice of a Zen master; Ione Skye is a dream girl who comes off as completely three-dimensional. In yet another daring innovation for a teen film, she's got a brain in her head. Is Skye ready for Cusack, who is clearly the right guy for her? The gentle, wise script poses that simple question and keeps you hooked for the film's entire running time. A great couples movie.

★ 1989, 100 minutes, color, PG-13.

★ With: John Cusack, Ione Skye, John Mahoney. Director: Cameron Crowe.

★ *Name the hit song that is featured in the movie's soundtrack.* (Answer on page 164.)

"I'm looking for a dare-to-be-great situation."
—John Cusack thinks Ione Skye might just be the opportunity he's been looking for.

For a great double feature, rent it with
The Breakfast Club.

Seen it but in the mood for something similar? Try
Pretty in Pink.

Answer to page 274 trivia question:
California Suite.

Sayonara

Who would have guessed that Brando could be upstaged by Red Buttons?

"I believe that maybe you've forgotten what an American girl looks like."

—Marlon Brando tries to set Red Buttons straight.

For a great double feature, rent it with

Teahouse of the August Moon.

Seen it but in the mood for something similar? Try

A Patch of Blue.

Answer to page 152 trivia question:

Polyester was in "Odorama."

Marlon Brando had a lot to say about the making of *Sayonara*; tempered by the director's fear of losing the air force's cooperation in the making of this surprisingly daring story of interracial love, Brando chose to undercut his leading role by insisting on script changes that let him portray his character as a bigoted southerner. That upped the ambiguity level a bit, and the military people didn't squawk too much.

Brando comes to Japan to meet with his beautiful blond fiancée, the daughter of an important general. A fast-track career awaits him; Brando's got the air force system pretty much beaten—until he meets a beautiful Japanese actress, played by Miiko Taka. Her elegance and tranquil beauty soon convince Marlon to put his career ambitions on hold and settle in for a struggle with the air force bureaucracy over his illegal interracial love affair.

Red Buttons turns in a strong performance as Brando's subordinate; Brando must assist if Buttons is to marry the Japanese woman for whom *he* has fallen (Miyoshi Umeki). And the casting of Ricardo Montalban as a Japanese star of the Noh theater misfires, but never in anything other than an interesting way.

★ 1957, 147 minutes, color, not rated.

★ With: Marlon Brando, Red Buttons, Miiko Taka. Director: Joshua Logan.

★ *In what role did Miyoshi Umeki win U.S. television fame?* (Answer on page 287.)

The Secret Policeman's Other Ball

*Mad rockers and Englishmen come out
for a midnight show.*

Way back in the eighties, English comedian John Cleese assembled a few of his friends for two fund-raising concerts to benefit Amnesty International; this indispensable cassette offers the highlights from both unforgettable evenings. Musical performers from Cleese's ample Rolodex include people like (ho-hum) Pete Townshend, Jeff Beck, Eric Clapton, and Sting; comedic performers who show up include (yawn) Graham Chapman, Michael Palin, Terry Jones, Rowan Atkinson, and, as an added bonus, the brilliant Peter Cook, whose immense talents merited far more than to be known for most of his career as either "Dudley Moore's partner" or "Dudley Moore's former partner."

Part of the appeal of *The Secret Policeman's Other Ball* is watching the talented assemblage strut their stuff without a net; there's that special crackle in the performance that only a live audience can bring, and Cleese nearly cracks up once or twice. If this video's musical numbers don't make you tap your toes, you've probably got a hearing problem; if its comedy sketches don't make you laugh, you're probably dead. Python fans: this one's got the Cheese Shop skit.

★ 1982, 91 minutes, color, R.

★ With: John Cleese, Graham Chapman, Michael Palin, Terry Jones, Peter Cook, Rowan Atkinson, Eric Clapton, Sting. Directors: Julien Temple, Roger Graef.

★ *What was the name of the sequel?* (Answer on page 286.)

"Did you know you've got four feet of tubing in your stomach?"
—Peter Cook appears to have done all the necessary research.

For a great double feature, rent it with
Black Adder III, Parts One and Two.

Seen it but in the mood for something similar? Try
Monty Python's The Meaning of Life.

Answer to page 88 trivia question:
Bud on "Father Knows Best."

Comedy

Tom Ewell's trying very hard not to scratch.

"I keep my undies in the icebox."
—Marilyn's clever solution to the New York summer weather.

For a great double feature, rent it with
Breakfast at Tiffany's.

Seen it but in the mood for something similar? Try
How to Marry a Millionaire.

Answer to page 188 trivia question:
1974's *One Flew Over the Cuckoo's Nest.*

Tom Ewell is an average Joe whose wife heads out of town for a while during a blisteringly hot New York summer. This leaves him vulnerable to the charms of his upstairs neighbor, Marilyn Monroe, who is, as usual, blissfully innocent of the effects of her bombshell persona on unprotected men. She's happy to have some company, and so is he—but for a different reason.

Ewell spins out elaborate fantasies of what his encounters with his voluptuous neighbor will be like, but the two never quite connect romantically. Ewell plans a romantic dinner for two with cocktails and Chopin but ends up falling gracelessly from his piano bench. The guy really loves his wife, but he needs a little practice in the real world to figure it out.

As usual, Monroe's appeal transcends simple sexuality—her laugh somehow carries a little more vulnerability and charm than, say, Jayne Mansfield's insipid giggle. This film maintains big-league comic tension, in part because it's Monroe who ultimately offers Ewell the hand he needs to make sense of his life and his marriage. The consistently sparkling dialogue and Monroe's unforgettable performance help make this one of her strongest comedies. Yes, this is the one with the subway-grate scene that made Joe DiMaggio so angry.

★ 1955, 105 minutes, color, not rated.

★ With: Tom Ewell, Marilyn Monroe, Evelyn Keyes. Director: Billy Wilder.

★ *In what Wilder picture was Marilyn described as "like Jell-O on springs"?* (Answer on page 232.)

Comedy

I don't know about you, but when I think of the Declaration of Independence, I think of show tunes!

File under "pleasant surprises." The film adaptation of the patriotic Broadway smash is a whole lot of fun—and, at no extra charge, it's historically responsible as well! Sherman Edwards and Peter Stone chart the profound political and personal struggles that preceded the signing of the Declaration of Independence, and darned if they don't make a whale of a musical out of the material.

Rather than propose sainthood for all the participants in the historic meetings that led up to the Declaration's signing, *1776* has the good dramatic sense to point up the incredible risks the Founding Fathers were courting by formalizing a split with the mother country, and it reminds us that enthusiasm for that split was by no means universal among the colonists. This is no poli-sci lecture, though; it's got some great musical numbers, and it leaves you feeling as though you've made a human connection with the historical figures who helped Thomas Jefferson get his proclamation through Congress with a song in his heart and a tap from his buckled shoes.

Excellent family viewing, with strong performances by William Daniels and Howard da Silva.

★ 1972, 141 minutes, color, G.

★ With: William Daniels, Howard da Silva, Ken Howard. Director: Peter H. Hunt.

★ *What Audrey Hepburn–Albert Finney film does William Daniels appear in?* (Answer on page 160.)

"When in the course of human events. . . ."
—Redhead with a quill makes a point.

For a great double feature, rent it with
Drums Along the Mohawk.

Seen it but in the mood for something similar? Try
Northwest Passage.

Answer to page 242 trivia question:
West invited Grant to come up and see her sometime in 1933's *She Done Him Wrong.*

Musical

The Seventh Seal

A run-in with the black plague can ruin your whole day.

"I have nothing to tell."

—Death, in response to Max von Sydow's request that he divulge his secrets

For a great double feature, rent it with

Bill & Ted's Bogus Journey.

Seen it but in the mood for something similar? Try

Wild Strawberries.

Answer to page 259 trivia question:

At one point Connery's computer screen bears the warning "For Your Eyes Only"—which happens to be the title of the Roger Moore Bond film released the same year as *Outland.*

A medieval knight manages to make it back alive from the Crusades, only to find that he has to play a game of chess with Death, with his own life in the balance. Leave it to Death to pick a game that's virtually impossible to cheat at. It's all just a little like this crazy thing we call existence, isn't it?

Ingmar Bergman's much-parodied masterpiece features a black-robed character who became one of the icons of modern cinema, but with the passage of time that icon has become something of a running gag. Woody Allen wrote a memorable skit in which the chess game became a spirited gin rummy session; see also this book's review of the laudably daffy *Bill & Ted's Bogus Journey* (page 37), where Death has a little trouble with Twister and Battleship.

Nothing against running gags, of course, but *The Seventh Seal* is a cinematic landmark that deserves to be seen on its own terms, too. This powerful examination of spiritual disillusionment reminds us that death awaits us all. Magnificent cinematography and unforgettable performances (particularly Max von Sydow's as the knight) make this one you should see every year or two.

★ 1957, 96 minutes, B&W, not rated.

★ With: Max von Sydow, Gunnar Bjornstrand, Bibi Andersson. Director: Ingmar Bergman.

★ *In what horror classic did von Sydow play an elderly priest?* (Answer on page 32.)

Man risks all for egg. Talk about your Freudian overtones.

A solid, entertaining adventure yarn that soars to the heights thanks to the wonderful Ray Harryhausen special effects. Torin Thatcher plays an evil sorcerer who reduces princess Kathryn Grant to something close to Hot Wheels scale; her boyfriend, Kerwin Matthews (as Sinbad) goes out looking for the egg that can get her back to normal size. Sweet talk whispered in one's ear from a pint-sized sweetheart is nice, but I think Matthews wants more from the relationship.

The stop-action animation is, as usual, great fun to watch; it's executed with so much energy and color that you'll forget, for a moment, how far the technology has advanced in the years since the picture was released. This is a zippy, engrossing adventure that everyone in the family will enjoy; nice score by Bernard Herrmann, too.

★ 1958, 87 minutes, color, not rated.

★ With: Kerwin Matthews, Kathryn Grant, Richard Eyer. Director: Nathan Juran.

★ *What action film features Harryhausen's famous battling-skeleton sequence?* (Answer on page 111.)

"From the land beyond beyond, from the world past hope and fear, I bid you, Genie, now appear."

—When he does, you have just the faintest bit of disappointment that he doesn't sound anything like Robin Williams, but them's the breaks.

For a great double feature, rent it with *Gulliver's Travels.*

Seen it but in the mood for something similar? Try *Thief of Bagdad.*

Answer to page 289 trivia question: Zero; he never wanted the responsibility.

Fantasy

Shadow of a Doubt

And you thought your family reunions were tough.

"I know a wonderful person who'll come and shake us all up."
—Teresa Wright should be careful what she wishes for.

For a great double feature, rent it with
Rope.

Seen it but in the mood for something similar? Try
Strangers on a Train.

Answer to page 324 trivia question:
Jessica Tandy, who appeared in *The Birds.*

So it turns out that Uncle Charley is a serial murderer; his niece is the only one in the family who suspects the truth about his mysterious past. Her name's Charley, too. This pair of Charleys is only the first in a seemingly endless list of doubles, twins, and doppelgangers in Alfred Hitchcock's piercing study of repressed evil. The niece, after all, sees her uncle as her twin, her soul mate. And as the restless younger Charley gets closer and closer to the truth about her uncle, she begins to wonder about just how much of her uncle's decadence lies dormant in her—and how much she has accepted of her own volition.

Check out all the fun Hitchcock has with the theme of duality in this film; try to count all the pairs, the doubles, and the references to the number two. I found 32 references, and I know I must have missed at least . . . a couple. By the way, I know where Hitchcock is, and I'm not telling.

★ 1943, 108 minutes, B&W, not rated.

★ With: Joseph Cotten, Teresa Wright, Macdonald Carey. Director: Alfred Hitchcock

★ *Name the club Uncle Charley takes his niece to.* (Answer on page 363.)

She's Gotta Have It

And the men have to figure out exactly what "it" is.

Have you ever noticed that you never seem to see African-American people making love with other African-American people in mainstream motion pictures? Spike Lee's *She's Gotta Have It,* an examination of a woman's search for her own sexual identity, is one picture that takes on this previously uncharted territory, and the stark, dazzling results went a long way toward establishing him as one of the country's top directors.

Tracy Camilla Johns is the woman on the verge of the choice that will begin a long-term commitment; of the three suitors she puts through various paces, Spike Lee (in his memorable incarnation as Mars Blackman) adds the most energy and persistence to the film.

An effective, modestly scaled film, *She's Gotta Have It* was shot on a shoestring budget; it uses an aggressive, pseudodocumentary style to retain the intimacy its subject matter demands. The picture succeeds in conveying the courage, strength, and independence of its central character without losing sight for a moment of the emotional land mines she has to negotiate to find herself.

★ 1986, 84 minutes, B&W, R.

★ With: Tracy Camilla Johns, Redmond Hicks, Spike Lee. Director: Spike Lee.

★ *What is the name of Spike Lee's production company?*
(Answer on page 229.)

"Please baby, please baby, please baby, baby, baby, please."
—Spike Lee probably just wants to borrow a cup of sugar or something.

For a great double feature, rent it with *Jungle Fever.*

Seen it but in the mood for something similar? Try *Do the Right Thing.*

Answer to page 345 trivia question: *Strangers on a Train.*

Drama

Shirley Valentine

It's like she's been talking to a wall.
Actually, she has *been talking to a wall.*

"I think you've gone round the bend."
"Good. I've always wanted to travel."

—Pauline Collins tells her husband that her boots are made for walking.

For a great double feature, rent it with

Educating Rita.

Seen it but in the mood for something similar? Try

Hannah and Her Sisters.

Answer to page 161 trivia question:

Jack Lemmon, Walter Matthau, and Carol Burnett. Sounds like it should be great, doesn't it? Don't bother. It isn't.

This is a rental must for any woman who finds herself at that time of life when the children have left home and that man sitting across the breakfast table doesn't look as familiar as he once did. That what's happened to Shirley, played by Pauline Collins.

She talks directly to the audience, confiding in us just as easily as she does to the wall in her kitchen. Don't worry; she's not crazy. Collins is just very good at verbalizing her feelings. The problem is that no one around her is very good at listening.

When she gets a chance to go to Greece with a girlfriend, she's reluctant. But after a good talk with her husband over thrown eggs one night at dinner, she makes up her mind, packs her bags, and sets off to find whatever comes her way. Who knows? Maybe she'll run into herself.

★ 1989, 108 minutes, color, R.

★ With: Pauline Collins, Tom Conti, Julia McKenzie. Director: Lewis Gilbert.

★ *In what "Masterpiece Theater" production did Pauline Collins appear?* (Answer on page 364.)

The Shootist

Wayne's last stand.

Moviegoers are used to being able to count on the Duke quickly dispatching any pointy-toed, black-hatted, yellow-bellied sidewinder who dares to pull a Colt on him. *The Shootist* sends a shiver down your spine by making Hollywood's ultimate survivor take a long, unflinching look at his own mortality.

Wayne's quick-drawing, all-conquering rugged individualism seemed a little out of place in the post-Watergate, post-Vietnam period in which the film was released, so there's an interesting twist on his character here. *The Shootist*'s custom-fitted script casts the Duke as an aging gunfighter who knows he's about to die of cancer and wants only to end his days peacefully. (Sadly, Wayne himself died of cancer three years afterward.)

In his last picture, the big guy's trademark swagger is more than a little creaky; he must come to terms with a 20th century in which "frontiers" are quickly vanishing. *The Shootist* provides a legendary screen presence with the perfect exit; it seems to know it's both a piece of history and a piece of entertainment.

The Duke, never a particularly subtle actor, delivers an unexpectedly poignant performance in his last role, and the supporting cast all appear to know full well that this is a once-in-a-lifetime project and deliver accordingly.

★ 1976, 99 minutes, color, PG.

★ With: John Wayne, Lauren Bacall, Ron Howard, James Stewart. Director: Don Siegel.

★ *What was John Wayne's real name?* (Answer on page 62.)

"It isn't always being fast, or even accurate, that counts. It's being willing."
—John Wayne, on the secret of successful gunfighting

For a great double feature, rent it with
Rio Bravo.

Seen it but in the mood for something similar? Try
The Grey Fox.

Answer to page 196 trivia question:
"Soap."

Western

The Shop Around the Corner

Love blooms in Budapest.

For a great double feature, rent it with

The Philadelphia Story.

Seen it but in the mood for something similar? Try

Made for Each Other.

Answer to page 232 trivia question:

De Niro was named Best Supporting Actor for his performance as the young Vito Corleone in *The Godfather, Part II.*

O nly moments after you pop this one into the VCR you'll have the pleasant, unmistakable feeling that you're among friends. The story concerns a group of people who have been working together for years in a leather goods shop (in, of all places, Budapest). The only new member to the staff is a young saleswoman, Margaret Sullavan, who, much to Jimmy Stewart's dismay, has finagled a job in the shop. Stewart, the practical, efficient shop manager, is good at his job, but he has a romantic side. The only person who knows about his dreamy, poetic side is a female pen pal of several months' standing. Any guesses as to her identity?

This is a great romance, even though there's no earthly reason for it to be set in Hungary. It's about 2,000 times better than the Judy Garland musical based on the same material (*In the Good Old Summertime*), and that's reason enough to check it out.

May I make a daring suggestion? Next Christmas, when you're about to watch *It's a Wonderful Life*, watch this. It's just as heartwarming, even a touch more romantic, and the *whole film*, despite the title of Garland's remake, takes place during the holiday season.

★ 1940, 97 minutes, B&W, not rated.

★ With: James Stewart, Margaret Sullavan, Frank Morgan. Director: Ernst Lubitsch.

★ *In 1939, Frank Morgan played the title role in* The Wizard of Oz. *Who was slated to play the part before him, and why didn't he get it?* (Answer on page 103.)

Comedy

Slap Shot

Men in blades with big wooden sticks.

Remember *Field of Dreams,* that ethereal film about baseball and generational forgiveness? Remember how it showed us how the sport transcends a mere game but is a metaphor for life and the pure harmony that can be achieved in the larger game, the game of existence, if only it is played well?

Well, you can't make a movie like that about hockey. There's nothing ethereal about hockey. It's a spectacle, a blood sport that should be played in a coliseum with all the thumbs pointed down. That's the way we love it. Come on, admit it. If you love the game, you love the fights too.

Paul Newman is the player/coach of the Charlestown Chiefs, a losing team that's about to be disbanded. Times in the town are tough; the mill is about to close. The fast-talking coach knows full well this is the end of the road, and he's determined to make his swan song the greatest season the town has ever seen. What's more, he doesn't much care how he does it. This rude, extremely funny film was criticized at the time of its release for its profanity. The way I see it, the language is perfectly acceptable given the setting. The seventies wardrobe, however, is another matter. It can get quite ugly.

★ 1977, 122 minutes, color, R.

★ With: Paul Newman, Strother Martin, Jennifer Warren. Director: George Roy Hill.

★ *What dangerous sport did Newman, like Steve McQueen, once engage in?* (Answer on page 155.)

"You go to the box two minutes, and you feel shame."

—A contrite hockey player explains the rules of the game to a television reporter.

For a great double feature, rent it with
The Longest Yard.

Seen it but in the mood for something similar? Try
Semi-Tough.

Answer to page 270 trivia question:
Cole Porter.

Comedy

Slaughterhouse-Five

Ready for a little cinematic jet lag?

"I'm unstuck in time."

—Michael Sacks's admission doesn't do much to clarify things for his befuddled conversational partners.

For a great double feature, rent it with

The Naked and the Dead.

Seen it but in the mood for something similar? Try

Catch-22.

Answer to page 146 trivia question:

"Colonel Bogey March."

Director George Roy Hill, who later delivered *Slap Shot,* uses Kurt Vonnegut's extraordinary novel about a temporally dislocated World War II veteran as an opportunity to throw all *kinds* of bizarre curveballs the audience's way. The basic question is this: What would life be like if you lived it according to connections, obvious or subtle, among the events you experienced, rather than in chronological order?

The film's protagonist (Michael Sacks) ricochets between a Nazi POW camp and a vapid suburban wasteland in the white-bread America of the fifties. Which is the real prison? There are other, even stranger stops along the way, but the material is so strong, and Hill's ability to make visual and thematic connections is so impressive that it all holds together.

A superior but challenging screenplay, and some fine acting work from Sacks make this a powerful, multilayered kaleidoscope of a picture. You may want to watch it twice to get everything straight, but that's OK in my book. Fine supporting work from Ron Leibman and Valerie Perrine. The sequence set in the aftermath of the Dresden bombing, in which an American prisoner finds a doll in the rubble, is unforgettable.

★ 1972, 104 minutes, color, R.

★ With: Michael Sacks, Ron Leibman, Valerie Perrine. Director: George Roy Hill.

★ *What supremely accessible, chronologically orthodox film set in the thirties did Hill direct shortly after this one?* (Answer on page 285.)

Drama

Sleuth

Terrific star duo benefits from solid work from the supporting cast.

If you're the sort who likes to be kept guessing, you'll feel as though you've died and gone to heaven when you hook up with this brilliant, invigorating mystery thriller. Michael Caine and Laurence Olivier star in this faithful adaptation of Anthony Shaffer's stage hit, which pits a game-playing veteran mystery writer against the younger man who's having an affair with his wife.

The plot is an intricate, red-herring-laced model that spins and snorts its way through several masterful plot twists; Olivier and Caine add peerless, high-energy acting technique to the project. Their work pushes *Sleuth* over the line from solid mainstream thriller to double-barreled tour de force. It's like watching Frank Sinatra and Elvis Presley at peak form in a joint concert in which they offer alternating showstoppers all night long.

I won't give away any plot points, but I will say that the movie concerns itself with the winning of games and isn't at all shy about trying a few out on the audience.

★ 1972, 138 minutes, color, PG.

★ With: Laurence Olivier, Michael Caine. Director: Joseph L. Mankiewicz.

★ *Who is Anthony Shaffer's playwright brother?*
(Answer on page 227.)

"I understand you want to marry my wife."
—Laurence Olivier tries to break the ice with visitor Michael Caine.

For a great double feature, rent it with *Murder by Death.*

Seen it but in the mood for something similar? Try *Ten Little Indians.*

Answer to page 182 trivia question: *Fahrenheit 451.*

Suspense

Smile

*She may be beautiful, but she has
Vaseline on her teeth. Eeeuw.*

Yet another fine film from director Michael Ritchie about cutthroat competitions and the incredible things people are willing to do—or even become—to win. (See *The Candidate*, page 60, and *Downhill Racer*, page 99.)

This is a wry, behind-the-scenes look at the fictional "Young American Miss" pageant; it's smart enough not to go for the most obvious joke, the contestants themselves. Ritchie positions the young girls as innocents, saving his barbs for the planners, organizers, and audience members at these spectacles. It's as if he's asking, "Why are you putting these poor kids through this degradation?" Of course not all the girls are sweet and innocent; some are real pros at the pageant game, but the picture skims over their story.

The head judge and promoter is played by Bruce Dern. 'Nuff said? Barbara Feldon, whose character was a Young American Miss herself years earlier, offers the girls a glimpse of what they may become if they're really, really lucky.

★ 1975, 113 minutes, color, PG.

★ With: Bruce Dern, Barbara Feldon, Michael Kidd. Director: Michael Ritchie.

★ *What daughter of a major Hollywood actress shows up as a nonwinner in the film?* (Answer on page 152.)

Comedy

The Snake Pit

*They just don't make insane asylums
like they used to.*

Just as 1945's *The Lost Weekend* helped audiences come to terms with some of the real-world implications of alcoholism, this stark, unflinching look at life in a mental institution went a long way toward correcting some of the abuses of the day in dealing with the mentally ill.

Olivia de Havilland stars in a searing examination of one woman's harrowing journey through a less-than-perfect treatment system after a nervous breakdown. As it turns out, her emotional collapse is only the beginning of her problems. It's what happens after she's committed that will give you the chills.

De Havilland is brilliant, and the film's innovative visual approach to its disturbing subject is consistently powerful. Keep an eye out for the unforgettable overhead sequence of writhing inmates that provides the image for the film's title.

★ 1948, 108 minutes, B&W, not rated.

★ With: Olivia de Havilland, Mark Stevens, Celeste Holm. Director: Anatole Litvak.

★ *Who was Olivia de Havilland's actress sister?* (Answer on page 115.)

"I heard a scream, and I didn't know if it was me who screamed or not—if it was I or not."
—Olivia de Havilland isn't the type of mental patient to let an incorrect pronoun slip by uncorrected.

For a great double feature, rent it with
What Ever Happened to Baby Jane?

Seen it but in the mood for something similar? Try
Suddenly, Last Summer.

Answer to page 252 trivia question:
Ira Levin.

The Snapper

Up the pole without a paddle.

"You're pregnant, y'said? That's lovely, that is."

—Colm Meaney is less than thrilled with the news he gets from his daughter.

For a great double feature, rent it with

The Commitments.

Seen it but in the mood for something similar? Try

Love with the Proper Stranger.

Answer to page 154 trivia question:

He played Ilya Kuryakin on "The Man from U.N.C.L.E."

In a working-class Irish neighborhood a young girl gets herself pregnant, faces a barrage of ruthless insults from her neighbors and former friends, and nearly drives her dad over the edge. *The Snapper* may not *sound* much like a comedy, but this gentle, wise, and touching exploration of a father-daughter relationship will keep you thinking for a long time. The film sets out to demonstrate the true meaning of the word *family*—it's the group of people who are willing to support you during tough times.

Frank, outspoken, and not above the occasional refreshing bit of lewd humor, the film is both an embrace of earthy sensuality and a meditation on its consequences. Through the course of the movie both the father (Colm Meaney, who is superb) and the daughter (Tina Kellegher, who is, too) learn that how you *react* to a mistake is, in the end, more important than the mistake itself. We may cringe every now and then—when a young boy earnestly commands his sister to stick a piece of metal into an electrical outlet, say, or when the young mother-to-be gleefully downs what seem to be gallons of stout in the local pub—but *The Snapper* is definitely worth the effort.

★ 1993, 90 minutes, color, not rated.

★ With: Tina Kellegher, Colm Meaney, Ruth McCabe. Director: Stephen Frears.

★ *To what does the phrase* the snapper *refer, and what is the term's derivation?* (Answer on page 64.)

Something Wild

*News flash: sometimes life on the edge
really sucks.*

Conservative suit-and-tie-bound Jeff Daniels doesn't seem like the kind of guy who has much of a dark side, but when Melanie Griffith spots him dashing out the door of a restaurant without paying the check, she suspects he's up for, well, something wild. So she takes him to a motel and seduces him. Life could be worse, right?

As it happens, it could; this picture starts out as a harmless enough exercise in male fantasy fulfillment, but as it picks up speed its plot reveals a harrowing edge that's enough to make you think twice before stiffing that waitress.

Griffith's performance as a sexy, over-the-top embodiment of rebellion for its own sake will make you sit up and take notice; Daniels is both hilarious and convincing as a straight arrow who realizes he's about to pay the price for breaking the rules.

Something Wild is an ingenious, well-crafted study of the pros and cons of choosing to get in over your head; it's well appointed with laughs, thrills, and the occasional unexpected insight. The picture is also notable in that it showcases Ray Liotta in his first major role; he's great here as the heavy.

★ 1986, 113 minutes, color, R.

★ With: Jeff Daniels, Melanie Griffith, Ray Liotta. Director: Jonathan Demme.

★ *In what film did Liotta star with Robert De Niro and Joe Pesci?* (Answer on page 16.)

"You're a closet rebel."
—Melanie Griffith has found a kindred spirit in Jeff Daniels.

For a great double feature, rent it with
Body Double.

Seen it but in the mood for something similar? Try
Local Hero.

Answer to page 189 trivia question:
Richard Dawson.

Sorcerer

If they hit a bump, the truck blows up.
What would you do?

"You gonna tell me where I'm going?"
—Roy Scheider's not as clear on his destination as he would like to be, but he doesn't have much of a choice—it's time to get out of town.

For a great double feature, rent it with

Casablanca (and while you're at it, count the oblique visual and verbal references to the Bogart classic in *Sorcerer*).

Seen it but in the mood for something similar? Try the film that inspired it,

Wages of Fear.

Answer to page 225 trivia question:

Ferris Bueller's Day Off.

A different kind of road picture. This harrowing Roy Scheider thriller, directed by William Friedkin of *The Exorcist* fame, isn't a horror fest; it's a portrait of men caught in a world that makes no sense, and it's their own damned fault.

Sorcerer starts out looking like three movies; it follows three vary shady characters through three blown power plays that backfire spectacularly, but other than that nothing in any one strand seems to connect to anything else for about 30 minutes. You wonder if Friedkin's going to be able to pull this film off. He does. All three end up exiles and make their separate ways to an obscure Latin American hellhole, where former Nazis hang out and call themselves Carlos and Juan.

The only economic activity to speak of in this anti-*Casablanca* village is an oil refinery; when it ignites, the powers that be have to use explosives to stem the inferno. Problem: the nitroglycerine is 200 miles away, and it's been so poorly maintained that anyone who transports it stands a good chance of blowing himself up. Our three fugitives volunteer for the job.

A spellbinding, unforgettable movie, *Sorcerer* showcases Scheider and Friedkin at the very top of their respective games. A nice watch.

★ 1977, 122 minutes, color, PG.

★ With: Roy Scheider, Bruno Cremer, Francisco Rabal. Director: William Friedkin.

★ *In what 1976 picture did Roy Scheider costar with Dustin Hoffman?* (Answer on page 2.)

Suspense

Sorry, Wrong Number

Talk about your call waiting!

One dilemma the producers of this film faced was that *Sorry, Wrong Number* was initially a very scary, very successful radio drama set in a single room. How do you retain the essential claustrophobic feel of the story, make the film visually interesting, and still scare the bejesus out of people? The solution: get the same writer (Lucille Fletcher) to write the screenplay and film all the important phone conversations that do not take place in the heroine's bedroom in tight, confined spaces (phone booths, narrow corridors, busy subway platforms, and the like).

Barbara Stanwyck brings a marvelously edgy, near-hysterical flavor to her part even before she overhears a murder plot as the result of crossed phone lines. Stanwyck plays a wealthy, bedridden woman who is predatory, manipulative, and likes collecting trophies of her own, no matter what it takes. She's driving Burt Lancaster nuts, and something's gotta give. It does.

★ 1948, 89 minutes, B&W, not rated.

★ With: Barbara Stanwyck, Burt Lancaster, Ed Begley. Director: Anatole Litvak.

★ *Stanwyck's character goes by what nickname?* (Answer on page 30.)

"My good woman, you probably don't understand, but a human being, a woman, is going to be killed—somewhere, somewhere in this very city."

—Barbara Stanwyck brings her own uniquely obnoxious style to the emergency that has presented itself to her.

For a great double feature, rent it with *The Conversation.*

Seen it but in the mood for something similar? Try *Dial M for Murder.*

Answer to page 260 trivia question: *The Treasure of the Sierra Madre.*

Suspense

Slip sliding away.

"There's only one rule—expedience."

—Questions of morality get put on the back burner in the world inhabited by Richard Burton and Oskar Werner.

For a great double feature, rent it with

The Ipcress File.

Seen it but in the mood for something similar? Try

Eye of the Needle.

Answer to page 167 trivia question:

Jim Hutton starred in "Ellery Queen."

I n a career filled with notable performances, this one is undeniably one of Richard Burton's finest. He plays an alienated cold war spy whose best days are behind him, and there's something uncanny about how well he fits into the role.

This fellow is a shattered player in a vast, mind-numbing game, a tired but brilliant warrior who can't do a thing about the fact that his world is crumbling under his feet. If the emotional tone of the piece is a little reminiscent of Burton's own troubled personal life in the years that followed, that may be yet another strange case of life imitating art.

The superior supporting cast includes Claire Bloom and Oskar Werner; Martin Ritt's taut direction is very nearly perfect. Considered by many to be the finest spy movie ever made.

★ 1965, 112 minutes, color, not rated.

★ With: Richard Burton, Claire Bloom, Oskar Werner. Director: Martin Ritt.

★ *What film features Burton's final screen performance?*
(Answer on page 70.)

Suspense

Start the Revolution Without Me

Memo to Gene Wilder: Try the decaf.

This gloriously silly send-up of the French Revolution consists of equal parts non sequitur, funny character names, heaving bosoms, and unforgivable levels of overacting. The picture makes fun of itself from beginning to end, spoofing a raft of cliches from historical epics of years past.

Donald Sutherland and Gene Wilder play both sets of mismatched twins, erroneously swapped at birth. (Don't ask.) The brothers in one mismatched pair turn out to be snobby, elitist fops; the other two are part of the downtrodden masses—complete with quasi-cockney accents (don't ask)—about to overthrow the corrupt monarchy.

Wilder gives one of the hilariously unrestrained performances typical of his early career; he gives *over the top* a good name. If only everyone could get away with it the way he did in the late sixties and early seventies. If only *he* could get away with it the way he did in the late sixties and early seventies.

The picture is gleeful, self-puncturing fun from beginning to end; its ridiculously overwrought metaphors, speeding text scrolls, and elaborately stupid names bring to mind the best of Monty Python.

★ 1970, 91 minutes, color, PG.

★ With: Gene Wilder, Donald Sutherland, Orson Welles (sort of). Director: Bud Yorkin.

★ *Billie Whitelaw, who plays Marie Antoinette here, plays the overbearing mother of two vicious English mobsters in what movie?* (Answer on page 101.)

"Liberty, equality, frater—I don't find that amusing."
—Gene Wilder isn't crazy about the new ideas he's reading about.

For a great double feature, rent it with
Long Day's Journey into Night. (No, seriously, rent it with *Monty Python and the Holy Grail.*)

Seen it but in the mood for something similar? Try
Big Business.

Answer to page 201 trivia question:
Jezebel and *The Little Foxes.*

Comedy

Still of the Night

Sometimes a cigar is just a cigar.

"What have I got? A green box and a little girl who's mean to her teddy bear."

—Scheider, contemplating the "evidence" of his murdered patient's dream.

For a great double feature, rent it with

Marnie.

Seen it but in the mood for something similar? Try

Dressed to Kill.

Answer to page 237 trivia question:

Our Town.

Glenn Close may have seared her way into the national subconcious as the lethal love object in *Fatal Attraction*, but Meryl Streep racks up some hair-raising points of her own in this often-overlooked 1982 thriller. She plays an art curator who tempts psychiatrist Roy Scheider. One of Scheider's patients has just been murdered, and because confidentiality issues prevent him from going to the police, the good doctor must follow whatever leads he can to get to the bottom of the crime. These include the patient's last harrowing dream, described immediately before the crime; a few tantalizing references to Streep as "just your [Scheider's] type" during the murdered man's final therapy session; and a strange visit from Streep herself after the murder.

Watch for director Robert Benton's skillful use of color in building character and for his recurring use of hallways, passages, and other mazelike paths, which serve as steadily more ominous hints of evildoings to come.

As imitations of—sorry, homages to—Hitchcock go, this entry has to be placed in the top tier. Streep has a remarkable monologue near the end that is a tribute to her own considerable talent and to great chunks of *Vertigo*.

★ 1982, 91 minutes, color, PG.

★ With: Roy Scheider, Meryl Streep, Jessica Tandy. Director: Robert Benton.

★ *What member of the cast had a featured role in an Alfred Hitchcock classic—and what was the film?*
(Answer on page 308.)

Suspense

Crook can't play by the book.

Dustin Hoffman turns in a spectacular, Oscar-caliber performance that went more or less unnoticed when this film was released. Hoffman plays an ex-con who gives life on the outside what he considers a fair shot. But when his parole officer lets a judgment call go the wrong way, Hoffman gives up on the rules and returns to his longtime vocation: professional thief.

This gripping, impossible-to-ignore film offers some fascinating meditations on the perils of those whose true calling leaves them on the outside of society looking in. It features some soberingly apropos lessons in trust, honor, and the foundations of a working system of morality—not exactly issues you associate with career criminals and their culture-outside-the-culture, but that's part of this remarkable film's appeal.

Hoffman's unnerving, intense work sizzles from beginning to end; the supporting cast offers a number of superb performances, especially Harry Dean Stanton's as Hoffman's partner in crime. Not to be missed.

★ 1979, 114 minutes, color, R.

★ With: Dustin Hoffman, Harry Dean Stanton. Director: Ulu Grosbard.

★ *For what film did Hoffman win his first Academy Award as Best Actor?* (Answer on page 239.)

"Maybe it would be better if you didn't ask me any more questions."
—Dustin Hoffman's girlfriend has started asking awkward questions.

For a great double feature, rent it with *Raging Bull.*

Seen it but in the mood for something similar? Try *Scarface* (1932).

Answer to page 275 trivia question: After having tried all manner of artificial stuff, they used real food. It worked.

Stranger than Paradise

You have to admire a picture that makes you laugh when nothing happens.

"What kind of meat is that?"

—Eszter Balint is uncertain about the contents of a TV dinner.

For a great double feature, rent it with

Bagdad Cafe.

Seen it but in the mood for something similar? Try

Night on Earth.

Answer to page 8 trivia question:

The Eiffel Tower.

The characters in this blessedly offbeat Jim Jarmusch comedy have a simple aim in life: do something, anything, to keep from dying of boredom. That sounds like an impossible premise for a full-length motion picture, and for most filmmakers it would be, but Jarmusch mixes in just enough in the way of laconic wit, extended pauses, and Screaming Jay Hawkins tracks to keep you hooked.

The plot, such as it is, involves two very nearly nonexistent loafers, Willie and Eddie, and Eddie's cousin Eva, recently arrived from Hungary. Eva sticks around for a while, then leaves for—get this—Cleveland. Time passes. There's some trouble involving a poker game. Willie and Eddie head to Cleveland to hook up once again with Eva. If it sounds dull, well, that's kind of the point, but the weird thing about this low-budget anti-movie is its ability to sustain surprisingly large amounts of comic tension with virtually no content.

In *Stranger than Paradise,* Jarmusch turns killing time into something truly funny—and even a little bit noble. Check it out.

★ 1984, 90 minutes, B&W, R.

★ With: John Lurie, Richard Edson, Eszter Balint. Director: Jim Jarmusch.

★ *Name another director who attempted, with less commercial success, to make films in which nothing happened.* (Answer on page 171.)

Suddenly, Last Summer

Any woman stupid enough to get a white bathing suit wet deserves whatever she gets.

This gothic Tennessee Williams treatment of mistargeted sexuality isn't exactly *pleasant* to watch, but I'll bet you can't take your eyes off it once you pop it into the VCR. The picture, which features strong performances from Elizabeth Taylor and Katharine Hepburn, focuses on the mysterious Sebastian, Hepburn's son, whose face we never see.

Hepburn doesn't want the startling (and, in places, disgusting) truth about the days leading up to her son's death to get out, so she'd like Montgomery Clift to give Elizabeth Taylor a lobotomy. Cheery plotline, eh? This grippingly weird piece of moviemaking is an expanded version of Tennessee Williams's off-the-wall play; even though it was released in 1959, the picture hints with unusual confidence at the theme of homosexuality that Williams's writing was often forced to suppress.

The picture is not exactly a model of perfect dramatic structure, but it does pack a heck of a wallop, especially at the end. It features an underutilized Montgomery Clift in the thankless role of the doctor; he spends most of the picture looking as though he wishes he were somewhere else. Maybe he was just uncomfortable with the plot for some reason.

★ 1959, 114 minutes, B&W, not rated.

★ With: Elizabeth Taylor, Katharine Hepburn, Montgomery Clift. Director: Joseph L. Mankiewicz.

★ *For what Tennessee Williams role did Vivien Leigh win her second Oscar?* (Answer on page 67.)

"Is that what love is? Using people?"
—Elizabeth Taylor's not eager to be used—or lobotomized for that matter.

For a great double feature, rent it with
Soylent Green (be sure to serve steak tartare as an appetizer).

Seen it but in the mood for something similar? Try
Cat on a Hot Tin Roof (1958).

Answer to page 42 trivia question:
John Griffin's.

Sunday, Bloody Sunday

No, it's not a slasher movie.

"Too late to start again."

— Peter Finch, after finding out that everything hadn't turned out quite as he had planned.

For a great double feature, rent it with

Damage.

Seen it but in the mood for something similar? Try

Husbands and Wives.

Answer to page 76 trivia question:

The Player.

Seldom has a good movie been done more damage by a misleading title than this penetrating, insightful study of the complicated private lives of three Londoners. Either people confuse it with the mediocre thriller *Black Sunday,* or they think it's a cheap horror flick. In fact, it's a showcase for superb performances from Peter Finch and Glenda Jackson, each of whom has a romantic interest in the attractive young Murray Head.

The dense script and hypnotic editing keep you hooked in, and even with its acres of ambiguity the picture manages to leave you feeling like you've learned something important about making the most of the romantic cards you draw in this chaotic world.

Finch and Jackson each turn in some remarkable work here; anytime you feel lost in the labyrinth of the film's artifice, one or the other of them checks in with a moment of such impressive emotional validity that you stay tuned for a little more random weirdness. Let's face it; sometimes love is pretty damn complicated.

★ 1971, 110 minutes, color, R.

★ With: Glenda Jackson, Peter Finch, Murray Head. Director: John Schlesinger.

★ *For what films did Glenda Jackson win the Academy Award as Best Actress?* (Answer on page 19.)

Drama

Sunset Boulevard

American gigolo.

B illy Wilder's 1959 masterpiece concerns a down-on-his-luck screenwriter (William Holden) who accepts what seems to be a heaven-sent assignment: a ghost-writing job for a rich, weird diva from the silent era. He thinks it's a chance to get his car out of hock; instead the gig turns him into a gigolo. Holden turns in one of his very finest performances; Gloria Swanson lets loose a gloriously campy Norma Desmond. The role, a brave choice for the former silent queen, marked Swanson's first screen appearance in nearly a decade.

This tightly constructed gothic drama may be the best picture Hollywood ever made about its own uniquely cannibalistic world view. Watch for the bridge game; the silent card players at Swanson's table are Buster Keaton, Anna Q. Nilsson, and H. B. Warner, all veterans of the pretalkie era; they're members of a remarkable cast that also includes Erich von Stroheim and Cecil B. de Mille. *Sunset Boulevard* is an achievement that should not be overshadowed by the success of its recent Broadway adaptation.

By the way, the film that Swanson watches in her private screening room is *Queen Kelly,* an unfinished 1928 Swanson vehicle by von Stroheim.

★ 1950, 110 minutes, B&W, not rated.

★ With: William Holden, Gloria Swanson, Erich von Stroheim. Director: Billy Wilder.

★ *Name the star who was to play Holden's role but backed out because of the picture's scandalous story line.* (Answer on page 36.)

"The poor dope; he always wanted a pool. Well, he got one—but the price was a little high."

—William Holden's talking about a dope he knows quite well.

For a great double feature, rent it with
The Player.

Seen it but in the mood for something similar? Try
The Barefoot Contessa.

Answer to page 110 trivia question:
Across the dining room table. The role of the son is played by Boorman's own son, Charley.

Drama

Sweet Liberty

History's fascinating, especially when you rewrite it.

> "*I never eat anything that hasn't been sitting on the TV for at least 24 hours. The radiation kills anything they* put into it."
>
> —Lillian Gish knows that proper food safety procedures are vital.

For a great double feature, rent it with
Paper Lion.

Seen it but in the mood for something similar? Try
Barton Fink.

Answer to page 18 trivia question:
Edgar Bergen.

In the mood for a sweet, unassuming romantic comedy that boasts an endearing script, great location shooting, and, as an added bonus, a hilarious appearance from Lillian Gish in one of her final screen appearances?

Alan Alda plays a professor at a New England college; he's written a nice little book about the true accounts of a notable colonial rascal—and the morally upstanding colonist who stood her ground against the rogue while her husband was off bravely fighting the British. Alda has it pretty lucky. He's a published professor. He's got a smart, great-looking girlfriend. Life is good—until the movie rights to his book are sold, and Hollywood comes to town. Michael Caine plays the star of the picture based on Alda's book; when he's not seducing every woman in town, he's drinking. Michelle Pfeiffer is set to play the brave heroine of Alda's book: she's the very image of the historical woman Alda secretly fell in love with while writing his book. Temptation looms. Then there's Bob Hoskins, the fellow sent to rewrite—er, adapt—Alda's book: "You know; jazz it up a bit." Writers love that.

★ 1986, 107 minutes, color, PG.

★ With: Alan Alda, Michael Caine, Michelle Pfeiffer, Lillian Gish. Director: Alan Alda.

★ *What star originally played Hawkeye in the movie M.A.S.H.?* (Answer on page 109.)

Swept Away

Man. Woman. Desert island. Despite what you may have been led to believe on "Gilligan's Island," the inevitable occurs.

A beautiful, wealthy, conceited woman from Milan finds herself shipwrecked on a remote island with her handsome Sicilian deckhand. Guess what? He's a dyed-in-the-wool Communist. Now then: who's in charge?

Considerable effort is expended resolving this crucial question, and the result is a culture clash for the ages. This well-crafted, provocative love story is a funny, fiercely intelligent examination of personal and political power games. It's a little like *The African Queen* with a progressive agenda.

Lina Wertmuller directed; Mariangela Melato (as the snobby society queen) and Giancarlo Giannini (as the left-wing firebrand) turn in extraordinary performances. The picture is also known by the more cumbersome title *Swept Away . . . by an unusual destiny in the blue sea of August.* (Whew! That's a bit heavy. I'll take the low-calorie title, please.)

★ 1975, 116 minutes, color, R.

★ With: Giancarlo Giannini, Mariangela Melato. Director: Lina Wertmuller.

★ *In what Lina Wertmuller film did Giancarlo Giannini mount an unlikely seduction in a Nazi prison camp?*
(Answer on page 168.)

"The world was changed by people with servants. I'll bet Marx had at least three."

—Mariangela Melato's astute observation doesn't score any points with Giancarlo Giannini.

For a great double feature, rent it with
From Here to Eternity.

Seen it but in the mood for something similar? Try
The African Queen.

Answer to page 52 trivia question:
Dangerous (1935) and *Jezebel* (1938).

Foreign

Swimming to Cambodia

Here's your assignment. Just sit down, talk about the Khmer Rouge for a good hunk of the evening, and make people laugh.

"Whenever I travel, if I can take the train, I travel by train."

—Spalding Gray likes to keep low to the ground when he can.

For a great double feature, rent it with

The Killing Fields.

Seen it but in the mood for something similar? Try

Monster in a Box.

Answer to page 86 trivia question:

Mary Pickford.

Spalding Gray's one-man stage hit settles into the screen with unexpected power and humor, thanks in no small measure to the inspired direction of Jonathan Demme. (For other surprisingly enthralling examples of one- and two-character moviemaking, see *Give 'Em Hell, Harry* [page 142], *My Dinner with Andre* [page 246], and Gray's *Monster in a Box* [page 237].

The film is basically a series of reminiscences about Gray's journeys, physical and emotional, during the shooting of *The Killing Fields,* in which he was a cast member. The topics of his offbeat monologues are wildly divergent (politics, insider film gossip, exotic massages, genocide, tourist tips . . .). They seem, at first, in danger of not holding together as a whole. The real journey Gray is making, however, is the one to find out exactly who he is, even in the midst of chaos. It's a tricky question, one that resonates powerfully as he explores it from every conceivable angle and even a few angles you probably wouldn't have conceived of.

Occasionally dense, but quite rewarding indeed if you stick with it, *Swimming to Cambodia* demonstrates just how riveting one man's observations on the elusive quest for the self can be.

★ 1987, 85 minutes, color, not rated.

★ With: Spalding Gray. Director: Jonathan Demme.

★ *In what rock concert movie did Demme work with a guy in a really big suit?* (Answer on page 342.)

Swing Time

Astaire as a gambler with two left feet.
Yeah, right.

Oh, if only today's musicals had the good sense to wrap a movie around a plot that fits like a comfortable old shoe. Rogers meets Astaire and hates him; Rogers is forced by some contrivance of circumstance to dance with Astaire; Rogers decides Astaire might not be so bad after all—at exactly the time Rogers is starting to get on Astaire's nerves; Rogers and Astaire stun the public with a magnificent dance number; Rogers and Astaire realize they're meant for each other after all.

Yes, it's that same familiar formula that worked for the first five films, filled out with more magnificent dance numbers than you can shake a stick at and bedecked with a big-budget ornateness only the Great Depression (and box-office clout) could summon up. Padded satin walls, mirrored black floors, dual staircases ascending to the heavens, white lamé gowns—they're all here, in glorious black and white.

If you watch only one Astaire-Rogers film in your entire life, this is the one to pick; it's got a witty, upbeat script, it spends no more time than necessary on the negligible plot, and Fred sings "The Way You Look Tonight" to Ginger while she has shampoo in her hair. The dance-instruction-studio scene is considered one of the finest numbers Astaire and Rogers ever filmed.

★ 1936, 103 minutes, B&W, not rated.

★ With: Fred Astaire, Ginger Rogers, Helen Broderick, Victor Moore. Director: George Stevens.

★ *Whom did Fred Astaire identify as his favorite dancing partner?* (Answer on page 361.)

"Hoofing's all right, but there's no future in it."

—Fred Astaire figures it's time to get a real job.

For a great double feature, rent it with *Daddy Long Legs.*

Seen it but in the mood for something similar? Try *Top Hat.*

Answer to page 121 trivia question: *The Great Escape.*

Musical

The Taming of the Shrew (1967)

*Liz, darling, I hate to say it, but
I'm really enjoying this.*

*"I would not wed her
for a mine of gold."*
—Yeah, but Richard Burton
would.

**For a great double
feature, rent it with**

*Who's Afraid of
Virginia Woolf?*

**Seen it but in the mood
for something similar?
Try**

Romeo and Juliet.

**Answer to page 22
trivia question:**

The Right Stuff as
Chuck Yeager.

Having earned critical and popular acclaim for their eerily realistic marital detonations in *Who's Afraid of Virginia Woolf?* in 1966, Richard Burton and Elizabeth Taylor made an inspired choice of material the following year. They signed on with director Franco Zeffirelli for another spellbinding art-imitates-life session but one that went for laughs instead of leaving the audience pondering the deeper significance of domestic trainwrecks. They got hold of a pretty good script, too.

The letter-perfect casting of the Bard's classic battle of the sexes is just too good to pass up; something very close to comic magic happens when you can tell the participants are taking perhaps a little *too* much glee in roles like these. Taylor's fiery, independent Kate retains a measure of self-respect at the conclusion that pushes the tricky ending a little closer to the "acceptable" level for modern audiences. (Not that anyone's claiming Shakespeare was a closet feminist, mind you.)

Solid direction from Zeffirelli, and sizzling comic turns from the two principals make this essential viewing. I wonder what the ride back home after a long day of shooting was like for the two leads.

★ 1967, 126 minutes, color, not rated.

★ With: Richard Burton, Elizabeth Taylor, Michael Hordern. Director: Franco Zeffirelli.

★ *What actress played both Juliet and the Virgin Mary for director Zeffirelli?* (Answer on page 236.)

Comedy

A Taxing Woman

*She's Steven Seagal with
a calculator.*

During the 1980s Japanese tax rates skyrocketed; some upper-bracket types found themselves subject to an 80 percent charge on their earnings. Not surprisingly, people found some pretty inventive ways of stashing money away from the prying eyes of the government.

Nobuko Miyamoto, so radiantly beautiful in *The Funeral*, here plays a decidedly plain-looking tax collector who proves herself the match of any man in her division. She's a divorced single mother working in an agency of perhaps 100 men; more to the point, she's working in a society in which the odds against female individual achievement are pretty long.

This is a person who doesn't quite fit into the societal pigeonholes reserved for her. The only way she manages to climb the ladder of success is to eliminate any trace of sexuality from her identity and to outthink the competition. When Miyamoto has to track down a slick hotel owner's suspected hidden loot, she has to bring her considerable powers of intuition and analysis to bear. The results are both amusing and thought-provoking. A pleasantly unpredictable character study.

★ 1987, 126 minutes, color, not rated.

★ With: Nobuko Miyamoto, Tsutomo Yamazaki. Director: Juzo Itami.

★ *The son of the hotel owner plays a Nintendo game called Attack of the Mushrooms. By what name is this game better known in the United States?* (Answer on page 106.)

"A female agent? They are so rare! She will be very useful to us."
—Nobuko Miyamoto doesn't mind how the boys talk; she's got a job to do.

For a great double feature, rent it with
Tampopo.

Seen it but in the mood for something similar? Try the sequel,
A Taxing Woman's Return.

Answer to page 56 trivia question:
Buck Privates Come Home.

Foreign

They Shoot Horses, Don't They?

Shall we dance?

"From what I've seen lately, I've been letting the wrong sex try and make me."

—Jane Fonda, contemplating a new approach to things.

For a great double feature, rent it with

Pennies from Heaven.

Seen it but in the mood for something similar? Try

Klute.

Answer to page 123 trivia question:

Tommy.

Here's a movie filled with color, action, music, and a *whole* lot of dancing—but don't go pulling out the Fred and Ginger costumes just yet. This powerful study of the contestants in a Depression-era dance marathon won Jane Fonda some of her first positive notices as a serious lead actress, and she deserved 'em. After the whole *Barbarella* thing, it's fair to say that no one expected to see Jane put on some serious star moves as a bitter, down-on-her-luck dancer who brings new meaning to the phrase *hard-bitten*. This movie was definitely a step up; she didn't even have to wear anything that incorporated large plastic bubbles.

They Shoot Horses, Don't They? latches on to a potent, unrelenting metaphor: America as a cannibalistic marathon race that leaves even the "winners" spiritually bankrupt. The idea is well executed and still carries a good deal of power, even though it's clearly rooted in the anti-Establishment ethos of the time. The supporting cast is excellent, especially Red Buttons and Gig Young, who plays the MC. (And just in case you were wondering, no, you're not supposed to make any sense of the title until the very end of the picture.)

★ 1969, 121 minutes, color, PG.

★ With: Jane Fonda, Gig Young, Michael Sarrazin, Red Buttons. Director: Sydney Pollack.

★ *Name the cast member who won an Oscar for his or her performance in the film.* (Answer on page 228.)

The Thing (1982)

As if the thought of being stranded in the Arctic with Wilford Brimley weren't scary enough.

The original (1951) picture is a great movie, too; I recommend renting them together if you possibly can, because the resonances are great, and the second film can serve as a sequel to the first. The original is a classic, scary piece of fifties Communist-metaphor paranoia about a rampant morphing, well, *thing* that can turn into anything it wants to. The only weapon that works against it is fire. Other than that, you're pretty much doomed.

This eighties entry is a rougher—and, yes, grosser—ride. It's a darker film all around, and every inch the equal of its distinguished predecessor. No longer do we have a handsome, clean-cut hero; now a grim-looking Kurt Russell, who needs a shave (and, we suspect, a bath), guides us through the proceedings. He's as cool as antiheroes come in his Arctic scientific outpost. Everybody on duty there drinks too much and carries a gun. Think *that's* a bad idea? Wait till the monster shows up.

★ 1982, 108 minutes, color, R.

★ With: Kurt Russell, Wilford Brimley, Richard Dysart. Director: John Carpenter.

★ *Who played the original Thing?* (Answer on page 154.)

"Trust is a hard thing to come by these days."
—Kurt Russell's feelng a little uneasy about the company he keeps.

For a great double feature, rent it with
The Thing (From Another World) (1951).

Seen it but in the mood for something similar? Try
Alien.

Answer to page 9 trivia question:
Sweetie.

Sci-Fi

The Thomas Crown Affair

Bored? Rob a bank; date
Faye Dunaway.

"What a mind, what a man."
—Faye Dunaway wouldn't mind getting a little more intimate with Steve McQueen.

For a great double feature, rent it with
The Getaway (1972).

Seen it but in the mood for something similar? Try
$ (Dollars).

Answer to page 43 trivia question:
Vanessa Redgrave.

G ive this excellent crime drama a shot if only for the rare believable Boston accents. Steve McQueen is a wealthy, bored bank robber who pulls intricate jobs not because he has to but because he's bored. Enter icy, beautiful Faye Dunaway and her unfortunate hair. She's an insurance investigator willing to break the rules to get the job done. After the big heist, Dunaway is brought in to track down the perpetrator; she knows from the get-go who pulled the job, and she also knows before too long that she'd like to see a lot more of McQueen.

The cat-and-mouse game the two play through the course of the film is part dual admiration society, part romance, and part mutual sting operation. McQueen and Dunaway are perfectly matched: he knows every move she's about to make—or does he? This one will keep you guessing from beginning to end. Don't mind the hideous outfits; it was, after all, 1968.

★ 1968, 102 minutes, color, not rated.

★ With: Steve McQueen, Faye Dunaway, Paul Burke. Director: Norman Jewison.

★ *What song from the film was a Top 40 hit?* (Answer on page 116.)

Action

A Thousand Clowns

But isn't the guy in the center ring a little young to be running the show?

Can you think of *any* movie in which you come away feeling that Jason Robards would make a good father? I'm sure he's a nice enough man in real life. Herb Gardner wrote the screen adaptation of his own Broadway play about a 35-year-old kid and a 12-year-old father figure; the picture served as a high point for the early career of Jason Robards, who is extraordinary. Just as memorable is his brilliant young ward, played by Barry Gordon. The two have to find some way to outwit the welfare establishment if they're going to continue their nonconformist lifestyle.

This is a dead-on, often painfully true account of an unorthodox adult-child relationship that runs up against the unpredictable shoals of the workaday world. It's got its fair share of laugh lines, but you'll be surprised at the poignancy of some of the scenes.

Barbara Harris plays the lovely social worker Robards charms; Martin Balsam plays Robards's brother (he won an Oscar for the performance).

★ 1965, 118 minutes, B&W, not rated.

★ With: Jason Robards, Barbara Harris, William Daniels. Director: Fred Coe.

★ *Name the film in which Jason Robards played newspaper publisher Ben Bradlee.* (Answer on page 65.)

"I never answer letters from large organizations."
—Jason Robards offers a course in Denial 101.

For a great double feature, rent it with
Searching for Bobby Fischer.

Seen it but in the mood for something similar? Try
Little Man Tate.

Answer to page 77 trivia question:
The Spy Who Came In from the Cold.

Comedy

Time Bandits

It's not nice to tick off the
Supreme Being.

"Don't touch it. It's evil."

—The little kid's right—
Ralph Richardson has left a
piece of concentrated evil in
the microwave.

For a great double feature, rent it with

The 5,000 Fingers of Dr. T.

Seen it but in the mood for something similar? Try

Willy Wonka and the Chocolate Factory.

Answer to page 111 trivia question:

Journey for Margaret.

This inventive, imaginative fantasy film starts at full speed and picks up from there. Its appealing blend of visual anarchy, great physical humor, and time-warp speed raps are all more than a little reminiscent of the work of those troublesomely hilarious Monty Python boys. There's a reason—Pythons Terry Gilliam and Michael Palin are responsible for the deliciously goofy script, Palin and John Cleese show up in the cast, and Gilliam directs with more enthusiasm than discipline. Good for him, I say.

This is the farcical story of a lonely little daydreamer of a boy who suddenly finds himself appropriated by a band of robbers who happen to be time travelers. By default he becomes the brains of the operation. It's the best kind of fantasy film: colorful and event-packed enough to hold the kids and with enough of an irreverent edge to keep the grown-ups interested, too. Any picture with the guts to cast Ralph Richardson as a grumpy Supreme Being in an unpressed suit has my vote.

Listen closely when Cleese shows up as Robin Hood; he's doing a dead-on Prince Charles impersonation. It's one of a number of sublime moments in a relentless, unexpectedly satisfying picture. Weird ending, admittedly, but then again, they're weird guys.

★ 1981, 110 minutes, color, PG.

★ With: Craig Warnock, Peter Vaughan, John Cleese, Ralph Richardson. Director: Terry Gilliam.

★ *What do Michael Palin and Phileas Fogg have in common?* (Answer on page 17.)

Comedy

The Time Machine

Futureworld.

This thoroughly enjoyable adaptation of the classic H. G. Wells novel casts Rod Taylor as an optimistic scientist with a dandy new machine he takes out for a spin around the space-time continuum. His faith in mankind is sorely tested when he can't land anywhere (anywhen?) without encountering war on a massive scale. Eventually he puts the craft into overdrive and settles down in the year 802,701, where an oppressed, dehumanized people need his help in learning to defend themselves against their cannibalistic overlords.

Witty ideas and cool special effects abound in this inspired film fantasy. My favorite moment: a delightful parody of the world of fashion involving a mannequin in a store window during Taylor's trip out of his own era. Just as a side note: How come none of these people with time machines at their disposal ever put it in reverse, jam the accelerator, and figure out that chicken-or-egg riddle once and for all?

★ 1960, 103 minutes, color, not rated.

★ With: Rod Taylor, Yvette Mimieux, Alan Young. Director: George Pal.

★ *Why do the movie's automobiles look suspiciously like vintage 1960 models?* (Answer on page 3.)

"One cannot choose but wonder. You see, he has all the time in the world."
—Alan Young's response when questioned about Rod Taylor's whereabouts.

For a great double feature, rent it with
Back to the Future.

Seen it but in the mood for something similar? Try
Time After Time.

Answer to page 297 trivia question:
"St. Elsewhere."

Sci-Fi

To Be or Not to Be (1942)

Benny. Lombard. Need I say more?

"Heil myself."

—Fake Nazi Jack Benny figures he's got to keep up appearances.

For a great double feature, rent it with

My Man Godfrey (1936).

Seen it but in the mood for something similar? Try

To Be or Not to Be (1983).

Answer to page 332 trivia question:

Stop Making Sense; the guy was David Byrne of the Talking Heads.

This marvelous World War II comedy has aged amazingly well. As if to prove the point, Mel Brooks and Anne Bancroft starred in a faithful, nearly verbatim remake of the picture in 1983. That one's cute; this one's better. After all, there was only one Jack Benny, and there certainly was only one Carole Lombard. Here they star as members of a Polish acting troupe who use their theatrical abilities to undercut the Nazis. They're both spectacular. It's hard to imagine anyone doing a better, wittier job of earning laughs from potentially downbeat material than Benny, Lombard, and director Ernst Lubitsch do here.

Benny's hambone Hamlet is a one-of-a-kind treat; the picture's first scene has to be one of the most masterful comedic fakeouts in movie history. You'll probably watch this one more than once, if only to long for all the pictures Carole Lombard never got to make; shortly after this picture was completed, she died tragically in an airplane accident during a war-bonds drive. (She was a vehement anti-fascist, which was one of the reasons the script appealed to her so strongly.)

★ 1942, 102 minutes, B&W, not rated.

★ With: Jack Benny, Carole Lombard, Robert Stack. Director: Ernst Lubitsch.

★ *What keepsake did Clark Gable use to honor his wife Carole Lombard's memory?* (Answer on page 31.)

Tomorrow

*So good, you'll wonder where
the subtitles are.*

Robert Duvall gives a quiet, methodical, and altogether unforgettable performance as the winter caretaker of a lumberyard. He's uncomfortable with people and looking forward to some time alone, but the day before Christmas a very cold, very pregnant woman (Olga Bellin) arrives on his doorstep. Duvall takes her in, and the relationship that develops between the two is slow magic.

The movie sneaks up on you; before you realize it, you find yourself caring very deeply for the pair. Director Joseph Anthony's evocation of warmth through his use of light in the scenes with Bellin is nothing short of masterful; *Tomorrow* is a testament to the power of black-and-white filmmaking when undertaken by someone who knows what he's doing.

This memorable film is based on a William Faulkner short story. It's rendered with sublime delicacy and feeling; keep a box of Kleenex handy.

★ 1972, 103 minutes, B&W, PG.

★ With: Robert Duvall, Olga Bellin, Sudie Bond. Director: Joseph Anthony.

★ *What film does Duvall consider his best?* (Answer on page 71.)

"Human beings who just want to do the right thing. . . ."
—Robert Duvall happens to be one of them.

For a great double feature, rent it with
To Kill a Mockingbird.

Seen it but in the mood for something similar? Try
Tender Mercies.

Answer to page 353 trivia queston:
Three; the producers had only that many model spaceships.

Drama

True Believer

That's no hippie; that's my lawyer.

"He didn't do it."
—James Woods offers a fairly straightforward line of defense.

For a great double feature, rent it with
Hair.

Seen it but in the mood for something similar? Try
Flashback.

Answer to page 19 trivia question:
The Seventh Seal.

James Woods, once a sixties civil rights idealist, has lost his will to fight. Lately, he's taken to sitting back, blowing a little weed, and defending the easy cases. The only remnant of his days of glory is the long, graying ponytail he still wears. Without it he could be mistaken for just another lawyer, as opposed to someone who used to give a damn.

When Robert Downey, Jr., comes on the scene, as a young attorney whose love for the law has been inspired by Woods's civil rights work, he's crushed to find that his hero has given up. It will take an unignorable case of miscarried justice and a good deal of prodding from Downey to remind Woods that there's still a chance to be the lawyer he always wanted to be. Although the setup seems fairly standard, the fast-paced suspense story offers some great twists.

★ 1989, 103 minutes, color, R.

★ With: James Woods, Robert Downey, Jr., Margaret Colin. Director: Joseph Ruben.

★ *What silent screen legend did Downey portray?* (Answer on page 102.)

Truly, Madly, Deeply

Everyone who saw Ghost *12 times should be required by law to see this once.*

Tired of predictable Hollywood-formula screenwriting? *Truly, Madly, Deeply* has the guts to throw its viewers a serious curveball. For the first 20 minutes or so the depth of Juliet Stevenson's grief over the passing of her lover (Alan Rickman) is so profound that it seems to leave the film only one path to follow, and when Rickman tries to reenter her life as a ghost you'll assume, and with good cause, that the film is about to mine the same emotional lode as the megahit *Ghost*. Fortunately, you'll be dead wrong.

Truly, Madly, Deeply is a confident, refreshingly funny piece of moviemaking that, for my money, easily outshines its glitzy American counterpart. The movie's considerable delights arise from the idea that the one you *thought* was the perfect person just might not be . . . especially if he has an annoying habit of inviting his otherworldly friends over without checking first.

This gem incorporates all the best elements of a high-voltage love story, a get-your-life-back-on-track slice of domestic realism, and a deliriously silly comedy. Amazingly, all three seemingly disparate elements succeed.

★ 1991, 107 minutes, color, not rated (but some mature themes).

★ With: Juliet Stevenson, Alan Rickman, Bill Paterson. Director: Anthony Minghella.

★ *What film does Juliet Stevenson accidentally tape over, much to the consternation of her houseguests?* (Answer on page 309.)

"And the dead shall have no dominion. We know that, you and me."
—Alan Rickman talks a nice line, but he doesn't say anything about hogging the VCR.

For a great double feature, rent it with
The Ghost and Mrs. Muir.

Seen it but in the mood for something similar? Try
Kiss Me Goodbye.

Answer to page 53 trivia question:
Murder by Death.

Romance

Twelve O'Clock High

*The war movie for people who
don't like war movies.*

*"Stop making plans.
Forget about going
home. Consider your-
self dead already. Once
you've accepted that, it
won't be so tough."*

—Gregory Peck does his
Samuel Beckett imitation.

**For a great double
feature, rent it with**

Spellbound.

**Seen it but in the mood
for something similar?
Try**

Bridges at Toko-Ri.

**Answer to page 87
trivia question:**

The Dead Zone and
Needful Things.

This fine Gregory Peck World War II picture has more to do with dealing with people than with dusting Germans. Peck plays the tough-as-nails commander assigned to take over a faltering bomber squadron based in England; he drills his men unendingly, gets them to look their job square in the face, and proves that they'll be stronger when they don't try to cover up for one another than when they do. The difficult routine he imposes does the trick, and the squadron starts perform- ing as it should—but even Peck, who has argued from square one about the importance of keeping overemo- tional reactions from clouding one's decisions, finds that he's not immune to the problem of growing too close to the men.

A thoughtful examination of psychological reactions to stress, *Twelve O'Clock High* is a war movie that hardly emphasizes its battle scenes at all; at times you get the feeling that the filmmakers could just as easily have been engaged in a psychological study that had nothing to do with war whatsoever. (Indeed the film is often used in management training seminars as a useful case study.)

★ 1949, 132 minutes, B&W, not rated.

★ With: Gregory Peck, Dean Jagger, Gary Merrill, Hugh Marlowe. Director: Henry King.

★ *For what film did Gregory Peck win the Academy Award as Best Actor?* (Answer on page 240.)

Two for the Road

The roads not taken.

A clever idea executed with unerring skill by director Stanley Donen. Audrey Hepburn and Albert Finney are a married couple on vacation—at different periods of their lives, simultaneously. They spend much of the film's running time on the road; every time the camera follows another passing car, there's a time shift, and we see the couple at a different stage of their marriage. The movie is a compelling study of the phases of a modern marriage—both partners falter, and the pieces cast no one as a villain—but just as important, it is an excuse to see Audrey Hepburn show off some of the most memorable fashion excesses of the 1960s.

Albert Finney is probably at his best in this film. Jacqueline Bisset, as the distraction Finney may or may not have an affair with, does the best she can with what she's given. This was a groundbreaking movie for the era, which means that people actually have sex before they get married, and the word *virgin* can be uttered out loud. Featuring a notable score by Henry Mancini.

★ 1967, 112 minutes, color, not rated.

★ With: Audrey Hepburn, Albert Finney, Jacqueline Bisset. Director: Stanley Donen.

★ *What designer won the Oscar for Costume Design in Sabrina? (Hint: She's not French, and she didn't design any of Audrey Hepburn's clothes.)* (Answer on page 172.)

"The girls were putty about you, and heaven knows, so were you."
—Audrey Hepburn's honest appraisal of Albert Finney.

For a great double feature, rent it with
Who's Afraid of Virginia Woolf.

Seen it but in the mood for something similar? Try
Breathing Lessons.

Answer to page 122 trivia question:
Patriot Games.

Comedy

The Uninvited

When scary things happen to charming people.

"*Between you and me and the grand piano, I think father was a bit of a bad hat.*"

—Gail Russell, sharing a delicate observation with Ray Milland and a prominent piece of furniture

For a great double feature, rent it with

The Haunting.

Seen it but in the mood for something similar? Try

The Ghost and Mrs. Muir.

Answer to page 30 trivia question:

Brain Donors.

The early portion of this film might lead you to believe you're in for a Nick and Nora Charles rip-off, but keep watching. There's a lot more to *The Uninvited* than its initial smarmy banter and the rather predictable setup, which involves a brother and sister (Ray Milland and Ruth Hussey) who buy a beautiful yet abandoned house high atop some very treacherous cliffs.

The two seem to be the only ones in town (including the dog and cat) who are unaware of the presence of something otherworldly—but what *kinds* of ghosts are we dealing with? As the plot develops, you start to realize that there is indeed an evil entity in the environs, something dark and unavoidable that wouldn't fit into a Noel Coward farce but won't be ignored here.

Behind the prim facade of the siblings' seemingly controllable world lies a tale of seduction, adultery, and madness that won't be dismissed with reasoned interpretations. The explanations begin to ring hollow at about the same time the witty repartee does. (Keep an ear out for the deft between-the-lines treatment of what just *might* be a lesbian relationship in the house's deep, dark past.)

★ 1944, 98 minutes, B&W, not rated.

★ With: Ray Milland, Ruth Hussey, Gail Russell. Director: Lewis Allen.

★ The Uninvited *features the first popular love song to emerge as a hit from a horror film. Can you name the song?* (Answer on page 68.)

Up the Down Staircase

Long hours, low pay, no support.
God, I love this job.

This superior drama about an idealistic young teacher trying to make sense of the vexing New York City public school system—and maybe, just, maybe make a difference in the lives of her students—provided Sandy Dennis with one of her finest screen roles.

Take a look at what she's up against! Organizational gridlock and inefficiency, crippling social problems, widespread disaffection in the student body . . . boy, it's a good thing we took care of all these problems back in the sixties, when we first noticed them, huh? Otherwise we might have a *real* dilemma on our hands.

Told with wit, insight, and humor, this winning adaptation of Bel Kaufman's book is a memorable look at some very human problems that the reigning institutions fail spectacularly to resolve. Although the problems in the public school system have gotten a good deal grimmer over the years, this picture's basic message—the system doesn't work and doesn't want to work—is still every bit as relevant as it was the day it was released. That's too damned bad.

★ 1967, 124 minutes, color, not rated.

★ With: Sandy Dennis, Patrick Bedford, Eileen Heckart. Director: Robert Mulligan.

★ *Who adapted Bel Kaufman's book for the screen?*
(Answer on page 20.)

"Let it be a challenge to you."
—Sandy Dennis probably has enough challenges on her plate already.

For a great double feature, rent it with *Dead Poets Society.*

Seen it but in the mood for something similar? Try *To Sir with Love.*

Answer to page 64 trivia question: Tracy Pollen; the two met on the set of "Family Ties."

Drama

Vincent & Theo

Sunflowers, sunflowers, sunflowers.
Always with the sunflowers.

"I am the holy spirit. I am the whole spirit."
—Tim Roth, heading into the stratosphere.

For a great double feature, rent it with
Amadeus.

Seen it but in the mood for something similar? Try
Housekeeping.

Answer to page 98 trivia question:
Darling (1965).

Usually when you think of Robert Altman films, you think of movies with huge casts of very famous people doing some pretty weird things. Here, however, the gifted director focuses on Vincent van Gogh and his less famous, generally saner brother. The movie wisely assumes that the viewer knows who Vincent was in the first place and spends most of its energy exploring a comparatively intimate story.

Theo knows there is magic in what his brother is doing; he is there to rescue his brother time and time again, trying in vain to sell his paintings and offering whatever he can manage in the way of money. What Vincent needs is someone to keep him grounded while his mind and his craft go further into the unseen. That would be Theo, of course—but what becomes of such a person when his other half leaves for good?

★ 1990, 138 minutes, color, PG-13.

★ With: Tim Roth, Paul Rhys, Johanna ter Steege. Director: Robert Altman.

★ *OK, let's see how obsessive you were in art history class. What earlobe did Van Gogh cut off, anyway?*

(Answer on page 37.)

Biography

Viva Zapata!

Not to be confused with Viva Las Vegas.

A terrific collaboration between John Steinbeck and Elia Kazan, both of whom leaned to the left politically and didn't mind using a movie to make their points. They wanted to tell a story of a reluctant rebel who becomes a revolutionary—and falls prey to the corruption of power. The film is set in Mexico in the early 1900s; Zapata (Brando) is an undistinguished peasant farmer who takes a stand before the dictator to complain of unjust land policies.

From the moment Brando steps forward to voice his opinion, he's a marked man. When he quells a later attempt to massacre a group of peasants, Brando takes up arms against the government and, without ever meaning to, becomes the hero of the people. The relationship between Brando and Jean Peters is a touching one. Fate intervenes and changes forever the simple life they had planned; the needs of the people must come first.

The acting is uniformly superb, as are Steinbeck's screenplay and Kazan's direction. Let's face it: all involved were at the top of their game for this one.

★ 1952, 113 minutes, B&W, not rated.

★ With: Marlon Brando, Jean Peters, Anthony Quinn. Director: Elia Kazan.

★ *Can you name Zapata's horse?* (Answer on page 110.)

"You've looked for leaders. For strong men, without faults. There aren't any. There are only men like yourself. . . . There are no leaders but yourselves."

—Brando's speech only serves to convince people he's the man to lead them.

For a great double feature, rent it with *The Godfather.*

Seen it but in the mood for something similar? Try *The Grapes of Wrath.*

Answer to page 134 trivia question: 1959's *Ben Hur.*

Drama

Wait Until Dark

No kidding: watch it with all the lights turned off to get maximum creepiness out of the ending.

Talk about a change of pace: Alan Arkin, best known for his superb comic turns in such pictures as *The Russians Are Coming! The Russians Are Coming!* and *Catch-22,* here shows up as the heavy in this thriller. A blind woman (Audrey Hepburn) has inadvertently ended up with a doll stuffed with heroin and is terrorized by a gang of criminals as a result. Arkin is menacing in the extreme; Hepburn brings a welcome dash of intellect to the tried-and-true woman-in-jeopardy formula.

Director Terence Young sets up an intricate pattern of visual metaphors and uses light with great care and effectiveness. His superior craftsmanship, and the outstanding performances of the principals, make *Wait Until Dark* a thinking person's thriller that doesn't have to resort to blood-spattered slasher scenes to hold an audience's interest. You'll think twice about changing the light in the refrigerator after you see this one.

★ 1967, 108 minutes, color, not rated.

★ With: Audrey Hepburn, Alan Arkin, Richard Crenna, Efrem Zimbalist, Jr. Director: Terence Young.

★ *What did Audrey Hepburn do after this film and* Two for the Road *were released in the same year?* (Answer on page 169.)

*Chrmng plnt, ocn vu,
easy 2 inhbt.*

The classic H. G. Wells tale is retold here in a 1953 Technicolor production that resounds with style and panache. As the story opens, Martians come crashing to Earth; we silly humans mistake the arrival for a meteor shower, as we are wont to do in this genre. Actually, that meteor-shower theory is only the initial conclusion of a group of world-class physicists who happen, fortuitously enough, to be doing some fishing nearby.

The foremost of these scientists is Gene Barry, who flies his own plane, is a great dancer, is fun at a party, and has some cool tortoiseshell glasses lest anyone forget that he's the smartest guy in the group. Basically, the guy is a dreamboat; between him and the pastor's niece, we can be pretty sure that everything that can be done to rescue the planet Earth will be done.

For all the fifties-era stereotyping, this movie makes some fascinating points, among them the notion that religion could fail us in the face of an interplanetary invasion and that our government, and eventually even science, could prove powerless against these invaders. In short, this is the ultimate Eisenhower-era nightmare. Well-executed, campy fun throughout, with cool spaceships aplenty and enough intellectual fidelity to the original story to keep things interesting.

★ 1953, 85 minutes, color, not rated.

★ With: Gene Barry, Ann Robinson, Les Tremayne. Director: Byron Haskin.

★ *How many invading space ships do we see at any one time?* (Answer on page 343.)

"The Martians can conquer the world in six days." "The same number it took to create it."

—Who said scientists never read the Bible?

For a great double feature, rent it with

The Adventures of Buckaroo Banzai Across the Eighth Dimension.

Seen it but in the mood for something similar? Try

When Worlds Collide.

Answer to page 55 trivia question:

Kris Kristofferson.

Sci-Fi

The Waterdance

Dancing in the dark.

"*I am!*"
—The unending epiphany of a particularly annoying patient in the ward

For a great double feature, rent it with

Bodies in Rest & Motion.

Seen it but in the mood for something similar? Try

The Men.

Answer to page 90 trivia question:

The Boston Red Sox.

This study of a writer's adjustment to the new world that awaits him after he shatters his spinal cord is far, far more than your standard affliction-of-the-week biopic. Writer-director Neal Jimenez, who was himself left paralyzed from the waist down after a hiking accident, here draws on his own painful transition to self-sufficiency and renders an exquisitely detailed examination of exactly what happens when one must adapt to the unthinkable.

Although the film approaches its subject without flinching, this is not, repeat, *not* a "downer" of an evening. Thanks to its tight, unsentimental script and a batch of strong performances from its gifted cast, *The Waterdance* gets its points across with humanity, clarity, and, given the circumstances, a surprising amount of humor.

There is not a single weak performance. Eric Stoltz, in the lead, and Helen Hunt, as the unhappily married woman with whom he has been having an affair, are particularly notable, and Wesley Snipes, who has taken to brainless action pictures in recent years, delivers a finely crafted supporting character.

Inspiring, sensitive, and powerful, Jimenez's one-of-a-kind offering is a fiercely felt embrace of all that is worth living for. Don't miss it.

★ 1992, 110 minutes, color, R.

★ With: Eric Stoltz, Helen Hunt, Wesley Snipes. Directors: Neal Jimenez and Michael Steinberg.

★ *Whom did Stoltz play when he appeared on Hunt's show "Mad About You"?* (Answer on page 362.)

What's Up, Tiger Lily?

Much ado about egg salad.

ere's the plan. Buy the rights to a cheapo Japanese spy thriller for next to nothing. Take the prints of the deliriously lame flick to the dubbing room. Start making fun of the stupid movie you now own. Keep the microphone on at all times. Put it all together and release it.

OK, so the cool script behind Woody Allen's *What's Up, Tiger Lily?* probably took a little more work on his part to put together. But you get the basic idea. Allen transforms a pale Tokyo attempt to cash in on the James Bond craze into an hour and 20 minutes of inspired comic madness.

He does it by launching a pyrotechnic display of his own ability to develop one-liners out of just about any material and by feeling free to insert some monumentally bizarre ideas in the strangest places. So instead of battling an evil ring of bad guys out for world domination, the hero sets off on an international struggle for possession of the ultimate egg salad recipe. It's like that for the whole picture. Enjoy.

★ 1966, 80 minutes, color, not rated.

★ With: Tatsuya Mihashi, Miya Hana, Woody Allen. Director: Woody Allen.

★ *What was the picture called before Allen transformed it into a self-destructing parody?* (Answer on page 237.)

"I'm a jet plane!"
—What's more, he don't know when he'll be back again.

For a great double feature, rent it with *Godzilla vs. the Thing.*

Seen it but in the mood for something similar? Try *Everything You Always Wanted to Know about Sex (but Were Afraid to Ask).*

Answer to page 124 trivia question:
Terwilliker.

Comedy

Where the Green Ants Dream

But where do they wake up?

For a great double feature, rent it with

Mad Max.

Seen it but in the mood for something similar? Try

The Coca-Cola Kid.

Answer to page 59 trivia question:

"The Dentist."

Werner Herzog directed this fascinating culture-clash picture about Australian aborigines who make a stand against a powerful lobby of uranium-mining interests. Caught in the middle of it all is the chief engineer, who must somehow make sense of a situation that pits the relentless forward march of technology against an ancient tradition designating as sacred the spot he's supposed to dig up. Turns out, according to the aborigines' tribal council, that if the green ants said to live in the region are awakened, they will destroy all mankind, earth, and, in fact, the entire universe. No pressure, though.

A sleek, engrossing drama that raises some important questions about crosscultural relations, ecology, big business, and entomology. Any movie that can fascinate me through all that certainly has my vote.

★ 1984, 100 minutes, color, not rated.

★ With: Bruce Spence, Ray Barrett, Norman Kaye. Director: Werner Herzog.

★ *Bruce Spence appeared in which* Mad Max *film?*
(Answer on page 166.)

Where's Poppa?

What's the opposite of an Oedipus complex?

Every once in a while a movie produces a classic, crystal-clear premise for a comedy that is so utterly perfect that audiences will follow the picture pretty much anywhere it wants to go. In Mel Brooks's *The Producers* the idea was to produce a Broadway show awful enough that it would be guaranteed to flop, thereby allowing its crooked backers to reap a windfall. In *Where's Poppa?* the memorable setup has to do with George Segal, who has promised his late father never to commit his mother (Ruth Gordon) to an old-age home and is now stuck with her. She's beyond tough to live with; she's psycho. So Segal sets out to scare the bejesus out of her in the hopes of initiating a heart attack.

This inspired black comedy (which, like most black comedies, spends a good deal of time right on the edge of bad taste) features consistently deft mugging by George Segal and straight-ahead direction from Carl Reiner, who knows exactly what he's doing just often enough for the picture to work. Ruth Gordon is appropriately terrifying; if she were any less hideous to Segal at the beginning, you might feel sorry for her. Reiner makes sure there's no danger of that.

★ 1970, 82 minutes, color, R.

★ With: George Segal, Ruth Gordon, Trish Van Devere. Director: Carl Reiner.

★ *What instrument does Segal play professionally in real life?* (Answer on page 107.)

"You almost scared me to death!" "Almost doesn't count."
—Ruth Gordon and her son George Segal share a tender moment.

For a great double feature, rent it with
King Rat.

Seen it but in the mood for something similar? Try
Harold and Maude.

Answer to page 25 trivia question:
Sergeant York, Gary Cooper's classic, which was released in the same year.

Comedy

White Heat

Your mama.

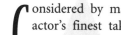

"How's mom?"
—James Cagney probably doesn't want to know.

For a great double feature, rent it with

Angels with Dirty Faces.

Seen it but in the mood for something similar? Try

GoodFellas.

Answer to page 93 trivia question:

Footlight Parade.

Considered by many Cagney aficionados to be the actor's finest take on the whole underworld-thug thing . . . and that's saying something. This time he's not just dangerous; he's completely out of it. Cagney plays a true *nutcase* of a hood—he's obsessed by his relationship with his mother—who's finally tracked down by a determined G-man.

There's plenty to like here: extraordinary black-and-white cinematography; lots and lots and lots of carefully mounted, exquisitely edited violence; and some unforgettable prison sequences. (Keep an eye out for the "whisper scene" in which Cagney inquires after Mom's health.)

The powerful finale is a high-powered, probably untoppable exercise in pedal-to-the-floor acting and impeccable production values; if a bigger, better exit scene has ever been filmed for a major star, I can't remember when.

★ 1949, 114 minutes, B&W, not rated.

★ With: James Cagney, Virginia Mayo, Edmond O'Brien. Director: Raoul Walsh.

★ *In what film did Cagney push a grapefruit half into Mae Clark's face?* (Answer on page 289.)

White Nights (1985)

Flashdance-vuh-danya.

aryshnikov dances avant-garde, ballet, and various painful modern Russian pieces; Gregory Hines, for his part, dances ballet à la tap and puts up an inspired scene from *Porgy and Bess*. And, of course, the two of them tap-dance together. This is a cold war drama? Well, yeah, but the aforementioned astonishing dance routines and Isabella Rossellini's customary cool line delivery and drop-dead looks are the real reasons to rent this film.

The plot, if you feel compelled to look for one, has to do with Hines, an American defector who sought refuge in the USSR during the Vietnam War. Baryshnikov is a defector in the other direction: he fled the Soviet Union for artistic freedom, but his plane crashed in the old country. Bummer, huh?

Plot contrivances aside, these two are probably the most inspiring male dance duo to hook up since Gene Kelly and Donald O'Connor did that "Moses Supposes" number in *Singin' in the Rain*. That one had just enough plot to get by, too. Rent *White Nights* for the exquisite dance moves, and the rest of it will glide by as an agreeable example of the cold war thriller.

★ 1985, 135 minutes, color, PG-13.

★ With: Mikhail Baryshnikov, Gregory Hines, Isabella Rossellini. Director: Taylor Hackford.

★ *What was Mikhail Baryshnikov's first picture?* (Answer on page 234.)

"You ever dance the Apollo? No. You dance on your tippy-toes over to the White House."

—An inebriated Gregory Hines doesn't think much of Mikhail Baryshnikov's style.

For a great double feature, rent it with *The Turning Point.*

Seen it but in the mood for something similar? Try *Running Scared.*

Answer to page 128 trivia question: The Royal North Surrey Regiment.

Action

The Wild One

Wind in your hair, bugs in your teeth. It just doesn't get any better than this.

Marlon Brando's electrifying performance as the original anti-hero—an anarchistic, leather-clad biker who hooks up with (gasp!) the sweetest girl in town—sent parental Middle America into a panic attack in the 1950s. The kids thought he was pretty cool, though. The Great Brooder is predictably awesome; he heads up a motorcycle gang called the Black Rebels that scares the hell out of a small town for no other reason than it looks like it might be fun. That's entirely juvenile, irresponsible behavior, of course. And it sure is fun to watch.

This is the great-granddaddy of the older-generation-doesn't-understand-us genre, and it still carries quite a charge. Cool jackets, huh?

★ 1954, 79 minutes, B&W, not rated.

★ With: Marlon Brando, Robert Keith, Lee Marvin. Director: Laslo Benedek.

★ *In what film did Brando push the whole Method thing a little too far by actually eating a fly?* (Answer on page 162.)

The Wind

Watch this spellbinder with someone who thinks silent films are dull.

Letty Manson (Lillian Gish) arrives in Texas to help her cousin manage the homestead. The family loves her—a little too much for the liking of Cousin Cora, who sees Letty as a threat and throws her out. Penniless and without prospects, Letty marries the pleasant, awkward Lige (Lars Hanson), who brings her to his remote desert cabin. The winds of the title soon make their presence known . . . and they prove to be as strong a character in the film as any of the principal personages. While her new husband is away, Letty is raped by an intruder, the beastly Wirt Roddy (Montagu Love).

The terrifying consequences of this act make *The Wind* a compelling, technically stunning examination of loneliness, guilt, survival, and imprisonment. If you've been looking for a silent film that meets modern standards for audience grabbing, this is it.

★ 1928, 88 minutes, B&W, not rated.

★ With: Lillian Gish, Lars Hanson, Montagu Love. Director: Victor Seastrom.

★ *What was Lillian Gish's last film?* (Answer on page 34.)

"Don't worry anymore, Cora—I know where I can go."
—Lillian Gish knows when she's not wanted.

For a great double feature, rent it with
The Scarlet Letter (1926). You'll be watching what are arguably Gish's two finest screen performances.

Seen it but in the mood for something similar? Try
Broken Blossoms.

Answer to page 333 trivia question:
Nobody. He was too tactful to single out any of his notable leading ladies and always dodged the question.

Wings of Desire

Angels in Berlin.

"At the Zoo-U-Bahn station, instead of the station's name, the conductor suddenly shouted, 'Tierra del Fuego!'"

—An angel shares an account of an unexpected event observed on a train.

For a great double feature, rent it with

It's a Wonderful Life.

Seen it but in the mood for something similar? Try

Nashville.

Answer to page 354 trivia question:

Her character's old boyfriend.

The film hailed by many critics as the single best film of the 1980s remains, for the most part, an unexamined masterpiece. Wim Wenders's evocative story of an angel who must choose whether or not to take on human form is patient, thoughtful, and unhurried, which is a tactful way of saying that it takes some time to build up power. Once it does, however, it's breathtaking.

The visuals are striking in the extreme; the film's conceit is that squads of angels in great long coats stride noiselessly among us and can read our thoughts; the masterful shots of public places filled with silent, gray-coated guardians next to the regular mortals will stay with you.

An unlikely but thoroughly delightful appearance by Peter Falk as Peter Falk pushes the movie into the outer stratosphere. If you stick with this one, it will pay off as few movies ever do. By the way, the current mania over angels had not yet reached shopping-mall levels of saturation when this delicate, carefully wrought film was produced; its thoughtful studies of the heavenly representatives are a good deal more profound than most of the recent New Age literature on the topic.

★ 1988, 130 minutes, color and B&W, PG-13.

★ With: Bruno Ganz, Solveig Dommartin, Curt Bois, Peter Falk. Director: Wim Wenders.

★ *What was the title of Wenders's sequel to* Wings of Desire? (Answer on page 113.)

Foreign

Without Love

Four movie stars, no waiting.

All right, we already knew Spencer Tracy and Katharine Hepburn had that great "couple" chemistry. But Lucille Ball and Keenan Wynn? Believe it. They wisecrack and leer in the background while Spencer and Kate make with the double takes and the witty repartee up front. It's a great combination. Hepburn, who was married blissfully for a short time, has been a widow for some time now; when she sees an opportunity to make herself useful by helping Tracy, a scientist working on a top-secret assignment for the war effort, she jumps at the chance. Even if that means she has to marry him to do it.

See, it's the forties, and it wouldn't have looked right for them to share the same house without . . . well, you get the idea. Spencer is the confirmed bachelor, quite content with the companionship his pet Scotty offers. Think they'll take to each other? An often-overlooked pairing of the famous screen duo.

★ 1945, 111 minutes, B&W, not rated.

★ With: Spencer Tracy, Katharine Hepburn, Lucille Ball. Director: Harold S. Bucquet.

★ *In what other film, about an ungainly vacation vehicle, did Wynn and Ball appear?* (Answer on page 157.)

"By gum!"
—Katharine Hepburn should really learn to tone down her language.

For a great double feature, rent it with
Woman of the Year.

Seen it but in the mood for something similar? Try
Desk Set.

Answer to page 308 trivia question:
The Till Two Bar.

Romance

The Women

Truth in advertising: there's not a man in sight.

I admit it. My first reason for recommending this film is Joan Crawford's bathroom. Don't you think it's just like hers must have been in real life?

Now then. This movie reminds us that there were once two kinds of women. What two kinds? If you have to ask, you're too young to have to worry about it.

Fast-forward over the mystifyingly obnoxious credits, which match each woman in the movie with a corresponding animal, and you have a prefeminist classic that boasts some powerful portraits of "modern" women. Some are jerks; some aren't. None of them have to stay married to a man they don't love or trust. They can get divorced and move on with their lives. Which, in this era, still means getting married to someone else. But hey, it was a start.

As if to prove the point that these ladies don't need men, not one shows up for the whole film. A glamorous, enjoyable movie that knows how to have a good time, if you get what I mean. By the way, there's a single Technicolor fashion segment thrown in for fun.

★ 1939, 132 minutes, B&W with color insert, not rated.

★ With: Norma Shearer, Joan Crawford, Rosalind Russell, Joan Fontaine. Director: George Cukor.

★ *In what film did child star Virgina Weidler, who plays Norma Shearer's daughter, appear as Katharine Hepburn's little sister?* (Answer on page 231.)

Zulu

Hakuna matata my butt.

OK, hypothetically now: If you had to face 10,000 or 20,000 Zulu warriors, and you had only 120 men, 15 of whom were in the hospital, too sick to fight, what would you do? Did I mention that you have plenty of notice that they're coming and that you know that they've just massacred another detachment of men? And that they've armed themselves with 12,000 of that detachment's rifles? What's that, you say? You'd high-tail it out of there? Sorry, that's not an option. You're British.

Michael Caine's first major film role is only one of the attractions of this fine dramatization of an amazing true story. The cast is superb, the screenplay is tightly contructed, and the direction is remarkably skilled. I'm not quite sure how Cy Endfield keeps us hooked on a movie whose final 90 minutes consist almost exclusively of fight scenes, but he does. Narrated by Richard Burton, *Zulu* is an extraordinary achievement.

★ 1964, 135 minutes, color, not rated.

★ With: Stanley Baker, Jack Hawkins, Michael Caine. Director: Cy Endfield.

★ *How many men received the Victoria Cross for their service in the battle of Rorke's Drift, chronicled in* Zulu? (Answer on page 159.)

"Usuto! Usuto! Usuto!" *(Kill! Kill! Kill!)*
—The natives have a message for Stanley Baker, Jack Hawkins, and Michael Caine, and it's not pleasant.

For a great double feature, rent it with
The Sand Pebbles.

Seen it but in the mood for something similar? Try
Zulu Dawn.

Answer to page 210 trivia question:
"Pennies from Heaven."

Drama

Index

To Be or Not to Be (1942)
Tomorrow
Truly, Madly, Deeply
Twelve O'Clock High
Up the Down Staircase
Waterdance, The
What's Up, Tiger Lily?
Wild One, The
Zulu

Beefcake (girls' night in)

Adventures of Buckaroo Banzai Across
   the Eighth Dimension, The
Arsenic and Old Lace
Awful Truth, The
Barefoot in the Park
Beau Geste
Big Easy, The
Bride Came C.O.D., The
Candidate, The
Captain Blood
Captain Horatio Hornblower
Charade
Coma
Compromising Positions
Count of Monte Cristo, The
Cyrano de Bergerac (1990)
Daddy Long Legs
Destination Tokyo
Divorce—Italian Style
Downhill Racer
Dracula

Dragon: The Bruce Lee Story
Dreamscape
El Mariachi
Elvis: One Night with You
Emerald Forest, The
Endless Summer, The
Eye of the Needle
Forbidden Planet
Fountainhead, The
Fourth Protocol, The
Getaway, The (1972)
Ghost and Mrs. Muir, The
Grey Fox, The
Gunga Din
Hair
Hearts of the West
His Girl Friday
Hud
Impromptu
Ipcress File, The
Jason and the Argonauts
Jezebel
Kings Row
Lady Eve, The
Laura
Love Comes to Andy Hardy
Love with the Proper Stranger
Map of the Human Heart
Mediterraneo
Now, Voyager
Oklahoma Kid
Operation Petticoat
Outland

Cheesecake (boys' night in)

Funny (guaranteed)

Good First-Date Material
(if you know what I mean)

Desk Set
Destry Rides Again (1939)
Educating Rita
84 Charing Cross Road
Enchanted Cottage, The
Everything You Always Wanted to Know
  About Sex (but Were Afraid to Ask)
Experience Preferred . . . but Not Essential
Eye of the Needle
Fantastic Voyage
Forbidden Planet
Four Feathers, The (1939)
Ghost and Mrs. Muir, The
Grey Fox, The
Gunga Din
Hear My Song
Heartbreak Kid, The
His Girl Friday
Impromptu
Jason and the Argonauts
Lady Eve, The
Laura
Libeled Lady
Little Romance, A
Lolita
Love Comes to Andy Hardy
Love with the Proper Stranger
Mediterraneo
Midnight Lace
Mystic Pizza
New Leaf, A
Now, Voyager
Pee-wee Herman Show, The

Picnic at Hanging Rock
Pillow Talk
Pirate, The
Play It Again, Sam
Rainmaker, The
Random Harvest
Sabrina (1954)
Say Anything
Sayonara
Shirley Valentine
Shop Around the Corner, The
Snapper, The
Swept Away . . .
Swing Time
Taming of the Shrew, The (1967)
Thomas Crown Affair, The
Truly, Madly, Deeply
Two for the Road
Wild One, The
Without Love

Guilty Pleasures
(well, I liked it, Ms. Kael . . .)

All of Me
American Dreamer
Baby Boom
Big Easy, The
Brain Donors
Bring Me the Head of Alfredo Garcia
Cactus Flower
Cat Ballou
Compromising Positions

Kid Stuff (hold the mouse, please)

Rent-to-Impress (intellectuals' night in)

Scary (and maybe not quite right if there are kids around)

Body Double
Bring Me the Head of Alfredo Garcia
Casualties of War
Conversation, The
Dark Half, The
In Cold Blood
Kafka
Krays, The
Naked Lunch
Of Mice and Men (1992)
Outland
Sorcerer
Thing, The (1982)

Scary (but not, you know, disgusting)

Abominable Dr. Phibes, The
Andromeda Strain, The
Bride of Frankenstein
Cat People (1942)
Charade

Coma
Creature from the Black Lagoon
Day the Earth Stood Still, The
Dead Zone, The
Don't Look Now
Dracula
Dreamscape
Duel
Fourth Protocol, The
Hospital, The
Invasion of the Body Snatchers (1956)
Manhattan Project, The
Midnight Lace
Nineteen Eighty-Four (1984)
Rope
Shadow of a Doubt
Sleuth
Snake Pit, The
Sorry, Wrong Number
Still of the Night
Suddenly, Last Summer
Uninvited, The
War of the Worlds